OpenNebula 3 Cloud Computing

Set up, manage, and maintain your Cloud
and learn solutions for datacenter virtualization
with this step-by-step practical guide

Giovanni Toraldo

[PACKT] open source *
PUBLISHING   community experience distilled

BIRMINGHAM - MUMBAI

OpenNebula 3 Cloud Computing

First published: May 2012

Production Reference: 1190512

Published by Packt Publishing Ltd.
Livery Place
35 Livery Street
Birmingham B3 2PB, UK..

ISBN 978-1-84951-746-1

www.packtpub.com

Cover Image by Asher Wishkerman (a.wishkerman@mpic.de)

Credits

Author
Giovanni Toraldo

Reviewers
Benoît Benedetti
Nick Zhu

Acquisition Editor
Kartikey Pandey

Lead Technical Editor
Arun Nadar

Technical Editors
Susmita Das
Merin Jose
Ameya Sawant

Copy Editors
Brandt D'Mello
Laxmi Subramanian

Project Coordinators
Kushal Bhardwaj
Vishal Bodwani

Proofreaders
Lydia May Morris
Chris Smith

Indexer
Monica Ajmera Mehta

Graphics
Manu Joseph

Production Coordinators
Melwyn D'Sa
Alwin Roy

Cover Work
Melwyn D'Sa
Alwin Roy

Foreword

It is a pleasure to write the foreword to a book which will guide you through the basics and internals of OpenNebula. In a world where the term Cloud Computing is clearly abused and overloaded, this book will be a valuable reference to both newcomers and Cloud professionals. The main steps to build Cloud infrastructures of any type, from public or hybrid to private clouds are described in this book in a practical, clear, and effective way using OpenNebula.

It is almost seven years since the first versions of OpenNebula were released in an embryonary phase as a University project, gathering the outcomes of our research in distributed Cloud infrastructures. OpenNebula by design is very light (in terms of its dependencies and components), and easy to extend and adapt. Its simple and quite effective design has proven (and is accepted) to be very scalable and "hackable" leading to flexible and agile Cloud deployments all around the world.

Since its first software release in March 2008, OpenNebula has evolved into an active open source project with an engaged community of users and developers that by many measures, is more than doubling each year. We are really excited with the wide adoption of the software, being downloaded several thousands times per month from our site, and being used in several very large scale deployments.

And now, you have the book in your hands. Giovanni has been a long-time contributor to OpenNebula in multiple and valuable forms. This book is just another great contribution from him, a must-have for every OpenNebula practitioner as well as a very interesting reference for anybody looking for hands-on knowledge in Cloud Computing. Thanks Giovanni for your valuable contributions!

OpenNebula could be difficult sometimes, but it provides you with a powerful and flexible technology. This book is your first step to master it.

Ignacio M. Llorente
Project Director, OpenNebula project

Rubén S. Montero
Chief Architect, OpenNebula project

About the Author

Giovanni Toraldo started to mess with Linux and free software during his early years at school, developing hobbyist websites with free CMS and maintaining the official Italian support site of PHP-Fusion. After a few unsatisfactory years at university, he decided to start working as a System Administrator and Web Developer at LiberSoft (http://www.libersoft.it), a start-up based in a technology park near Pisa (http://www.polotecnologico.it/). Nowadays, he has developed skills in designing and maintaining Open Source virtualization and clustering solutions, managing tens of hosts, servicing hundreds of requests — mainly web hosting stacks for Drupal and Symfony webapps.

I would like to thank everyone who participated on this project, especially LiberSoft, for sponsoring the hardware with which I tested the OpenNebula configurations.

About the Reviewers

Benoît Benedetti works as a Linux System Administrator, for the University of Nice Sophia Antipolis, where he graduated with a degree in computer science.

Before coming back to the university as a sysadmin, he worked for various companies ranging from banks to hosting providers, where he had to deal with different operating systems, but always promoted the use of open source software and Linux.

He is interested in resolving new problems, as it is always an opportunity to work on new technologies. Benoît loves helping users, teaching students, and he occasionally writes technical articles for French Linux magazines.

> I would like to thank every person who dedicates his/her time to developing free and open source software, and making them available for us to play with.
>
> Many thanks to the author and the entire staff at Packt Publishing, they helped me to be as efficient as possible as a Technical Reviewer.
>
> Last but not the least, I would like to dedicate all my accomplishments to my parents for their hope, patience, and support.

Nick Zhu is a professional Software Development Consultant and a journeyman Software Craftsman living and working in Greater Toronto, Canada. In his spare time he is an active open source contributor, and a Pragmatic and Agile advocate.

www.PacktPub.com

Support files, eBooks, discount offers and more

You might want to visit www.PacktPub.com for support files and downloads related to your book.

Did you know that Packt offers eBook versions of every book published, with PDF and ePub files available? You can upgrade to the eBook version at www.PacktPub.com and as a print book customer, you are entitled to a discount on the eBook copy. Get in touch with us at service@packtpub.com for more details.

At www.PacktPub.com, you can also read a collection of free technical articles, sign up for a range of free newsletters and receive exclusive discounts and offers on Packt books and eBooks.

http://PacktLib.PacktPub.com

Do you need instant solutions to your IT questions? PacktLib is Packt's online digital book library. Here, you can access, read and search across Packt's entire library of books.

Why Subscribe?

- Fully searchable across every book published by Packt
- Copy and paste, print and bookmark content
- On demand and accessible via web browser

Free Access for Packt account holders

If you have an account with Packt at www.PacktPub.com, you can use this to access PacktLib today and view nine entirely free books. Simply use your login credentials for immediate access.

Table of Contents

Preface

OpenNebula is one of the most advanced and highly-scalable open source cloud computing toolkits. If you ever wanted to understand what Cloud Computing is and how to realize it, or if you need a handy way to manage your messy infrastructure in a simple and coherent manner, this is your way.

This book guides you through the building and maintenance of your cloud infrastructure, providing real-world examples, step-by-step configuration, and other critical information.

What this book covers

Chapter 1, OpenNebula, and Why it Matters?, introduces us to the Cloud, OpenNebula, and its underlying technologies.

Chapter 2, Building Up Your Cloud, provides an overview of the most typical hardware and software requirements, and how to start configuring the basic networking and OpenNebula frontend.

Chapter 3, Hypervisors, helps you understand how to install, configure, and optimize all the three hypervisors supported by OpenNebula: KVM, Xen, and VMWare ESXi.

Chapter 4, Choosing Your Storage Carefully, provides an overview of all the common storage solutions for our infrastructure with a focus on using distributed file systems.

Chapter 5, Being Operational – Everything Starts Here!, launches the first VM instance and a full dive into the OpenNebula resource management process.

Chapter 6, Web Management, simplifies OpenNebula management tasks and monitoring using Sunstone, the OpenNebula cloud operations center.

Chapter 7, Health and Monitoring, helps us to understand how to effectively monitor and manage host and VM failures for our infrastructure, build custom hooks, and integrate with Ganglia, a scalable distributed monitoring system.

Chapter 8, Hybrid Cloud Computing: Extending OpenNebula, helps you to understand how to integrate OpenNebula with Amazon EC2 and burst your capacity!

Chapter 9, Public Cloud Computing and High Availability with OpenNebula, exposes the standard EC2 and OCCI interfaces to the public and helps manage large OpenNebula deployments with the oZone component.

What you need for this book

OpenNebula does not require any particular hardware or software configuration; you need to have at least a single server (or your laptop), with a recent GNU/Linux distribution installation of your choice. Personally, I prefer using Debian or Ubuntu.

Who this book is for

This handy guide to Cloud computing with OpenNebula will be of great help to a GNU/Linux system administrator with no experience in Virtualization or Cloud computing, but eager to learn about it, or for a commercial Cloud administrator thwarted by their currently virtualized infrastructure. The reader should have some basic knowledge of GNU/Linux and system configuration, including the basics of package management tools for their preferred GNU/Linux distribution.

Basic Shell scripting and Ruby are required only if you want to hack the OpenNebula internals.

Conventions

In this book, you will find a number of styles of text that distinguish between different kinds of information. Here are some examples of these styles, and an explanation of their meaning.

Code words in text are shown as follows: "You can check it by viewing the information contained in the /proc/cpuinfo file of your Linux box."

A block of code is set as follows:

```
VM_MAD = [
  name = "vmm_kvm",
```

```
     executable = "one_vmm_exec",
     arguments = "-t 15 -r 0 kvm",
     default = "vmm_exec/vmm_exec_kvm.conf",
     type = "kvm" ]
```

When we wish to draw your attention to a particular part of a code block, t
he relevant lines or items are set in bold:

```
SRC_PATH=`arg_path $SRC`
DST_PATH=`arg_path $DST`
fix_paths
```

Any command-line input or output is written as follows:

```
$ onequota show john -f
 uid        num_vms         memory         cpu        storage
  1          0/8                           0/0            0/0              0/0
```

New terms and **important words** are shown in bold. Words that you see on the
screen, in menus or dialog boxes for example, appear in the text like this: "clicking
the **Next** button moves you to the next screen".

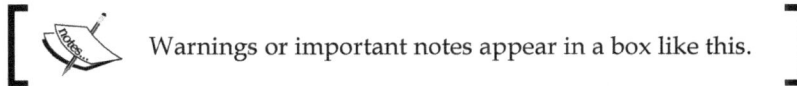

> Warnings or important notes appear in a box like this.

> Tips and tricks appear like this.

Reader feedback

Feedback from our readers is always welcome. Let us know what you think about
this book—what you liked or may have disliked. Reader feedback is important for
us to develop titles that you really get the most out of.

To send us general feedback, simply send an e-mail to feedback@packtpub.com,
and mention the book title via the subject of your message.

If there is a book that you need and would like to see us publish, please send
us a note in the **SUGGEST A TITLE** form on www.packtpub.com or e-mail
suggest@packtpub.com.

If there is a topic that you have expertise in and you are interested in either writing
or contributing to a book, see our author guide on www.packtpub.com/authors.

Customer support

Now that you are the proud owner of a Packt book, we have a number of things to help you to get the most from your purchase.

Errata

Although we have taken every care to ensure the accuracy of our content, mistakes do happen. If you find a mistake in one of our books—maybe a mistake in the text or the code—we would be grateful if you would report this to us. By doing so, you can save other readers from frustration and help us improve subsequent versions of this book. If you find any errata, please report them by visiting http://www.packtpub.com/support, selecting your book, clicking on the **errata submission form** link, and entering the details of your errata. Once your errata are verified, your submission will be accepted and the errata will be uploaded on our website, or added to any list of existing errata, under the Errata section of that title. Any existing errata can be viewed by selecting your title from http://www.packtpub.com/support.

Piracy

Piracy of copyright material on the Internet is an ongoing problem across all media. At Packt, we take the protection of our copyright and licenses very seriously. If you come across any illegal copies of our works, in any form, on the Internet, please provide us with the location address or website name immediately so that we can pursue a remedy.

Please contact us at copyright@packtpub.com with a link to the suspected pirated material.

We appreciate your help in protecting our authors, and our ability to bring you valuable content.

Questions

You can contact us at questions@packtpub.com if you are having a problem with any aspect of the book, and we will do our best to address it.

1
OpenNebula and Why it Matters?

In the last few years, many IT environments have been facing profound changes in how hardware infrastructure is designed and how software is being managed. This is thanks to what is popularly called The Cloud.

A cloud provides users with computation power, storage, and software services. It does not require knowledge of the physical location or the specific hardware configuration of where the services are running. It runs on the the same logic that applies to a power grid providing energy to different houses, where a consumer does not need to know how the power is produced or how it is delivered to the house. Services provided by a cloud can be subdivided into three main service layers, as follows:

- **Software as a Service (SaaS)**
- **Platform as a Service (PaaS)**
- **Infrastructure as a Service (IaaS)**

The Application layer is used when the user has access to a service without a need to know the physical infrastructure on which the application relies. The installation, configuration, and maintenance are completely managed by the provider itself, such as the popular Gmail service. The main advantages over legacy software are minor maintenance costs and no hardware costs at all.

The Platform layer is used when the user has access to a particular instance of an operating system or a software stack, with the desired amount of CPU power, memory, and storage available. Each instance is completely isolated from others running on the same hardware, and it is easy to scale out resources as they are needed. Take for example Google App Engine, where developers can deploy their own Python applications without the need to know how to configure a high-performance scalable stack. Also, they do not need to make long-term hardware provisioning plans to be prepared for future resource needs.

The Infrastructure layer is the most complex one. It involves different components that need to be orchestrated to be effective (for example, CPU power, memory allocation, storage, network, **Virtual Memory (VM)** instance management, and end-user access). It also allows complete outsourcing of IT infrastructure—the users pay for their effective usage, and even complex architectures can be managed without the need to have a bunch of physical systems. A typical example is Amazon EC2.

As there are situations where you cannot simply rely on external cloud providers (because of strict business policies), and you cannot afford proprietary virtualization solutions, cloud frameworks such as OpenNebula will be of great help. It will act as an effective open source toolkit, which can easily be adapted to work flawlessly even in heterogeneous environments, to build private, public, and hybrid IaaS.

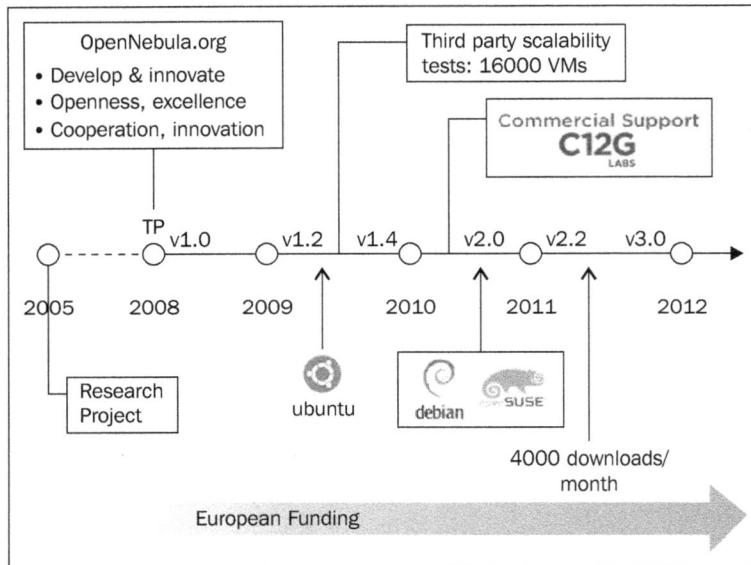

OpenNebula started as a research project by **Distributed Systems Architecture (DSA)** Research Group (http://dsa-research.org) with a few of the current features. Based in Madrid in 2005, and later released in 2008 as completely open source, it is now actively developed by the community that has grown around it. Today, OpenNebula has achieved a very neat feature set thanks also to its great modularity, which eases the integration with other solutions.

The main difference between OpenNebula and other commercial cloud solutions is that its true open source blood guarantees users complete interoperability with every existing infrastructure component already available. Thus, it avoids the vendor lock-in using common open industrial standards, such as EC2 API and **Open Cloud Computing Interface** (OCCI).

Unlike other open source alternatives, OpenNebula does not embrace a particular hypervisor. It also does not have any specific infrastructure requirements, fitting well into any pre-existing environment, storage, network, or user-management policies.

The plugin model on which OpenNebula is implemented, gave system integrators the ability to customize every aspect including virtualization, storage, information, authentication, authorization, and remote cloud services. Every action is managed by a bash script that can easily be modified or plugged with some other custom script or software written in any language and supported by your operating system.

The following diagram will help you to understand which components are involved in OpenNebula and also the level at which they operate (lower ones interact directly with the host's resources, higher ones interact with user interfaces).

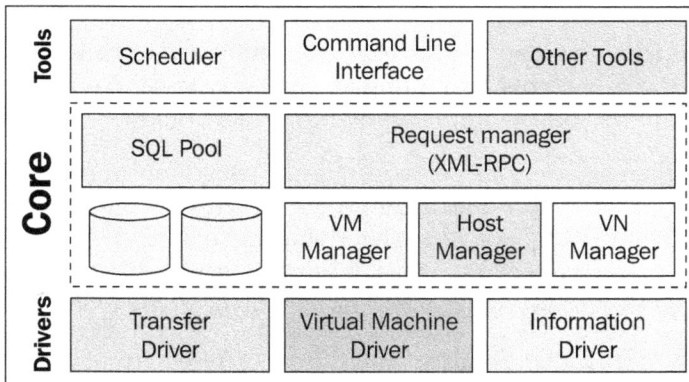

On the lowest level, there are drivers that directly talk to the underlying software OS components. They are as follows:

- **Transfer drivers**: These are used to manage the disk images on the current storage system — a shared one, such as **Network File System** (**NFS**) or **Internet Small Computer System Interface** (**iSCSI**), or on a non-shared one such as a simple copy over **Secure Shell** (**SSH**).

- **Virtual Machine drivers**: These are hypervisor-specific and they are used for managing the virtual machine instances on the current hosts.

- **Information drivers**: These are used to retrieve the current status of virtual machine instances and hosts. They are hypervisor-specific, too — they are copied and remotely executed in every physical host through SSH.

All the monitoring information collected from physical hosts and VM instances, along with the configurations of every VM, the available disk images (images catalog) and the virtual networks, is stored in a simple SQLite database or a replicated MySQL database. It can easily be retrieved or altered by custom scripts or software, depending on your infrastructure needs.

The user can take advantage of the native OpenNebula cloud API, available as Java, Ruby, and XML-RCP API. It gives access to all the functions available and permits an easy integration of custom procedures before or after the standard one.

For performance reasons, the core of OpenNebula is written in highly optimized C++ code, giving good scalability. A good example of its robustness is the CERN infrastructure prototype, initially managing 480 server hosts; in spring 2010, they reached an impressive figure of 16,000 virtual instances.

A hook system is implemented to give users the ability to execute custom scripts after a predefined set of events, providing an easy way to send e-mail notifications upon changes, or to provide a simple failover mechanism.

Security is also taken into serious consideration. Host communication takes place exclusively through secured connections protected with the SSH RSA keypairs and **Secure Socket Layer (SSL)**. Each virtual network is isolated with a firewall, **ebtables** (http://ebtables.sourceforge.net/). It works at the **Address Resolution Protocol (ARP)** level, also known as the data link layer in the OSI stack.

OpenNebula has a dedicated **Quality Assurance (QA)** team that deals with both unit and functional tests with a wide range of scenarios. This greatly reduces the number of bugs, or at least enables a greater user awareness of such bugs. There is also in use a continuous integration system, which carries on automatically building and testing every change-set pushed by OpenNebula developers, available at (http://hudson. opennebula.org/).

The OpenNebula project aims high, as its objectives are to develop the most advanced, scalable, and adaptable software toolkit with quality and stability checks for every release. It also actively searches for community support and contributes to the open source ecosystem — every bug request is analyzed by the team, and every bug found in the underlying software components is forwarded back to the respective project owner.

These kinds of operations are essential for maintaining a high profile and for attracting new people, to use and participate in the development of the project. Many third-party projects related to OpenNebula are directly hosted on the main site, emphasizing the work of every participating user, even for small contributions. The initial contributions arrived from the DSA research group (`http://dsa-research.org`) at the Universidad Complutense de Madrid, which has received funding from the European Union's Seventh Framework Programme, for the adoption of cloud solutions for scientific grid computing

Since mid-2010, OpenNebula has had official commercial support from C12G Labs, after numerous requests for support; this gave a boost in vitality to the project.

The core features

The first steps with OpenNebula are towards the realization of a private cloud. A **private** cloud does not expose any API, and every resource is used for internal purposes only. When cloud resources are available, whether exclusively or not, to third-party users through a predefined set of APIs, it is named a **public** cloud. When you use external resources to improve your cloud, or you expose to third-party users your own local resources or both, it is called a **hybrid** cloud.

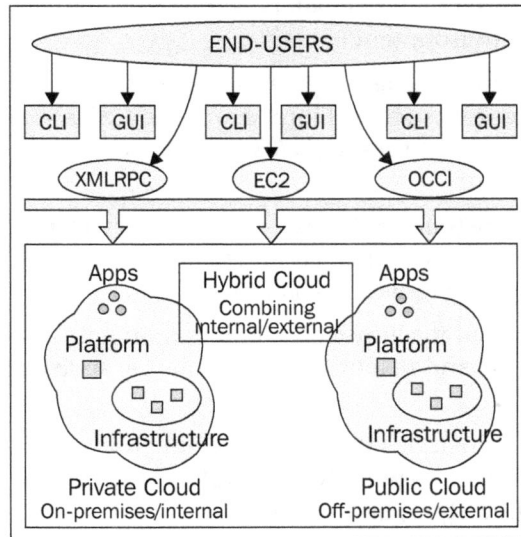

Starting with the private cloud, we can identify a set of features, as follows:

- **User management**: It is possible to configure multiple users, who will have access only to their own instances, the ability to account for used resources, and with limits enforced by quota

- **VM Image management**: Every disk image is registered and managed by a centralized image catalog

- **Virtual Network management**: It is possible to define multiple networks bonded to different physical interfaces, with either static or dynamic IP address assignment

- **Virtual Machine management**: Every machine has its own set of characteristics (for example, CPU, memory, disk storage, and virtual network) and can be launched under every available hypervisor of our cluster

- **Service management**: A group of virtual machines can be grouped for being deployed together at boot time, and every virtual machine can be configured at boot time, without the need to assign different disk images for similar machines

- **Infrastructure management**: The physical hosts can be managed alone or grouped on independent clusters, and it is useful when you have a heterogeneous environment

- **Storage management**: The support for most common storage solutions is found in data centers such as FibreChannel, iSCSI and shared storage such as **Network Attached Storage** (**NAS**) with specific support for optimal disk image management

- **Information management**: Every host and every virtual machine is actively monitored every few seconds, and it is already available in integration with standard monitoring tools such as Ganglia

- **Scheduling**: Virtual machines are deployed on host nodes following specific user requirements and resource-aware policies, such as packing, striping, or load-aware

- **User interface**: It includes the command-line tools available for managing every aspect of OpenNebula (for example, cluster status, virtual machines status, image repository, and so on)

- **Operations center**: Most of the information and tasks available from the command line are available on web interfaces browsable with any modern web browser on any operating system (even Android smartphones or tablets)

For a Hybrid cloud, which uses both local and remote resources, the two main features available are as follows:

- **Cloud-bursting**: It is the ability to add computing resources to your local infrastructure, using external resources, in order to meet peak demands or implement high-availability/disaster recovery strategies. This is essential for having a flexible and reliable infrastructure.

- **Federation**: It is the ability to combine together different clusters, dislocated in different physical positions, enabling higher levels of scalability and reliability.

For a Public cloud, the main feature is exposing the cloud resources to externals with one or more standard interfaces, such as the cloud interfaces that enable the reachability of cloud resources, in a secure way, to external users, with OCCI and EC2 standard API interfaces.

Standing on the shoulders of the giants

As in any other open source project, OpenNebula does not reinvent the wheel and makes efficient use of existing open source technologies for its foundations.

Xen

The first adopted OpenNebula hypervisor is Xen (http://www.xen.org/). It has been a unique leading open source virtualization technology for many years. Today, it is still one of the most advanced virtualization platforms, maintained by over 50 vendors, including AMD, Cisco, Dell, Fujitsu, HP, IBM, Intel, Novell, Red Hat, Samsung, and Citrix.

Besides its use as a hypervisor in OpenNebula, Xen is also used standalone by many Internet hosting companies such as Amazon EC2, Linode, and Rackspace Cloud. It was originally distributed as a Linux patchset, but is nowadays included in main GNU/Linux distributions such as SuSe, RedHat, and Debian.

Xen is composed of the following three modules:

- **Hypervisor**: The core component responsible for scheduling and executing all the virtual machine instances currently running.

- **Dom0**: It is a privileged virtual machine running the base system and having direct hardware access. It is used to manage all the other deprivileged instances.

- **DomU**: An unprivileged virtual machine running on the hypervisor and having access only to virtual resources exposed by Dom0.

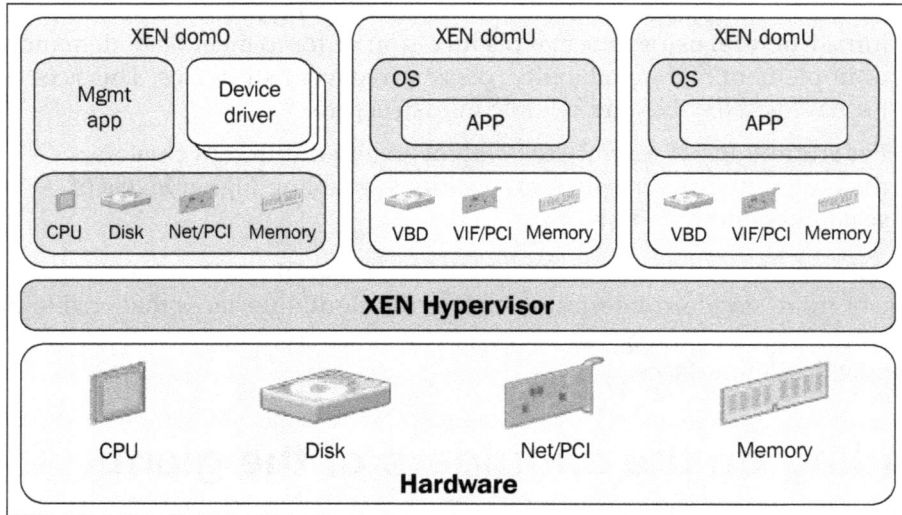

Before the introduction of specific Intel/AMD CPU support for virtualization, Xen used a form of virtualization known as **paravirtualization**, meaning that virtual machines required a modified operating system if they were to run well with negligible virtualization overhead.

Without specific Xen support it was not possible to execute arbitrary operating systems as virtual machines.

Nowadays, with the help of specific CPUs' virtualization support, the guest operating system does not need any modification to run. Hence, it is possible to run any Linux, Windows, *BSD, or Solaris version with good performance.

KVM

After the Xen dominance in the past, the **Kernel-based Virtual Machine (KVM)** has grabbed more attention from the public in recent years (http://www.linux-kvm.org/). It has been directly integrated into the mainline kernel sources from release 2.6.20 of February 2007 and has been readily available in every GNU/Linux distribution from that point on.

KVM was being initially developed by a techie start-up, **Quramnet**, bought in 2008 by RedHat, and is now actively maintained by Linux developers all around the world.

The KVM design is another interesting point, because KVM by itself is only an interface available to user space programs that can be called through the /dev/kvm special system file. For similar reasons, another open source project has been ported to support the KVM interface in gaining a full virtualization environment, QEMU.

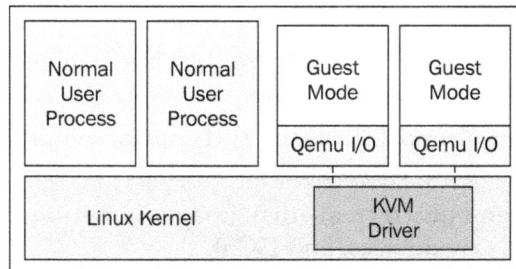

QEMU/KVM

Quick Emulator (QEMU), which can be accessed at http://wiki.qemu.org/, is a famous CPU emulator developed by Fabrice Bellard (one of the most surprising open source developers in the world). It has also laid the foundation for many other virtualization platforms, such as Xen and VirtualBox.

Over time, we have been introduced to the QEMU features. It includes support for the most common hardware devices, such as serial port, network card, PCI-ATA interface, USB controller and so on. Now, it has quickly become one of the first user space virtual machine emulators.

Thanks to the virtualization hardware support implemented by both Intel and AMD on their CPUs, the QEMU project forked in KVM to natively support those hardware extensions.

As in Xen, KVM supports paravirtualization thanks to the implementation of VirtIO devices. Instead of emulating real hardware like standard QEMU does, special devices using an API for virtual I/O result in better performances. Thus, the objective to provide a standardized set of hardware for every hypervisor is fulfilled. VirtIO devices are supported natively by recent Linux releases, and their downloadable drivers are available even for Windows. The usage of VirtIO for storage and network devices is strongly suggested.

Libvirt

Finally, the latest abstraction layer in a KVM/XEN virtualization stack is Libvirt (`http://libvirt.org/`). Libvirt is a collection of software, developed by RedHat, which provides an API interface for any major programming language that should be used for the following:

- **VM management**: To control the complete life cycle of a virtual machine, including monitoring and migration.

- **Remote machine support**: To reach and control remote hosts with a simple SSH tunnel or a more advanced SSL protocol.

- **Storage management**: To create disk images in various formats, management of LVM groups, raw devices, and iSCSI.

- **Network interfaces management**: To set up new bridges, VLANs, and bond devices. Automatically manage **iptables** for **Network Address Translation (NAT)** virtual machines.

In recent releases, `Libvirt` has included support for the major hypervisors available, becoming the de facto standard tool for managing virtual machine instances.

VMware

Finally, OpenNebula includes support for a range of VMware hypervisor versions (`http://www.vmware.com/products/datacenter-virtualization/`), that including the following:

- **VMware ESXi**: It is a free (not open source) hypervisor, the simplest of the whole family, and natively includes only a command-line interface, and runs on its own kernel (not on Linux, as Xen/KVM do). Hence, the hardware support is pretty limited or highly optimized, depending on how you see it.

- **VMware ESX**: It was the mainline product before ESXi. It includes a Java web interface, and it is available under commercial license only.

- **VMware Server**: It is a free (not open source) hypervisor, available for installation on Linux and Windows; it includes a Java web interface such as ESX, but with fewer features.

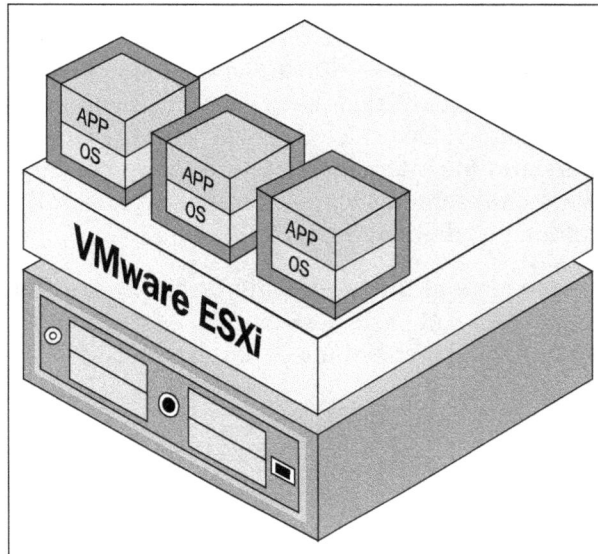

VMware hypervisors historically offer better performance and are better integrated with Windows virtual machines. However, nowadays there is practically no relevant difference from the other two open source hypervisors. Maybe, in some environments, VMware hypervisors are required due to strict software certification licenses, which are not so easy to circumvent in Enterprise software.

We will mainly take into consideration VMware ESXi because of its Xen-/KVM-like architecture than the other two VMware products considered independently. However, keep in mind that the infrastructure used by OpenNebula is common.

> Remember that VMware ESXi does not have out-of-the-box support for every kind of hardware that Xen/KVM has, thanks to the Linux kernel. Hence, you should check the online VMware compatibility guide at `http://www.vmware.com/resources/compatibility/search.php` or ask your hardware supplier before buying new hardware, otherwise you may not even be able to install it.

Summary

Now you have an overview of what the OpenNebula project is and how it fits into the cloud computing environment. Also, you have an idea about the underlying software components on which OpenNebula relies, and the components you need to know to fully understand the interactions within them. We can now focus more closely on the hardware requirements for your infrastructure and the basic operating system, and OpenNebula installation.

Get ready for a bird's-eye view of the most common hardware and software configurations, such as RAID and basic networking. At the end of the final chapter, we will have our first OpenNebula daemon running on our frontend node!

2
Building Up Your Cloud

Before you get started with the OpenNebula installation and configuration procedures, you need to get an overview about the hardware components that are used to build up the physical infrastructure that will host your cloud.

Typical cloud hardware

You need an overview of the typical hardware required for building up your cloud. However, keep in mind that the following advice will only give you an idea of the kind of hardware required. Every infrastructure will have its own requirements, so your mileage may vary.

CPU

One of the most interesting points is that there is no special hardware requirement for your cloud hosts other than having a CPU with virtualization support. You can check it by viewing the information contained in the /proc/cpuinfo file of your Linux box. You can search for the flags vmx for Intel and svm for AMD. The required command is:

```
$ egrep '(vmx|svm)' /proc/cpuinfo|wc -l
```

If the command returns 0, your CPU lacks virtualization support or you need to enable it under the BIOS setup (enabling procedures vary among hardware manufacturers; check the manual). Otherwise, it will return the number of CPU cores with basic virtualization support.

Virtualization support in CPUs is being improved continuously, and primary CPU vendors, such as Intel and AMD, have developed specific features that increase the performance in virtualized environments.

A summary table of the common CPU flags from both vendors with short descriptions is as follows:

CPU Flag	Vendor	Description
vmx	Intel	VT-X: Basic virtualization support
svm	AMD	AMD-V: Basic virtualization support
ept	Intel	VT-D: Extended Page Table: Decreased overhead for virtual memory management
npt	AMD	AMD-Vi: Nested Page Tables: Decreased overhead for virtual memory management

Before buying new hardware, you should look up the model number of your CPU on the manufacturer's site for available features. The links are as follows:

- Intel: http://ark.intel.com/

- AMD: http://products.amd.com/

If you do not know the model number of your CPU, you can still check it in the /proc/cpuinfo folder with the following command:

```
grep 'model name' /proc/cpuinfo
```

Memory

The second thing to take into consideration when planning your hardware infrastructure is the amount of memory your servers will have. It really depends on what kind of applications, and how many of their instances, will run on your cloud. Based on the memory size, we can classify them as follows:

- For small virtual machines, such as slow-traffic web applications, 256 MB per VM is sufficient.

- For medium-size machines, such as a database server that relies on a small memory cache for serving its request, 1 GB per instance is sufficient.

- For large-size virtual machines, such as those running Java application servers, 2 GB per instance is often required.

With these simple examples, you will begin to get an idea about the total amount of memory you will need. However, keep in mind that 4 GB is a good starting point, but you can easily increase it while you are trying to maintain an optimal level of balancing with the available CPU power.

In order to check for the currently available memory on your machine, execute the following command:

```
free -m
```

The `-m` parameter is used to return values with MB as the current unit of measurement. You can use the parameters `-k` or `-g` if you want values in kB or GB respectively.

Disk and RAID

If you already have experience with virtualization, you probably know that the bottleneck in such environments is often disk I/O. With a high number of concurrently running virtual machines, even with only short read and write requests, it is easy to reach the maximum **IOPS (Input/Output Operations Per Second)** supported by your storage devices.

Basic storage equipment choices could start with **Serial Advanced Technology Attachment (SATA)**-2 (7200 rpm), which has a better ratio of dollars to GB. Also, they are fast enough for CPU-bound or network-bound applications, such as frontend Java application servers, web servers, reverse proxies, and low-load databases.

As soon as you reach the SATA-2 bottleneck, you should switch to **Serial Attached SCSI (SAS)** storage devices (or equivalent) whose disk speed runs from 10k rpm up to 15k rpm. Unfortunately, you will get one-tenth lesser space availability than with SATA-2, for the same price. This kind of equipment is often required if you have high-traffic applications or large databases with thousands of queries per minute.

Nowadays, solid-state disks are becoming more affordable, and they can be a good compromise for having both speed and price. As they do not have movable read/write heads, they have zero seek time, and so they perform very well in environments with a high number of random reads/writes.

The SATA-2 hybrid drives, which have recently become available in the market, combine the features of an HDD and a **Solid-state Drive (SSD)** into one unit. They contain a standard hard disk, with a smaller SSD cache to improve the performance of frequently accessed files.

Apart from physical equipment, the most common technique used to improve the performance and reliability of disks is a **Redundant Array of Independent Disks (RAID)**. It is a set of multiple hard disks grouped as a single logical unit, with different configurations available. The various RAID levels, along with brief descriptions, are as follows:

- **RAID 0** (striping): All read and write operations are spread across all the drives, maximizing performance, but a single disk failure compromises the entire array.

- **RAID 1** (mirroring): Every disk in the array is identical to each other, providing very good reliability against disk failures and good read performances, but the write speed is comparable that of a single disk.

- **RAID 5**: At this level, a single data block is spread across *n-1* devices of the array and the *nth* device contains parity information to recalculate data lost due to a single disk failure.

- **RAID 6**: This is identical to RAID 5, but two disks are used to store parity information, which means it can tolerate the failure of two disks in a row.

- **RAID 10** (or **RAID 1+0**): This is a RAID 0 array of multiple RAID 1 mirrors. It needs an even number of disks (at least 4), can tolerate only a single disk failure in the worst case or two when lucky, and provides better performances than RAID 5.

A good starting point is using Linux software-RAID, which has been available for a long time (the early v2.2 already had software-RAID support) and has proven to be reliable even for enterprise-level use, without the additional costs of a dedicated RAID card. Every common GNU/Linux distribution contains support for configuring software-RAID during system installation.

Software-RAID provides some unique benefits. It has the ability to recover data using any common Linux distribution (even on a laptop, if you have a sufficient number of connectors), hot reconfiguration, and integrated status monitoring.

On the other hand, hardware-RAID gives the best performance. It can better handle disk failures. Sometimes, it may happen that a faulty drive slows down system booting or may crash a poor BIOS implementation, thus requiring on-site intervention.

Please beware that some vendors offer integrated RAID functionality within the system motherboard (for example, without a dedicated RAID card). These RAID implementations are called fake RAID and their use should be discouraged, because they combine the worst features of both worlds — lower performances and poor data recovery expectations on crash. Avoid them if you can.

In order to check your disk performance, you can use the hdparm utility:

```
hdparm -Tt <device>
```

In order to perform a simple read and write test on a mounted filesystem, use:

```
dd if=/dev/zero of=/mnt/volume/test.dat bs=4096 count=1M
```

The above command will write a file of 4 GB filled with zeros. When the operation gets executed, read it back with:

```
dd if=/mnt/volume/test.dat of=/dev/null bs=4096
```

Remember that to prevent the I/O cache from tricking your mind, you should write a file larger than your available memory.

Network card

The choice of network cards is highly dependent on your workload. However, it is advisable to have at least a gigabit Ethernet network or better, if you plan to use a shared storage configuration (for example, NFS, iSCSI, and AoE).

Keep in mind that Linux includes a bonding driver, which permits the bundling of several physical network devices into a bigger logical one, providing more performance or fault-tolerance.

Book conventions

Before starting with the OpenNebula installation, there are some points to be noted.

The platform of choice for this book is Ubuntu Server v10.04 (the current long-term support) due to its growing community (http://ubuntuforums.org/) and availability of documentation (https://help.ubuntu.com/), guides, and how-tos on the Internet, (such as wikis or blogs).

In order for the book to be used as a working step-by-step guide, I will provide the exact commands needed, but I will try to stay as distribution-independent as possible, so that you can use them as reference for every GNU/Linux distribution supported by OpenNebula.

You need to install sudo to allow normal administration tasks from your normal user account. Many of the configuration steps require `root` privileges, and with sudo, you do not need to switch between `root` and normal `user` accounts every now and then.

Monitoring the logfile is essential to detecting configuration problems. It would be nice to have a dedicated terminal continuously printing system log messages, such as the following command will achieve:

```
cd /var/log; sudo tail -f auth.log debug daemon.log  kern.log syslog
messages
```

The `-f` option is used to output the appended data as the file log grows. A good alternative to the standard `tail` command is `multitail`, which offers better readability when watching many different logs.

Install it by using the following command:

```
$ sudo apt-get install multitail
```

Launch it with, the following command:

```
cd /var/log; sudo multitail auth.log debug daemon.log  kern.log syslog
messages
```

I will mention more logfile names when needed, hereafter.

OpenNebula requires setting some particular shell environment variables to work, and you will see in the following chapters some commands such as the following:

```
$ echo export VAR=something >> ~/.profile
```

Altering profile scripts does not apply the changes immediately. You need to log out/in or to execute the following command:

```
$ source ~/.profile
```

Always remember to do it after executing a command that alters a profile script, or it will not work!

Basic OS installation and partitioning

We will start with the basic OS installation that can be carried on with different installation media. You can choose any of the options from the following:

- The first option is to download the installation ISO from the Ubuntu website, http://www.ubuntu.com/download/server/download.

- The standard 700 MB ISO is the second best option, but if you do not want to waste time downloading the entire ISO, you can use the mini edition available at https://help.ubuntu.com/community/Installation/ MinimalCD.

- A third option, the one I am used to, is to set up a Preboot eXecution Environment (PXE) environment to boot Ubuntu (or any other GNU/ Linux distribution installer) directly from the network, without the need to burn any CD-ROM. However, the setup is complex and is not advisable for newbie users. You will find a detailed guide for PXE configuration at https://help.ubuntu.com/community/PXEInstallServer.

Ubuntu installation is pretty straightforward and does not need any particular technical advice. You just need to follow the onscreen requests, and the default options are always good except for partitioning.

Partitioning is the act of (the art of, for most system administrators) subdividing the hard disk's available space into multiple logical units called partitions.

Each partition is used for specific purposes, such as a partition to contain operating system files, a partition for storing the users' data, and a swap partition used by the OS to manage its memory.

A lot of documentation is available for this argument, and it is under constant debate between novice and experienced system administrators. Hence, I will provide some common working setups that are not necessarily the best in every situation.

In the case of single disk availability (or if you are using hardware-RAID), you can create by manual partitioning mode the following partitions:

- A partition of 10 GB, `mountpoint /`, which can be used for the Ext4 filesystem, the general purpose and de facto standard in Linux
- A partition of 2/4/8 GB (directly proportional to your available RAM) that can be used as swap area
- A partition of the remaining space, `mountpoint /var`, that can be used as an Ext4 or XFS filesystem (the latter provides better performance when handling large files, such as disk images)

In the case of multiple disks without any hardware-RAID available, you can create RAID levels in manual partitioning mode for each disk:

- A partition of 10 GB that can be used as a physical volume for RAID
- A partition of 2/4/8 GB (directly proportional to your available RAM) that can be used as a physical volume for RAID
- A partition of the remaining space, that can be used as a physical volume for RAID

Once you have created these three partitions for every available disk, you can select **Configure Software RAID** and proceed with the creation of three different arrays, as follows:

- If you have two disks, you should create RAID 1 arrays.
- If you have three disks, you can create a RAID 1 arrays (that provides no additional space but provides high reliability).
- If you have four disks, you can create hybrid RAID create hybrid 10 arrays (that provides $n*2$ space availability, and is reliable in case of single drive failure or two drives, at the most).

Remember that is highly discouraged to use RAID 5/6 with software RAID, and also in hardware-RAID without battery backed caches, due to a common vulnerability called a write hole: in case of power loss, there is the possibility that not all drives have already physically written the last data block, and after reboot it is impossible to distinguish the old data from new at this RAID level.

Confirm the creation of the three arrays and configure each array's mountpoints similar to the creation of a single disk setup.

> After selecting the filesystem type, enable the `relatime` option to improve speed while reading files.

When the installation starts, you will be asked about the creation of a default user with sudo access. Insert `oneadmin` as the first system user; we will use it to configure and run our OpenNebula installation.

Commonly required configurations

OpenNebula requires a cluster-like setup with a single frontend, containing the management interface and a bunch of cluster nodes.

In a small infrastructure, it is OK to use the frontend node as a cluster node too. In bigger infrastructures, the frontend node could require a lot of CPU, memory, and disk resources that should be placed on a dedicated node. The following is a diagram representing an OpenNebula system:

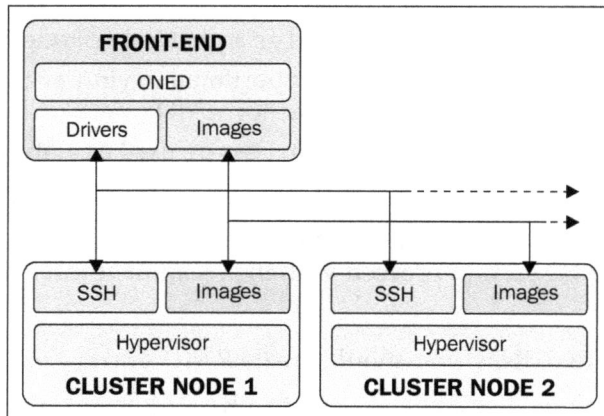

The basic components of an OpenNebula system are as follows:

- **Frontend**: This executes the OpenNebula services.
- **Hosts**: These are hypervisor-enabled nodes that will physically run the infrastructure.
- **Image Repository**: This holds the base images of the VMs.
- **Physical network**: This provides VLAN for the VMs infrastructure links (for example, storage).

Frontend software requirements

The machine that runs OpenNebula is called the frontend. OpenNebula package installation should be carried out only here!

This machine must be able to communicate with all the other hosts and have access to the network storage mounts.

OpenNebula services include the following components:

- Management daemon (oned)
- Virtual Machine scheduler (mm_sched)
- The monitoring and accounting daemon (onecctd)
- The web interface server (Sunstone)
- The cloud API servers (EC2-query and/or OCCI)

Keep in mind that these components communicate together through an XML-RPC interface and actually may be installed on different machines, for security or performance reasons.

The frontend needs to have the Ruby 1.8.7 software installed.

Host software requirements

The hosts are physical machines that will run the VMs. Hosts are managed directly by the OpenNebula daemons running on the frontend, using SSH for communication.

There is no need to install any particular OpenNebula package on the hosts, and the only software requirements for them are:

- An SSH server running with public key authentication enabled
- A hypervisor such as Xen/KVM (covered in detail in the next chapter)
- An open source programming language, Ruby 1.8.7

Image Repository and storage

OpenNebula has its own Image Repository to manage the VM image files. It has to be accessible through the frontend using any suitable technology, such as NAS, **Storage Area Network (SAN)**, direct attached storage, or any GNU/Linux distributed-network filesystem.

The OpenNebula Image Repository can work with or without shared storage between hosts, as follows:

- **With Shared Storage**: You can take full advantage of hypervisor capabilities, such as Live Migration, and speed up VM deployment time.
- **Without Shared Storage**: The VM image files will be transferred from one host to another before running or migrating the VM, and you will only be able to do cold migrations.

The Image Repository should be big enough to store all the VM images of your infrastructure. The VM can be configured to work with cloned copies of master images, when you start a VM, or to directly use an image available in the repository.

For example, a 64-core cluster will typically run around 80 VMs, and each VM will require an average of 10 GB disk space. Hence, you will approximately need 800 GB for the /var/lib/one directory. You will also want to store 10-15 master images, so approximately 200 GB for /var/lib/one/images will be needed. A 1 TB /var/lib/one directory will be sufficient for our needs.

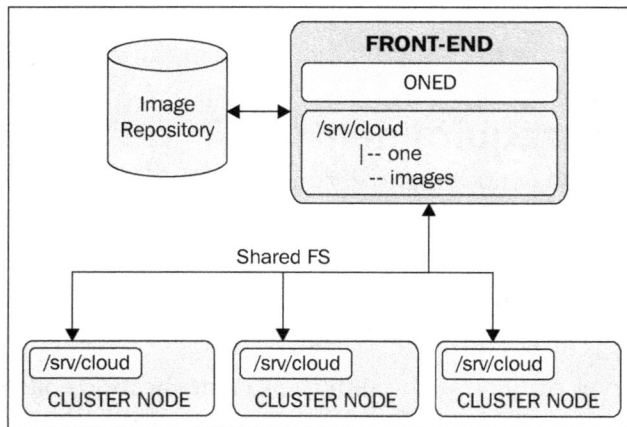

Networking

OpenNebula provides an easily adaptable and customizable network subsystem, in order to better integrate with the specific network requirements of existing datacenters.

However, hosts require the configuration of an Ethernet bridge for every physical network connected to them.

A typical host is attached to two different physical networks, one for public IP addresses and one for private LAN IP addresses.

On Ubuntu hosts, you need to install the `bridge-utils` package by using the following command:

```
$ sudo apt-get install bridge-utils
```

After the installation, you can configure the Ethernet bridges in `/etc/network/interfaces` by using the following block of code:

```
# The default loopback interface
auto lo
iface lo inet loopback
# The private LAN network
auto lan0
iface lan0 inet static
  bridge_ports eth0
  bridge_stp off
  bridge_fd 0
  address 192.168.66.97
  netmask 255.255.255.0
  gateway 192.168.66.1
  dns-nameservers 192.168.66.1
# The public (or DMZ) network
auto dmz0
iface dmz0 inet manual
bridge_stp off
  bridge_fd 0
  bridge_ports eth1
```

> A bridge does not require a configured network on the hosts (as with `dmz0`). It indeed is a good practice to not expose the hosts to external networks.

The oneadmin user

If during the frontend OS set up you did not create a dedicated OpenNebula user, you should do it now.

Create a de-privileged user with the following command:

```
$ sudo adduser –home /var/lib/one oneadmin
```

You can use whatever username you like; `oneadmin` is the common convention used for OpenNebula installations.

OpenNebula installation through sources

Directly building from sources is the most independent way to install OpenNebula and it will work on every supported platform. It can also be used if you want a self-contained installation that does not require `root` privileges (instead of a system-wide installation), if you want a customized installation of OpenNebula, or if you need to modify the OpenNebula source code (for example, by applying a custom patch).

However, this is not the recommended way for novice users, and in this case it is advisable to use distribution-specific packages for easy installation, upgrading, and removal of OpenNebula, on your frontend node.

To download the OpenNebula package:

1. Browse to the OpenNebula main site.
2. Click on the **Software** option.
3. Click on the **Download** option.

You can also download directly from `http://downloads.opennebula.org/`, and after this, select **Tarball** as **Source**.

Download the **Component, Open Nebula 3.2 tarball**

from `http://downloads.opennebula.org/`and copy it from your machine to the OpenNebula frontend host and unpack it.

Before you start building the package you need to install some required software libraries. You can find more information at the following link:

`http://opennebula.org/documentation:archives:rel3.2:build_deps`

For Ubuntu, you need to install the following libraries:

```
$ sudo apt-get install g++ libxmlrpc-c3-dev scons libsqlite3-dev
  libmysqlclient-dev libxml2-dev libssl-dev ruby
```

In order to start building the package, execute `scons`:

```
$ scons [option=value]
```

The available optional build options are:

Option	Value
sqlite_db	Path to SQLite install (if you needed, for whatever reason, to install this library in a non-standard system folder)
sqlite	**No**, if you do not want to build SQLite support
mysql	**Yes**, if you want to build MySQL support
xmlrpc	Path to xmlrpc install (if you needed, for whatever reason, to install this library in a non-standard system folder)
parsers	**Yes**, if you want to rebuild flex/bison files

The two main options when you want to build from sources would include enabling support for either SQLite or MySQL, as only one of them would be needed.

For `sqlite` support, build with:

```
$ scons
```

For `mysql` support, build with:

```
$ scons mysql=yes
```

> If you add the -j2 parameter, scons will use two threads to compile OpenNebula. Adjust to your current CPU-core availability to speed up the compilation phase.

Once building is successful, you can use the install.sh script to install OpenNebula on your Ubuntu system:

```
$ ./install.sh [options]
```

The available install.sh options are as follows:

Option	Value or function
-u	User that will run OpenNebula; defaults to user executing install.sh.
-g	Group of the user that will run OpenNebula; defaults to user executing install.sh.
-k	Keep configuration files of existing OpenNebula installation; useful when upgrading. This flag should not be set when installing OpenNebula for the first time.
-d	The target installation directory. If defined, it will specify the path for a self-contained install. If it is not defined, the installation will be performed system-wide.

Option	Value or function
-c	Only for installation of client utilities: OpenNebula CLI, OCCI and EC2 client files.
-r	Remove OpenNebula; only useful if -d was not specified, otherwise rm -rf $ONE_LOCATION would do the job.
-h	This prints installer help.

The most important switch is -d actually, which determines if you want a system-wide or self-contained install.

A system-wide install will use the common folder structure of the Unix system, for example, /etc for configuration files, /usr/bin for binaries and /usr/lib for libraries. This is also the mode you get when you install OpenNebula through pre-built binary packages available from the OpenNebula website. For completing a system-wide install, root privileges are required.

A self-contained install will copy the OpenNebula required files under a specific folder of your choice and does not require root privileges to install. It is also useful if you need to maintain different, installed versions of OpenNebula on the same system.

A good practice is to use a subfolder inside your home directory, as follows:

```
$ ./install.sh -d $HOME/one
```

You can also use a dedicated folder under /srv:

```
$ sudo mkdir /srv/cloud/one
$ sudo chown oneadmin:oneadmin /srv/cloud/one
$ ./install.sh -d /srv/cloud/one
```

As you can see from available options, scons can also be used to upgrade or uninstall OpenNebula, if you have already installed it through sources.

A great advantage of a self-contained installation is that we simply need to delete the top-level folder to uninstall that version of OpenNebula. For system-wide installs, use the -r switch to remove OpenNebula.

Ruby dependencies

Some of the OpenNebula components need specific Ruby libraries (called gems) installed on the system to run correctly. The following is a list of the Ruby libraries that are needed:

- **Ruby 1.8.7**: The main ruby interpreter
- **Sqlite3**: The SQLite3 development library
- **MySQL**: The MySQL client development library
- **Curb**: The Curb development library
- **Nokogiri**: The expat development library
- **Xmlparse**: The `libxml2` and `libxslt` development libraries

You will also need the Ruby development package in order to compile these gems.

OpenNebula provides a script to ease the installation of these gems. It is located at `/usr/share/one/install_gems` for system-wide installations, or at `path_to_opennebula/share/install_gems` for self-contained installations.

It can be executed without options to install all the available gems or for a specific one select from the following:

- `optional`: The libraries that make CLI and OCA faster
- `quota`: The quota system
- `sunstone`: The sunstone graphical interface
- `cloud`: The EC2 and OCCI interfaces
- `ozones_client`: The CLI for oZones
- `ozones_server`: The server part of oZones; both MySQL and SQLite support
- `ozones_server_sqlite`: The oZones server; only SQLite support
- `ozones_server_mysql`: The oZones server; only MySQL support
- `acct`: The accounting collector; both MySQL and SQLite support
- `acct_sqlite`: The accounting collector; only SQLite support
- `acct_mysql`: The accounting collector; only MySQL support

The tool can also be called without parameters, and all the packages will be installed.

In Ubuntu, for installing gems you need to first install `rubygems`, `ruby-dev`, and `rake`, using the following command:

```
$ sudo apt-get install rubygems libopenssl-ruby ruby-dev rake libxslt1-
dev
```

After this launch the `install_gems` script that is provided with OpenNebula:

```
$ sudo ~/one/share/install_gems
```

For system-wide installations use the following command:

```
$ sudo /usr/share/one/install_gems
```

The procedure will work for a couple of minutes. After the gems installation finishes, you will have a full-featured OpenNebula with all components installed.

OpenNebula installation through pre-built packages

The recommended way to install OpenNebula is through the distribution-specific packages.

You can download them directly from the OpenNebula website as you would do for a source **Tarball**, or you can check directly from your distribution repository.

For Ubuntu packages that are distributed by Ubuntu, you can check the available version directly at `http://packages.ubuntu.com/source/lucid/opennebula`. At the time of writing this book, Ubuntu provides only old OpenNebula packages, so the use of prebuilt packages available from the OpenNebula website is recommended.

The Ubuntu package filename will look like `opennebula_3.0.0-1_amd64.deb`.

In order to install it after downloading, use the following command:

```
$ sudo dpkg -i opennebula_3.0.0-1_amd64.deb
```

In order to fix the eventual package dependency, launch it now by using the following command:

```
$ sudo apt-get install -f -y
```

This method will install binaries, libraries, and configurations as you would do a system-wide install from source **Tarball**; remember it for following chapters!

Furthermore, depending on the availability of the Ruby libraries needed as binary packages on the distribution of your choice, you may need to execute the aforementioned `install_gems` script in order to ensure that the library dependency requirements are met.

Basic OpenNebula configuration

After the OpenNebula frontend installation, we can start to configure it using the system user we created previously, during setup (for example, `oneadmin`).

SSH public-key authentication

The first required step after installing OpenNebula on the frontend node is to configure passwordless SSH logins for the oneadmin user.

You can generate a new RSA keypair for oneadmin, with:

```
$ ssh-keygen
```

Stay with the default path option and empty passphrase.

This is required, because OpenNebula communicates with other nodes through SSH protocol and so needs to connect to all of them without the need of entering a password.

In the following chapters, we will see how to configure remote hosts to accept our newly created RSA keys for logging in.

One daemon per oneadmin user

Before starting for the first time with the OpenNebula daemon, you should configure the credentials for the default administrator user of OpenNebula.

```
$ mkdir -p ~/.one
$ echo "oneadmin:password" > ~/.one/one_auth
$ chmod 600 ~/.one/one_auth
```

The user oneadmin will be the main OpenNebula user with all privileges necessary to create new users, assign privileges to them, and manage the entire infrastructure.

Self-contained installations

If you have installed from **Source**, choosing a self-contained installation, OpenNebula sources the location where you have actually installed the file, by using an environment variable called $ONE_LOCATION.

You can set it to system-wide at /etc/profile for the oneadmin shell user, using the following command:

```
$ echo export ONE_LOCATION=$HOME/one | sudo tee -a /etc/profile.d/one
```

Otherwise, only for the oneadmin shell user (recommended if oneadmin will be the unique OpenNebula shell user), use the following command:

```
$ echo export ONE_LOCATION=$HOME/one >> ~/.profile
```

`$HOME/one` is the path where you have installed OpenNebula, corresponding to the path you passed to `install.sh`, which has the `-d` parameter.

In order to test it, log out, log in, and try:

`$ echo $ONE_LOCATION`

It should print the path to your OpenNebula installation.

Another useful trick is to add the OpenNebula `bin` folder in self-contained installations to the `$PATH` environment variable, so it is not needed to specify the full path for every OpenNebula executable:

`$ echo -e PATH="\$ONE_LOCATION/bin:\$PATH" >> ~/.profile`

Now, after logging out and logging in, you should be able to execute the `one` command simply with:

`$ one -h`

It should return the `one` command usage.

First start of oned

Now if you have correctly followed every installation step, you should be capable of executing the OpenNebula daemon, using `oneadmin` user, with the following command:

`$ one start`

If any error gets printed, OpenNebula is up and running!

Check the main `oned` process running with:

`$ ps ux | grep oned`

You can check logfiles for system-wide installs with:

`$ tail -f /var/log/one/oned.log`

For self-contained installs, use the following command:

`$ tail -f $ONE_LOCATION/var/oned.log`

Try to issue the command for listing running VMs:

`$ onevm list`

It should return an empty table with headings, such as, `id`, `user`, `group`, `name`, `stat`, `cpu`, and `mem`.

OpenNebula frontend configuration

Now that you have achieved starting the OpenNebula daemon with its default configuration, you need to change it to fit your infrastructure needs. The configuration file for the daemon is called `oned.conf`, and it is placed inside the `/etc/one` directory, for system-wide installs, and in `$ONE_LOCATION/etc`, for self-contained installs.

The process `oned` is where every OpenNebula action starts, and it is responsible for the management of hosts, virtual networks, virtual machines, users, groups, and the Image Repository.

In the first section of the configuration file, you will find these options:

- `MANAGER_TIMER`: This is the wake-up interval in seconds, for `oned` main functions.

- `HOST_MONITORING_INTERVAL`: This is the time in seconds at which host checks are performed (for example, host availability or resource availability check). A lower interval gives you more reactivity to certain events but consumes more resources (keep that in mind for large deployments).

- `HOST_PER_INTERVAL`: This is the number of hosts monitored in each interval. On very large deployments, it could be better to limit the number of hosts contacted on a single monitoring iteration.

- `VM_POLLING_INTERVAL`: This is the time in seconds during virtual machine monitoring (set to `0` to disable VM monitoring; not recommended if you care to know how healthy your running instances are).

- `VM_PER_INTERVAL`: This is the number of VMs monitored in each interval.

- `VM_DIR`: This is the path where VM images are stored in a shared-storage setup. This should be a shared directory between all hosts, for example, the NFS client `mountpoint`.

- `SCRIPTS_REMOTE_DIR`: This is the path where monitoring and VM management scripts are uploaded from the frontend to the hosts.

- `PORT`: This is the port where `oned` will listen for XML-RPC calls.

- `DB`: These are configuration attributes for the database backend.

- `VNC_BASE_PORT`: The VNC ports for each VM will be automatically mapped by adding this value to the `VM ID`.

- `DEBUG_LEVEL`: This sets the level of verbosity of the `oned.log` logfile. Possible values range from `0` (shows fatal errors) to `3` (shows verbose debug notices).

A suggested working configuration example is as follows:

```
HOST_MONITORING_INTERVAL = 20
HOST_PER_INTERVAL = 15
VM_POLLING_INTERVAL = 10
VM_PER_INTERVAL = 5
VM_DIR=/srv/nfs/images
SCRIPTS_REMOTE_DIR=/tmp/one
PORT=2633
DB = [ backend = "sqlite" ]
VNC_BASE_PORT = 5900
DEBUG_LEVEL=3
```

MySQL backend configuration

For large deployments with redundant frontends and for ease of integration with third-party software, it is often advisable to configure a MySQL backend instead of SQLite.

You can install the MySQL server on the frontend or use an existing one.

In order to install MySQL server on the Ubuntu frontend use the following command:

```
$ sudo apt-get install mysql-server
```

You will be asked for the mysql root password.

Now create a normal user for OpenNebula with access to a dedicated database:

```
$ mysql -u root -p
mysql> create database one;
mysql> CREATE USER 'one'@'localhost' IDENTIFIED BY 'onepassword';
mysql> GRANT ALL ON one.* TO 'one'@'localhost';
mysql> quit
```

In oned.conf, change the DB parameter to:

```
DB = [ backend = "mysql",
  server = "localhost",
  port = 3306,
  user = "one",
  passwd = "onepassword",
  db_name = "one" ]
```

Virtual network configuration

The second section of `oned.conf` contains two default parameters for virtual network configuration:

- `NETWORK_SIZE`: This is the default size for virtual networks (`netmask`). Available values are A, B, or C, respectively, for `/8`, `/16`, `/24` netmasks, or an integer representing the number of available hosts (such as 254 for C class networks).

- `MAC_PREFIX`: The default MAC prefix used to generate virtual network MAC addresses. Default value is fine for every install; change it only if you know what you are doing.

A working example is as follows:

```
NETWORK_SIZE = 254
MAC_PREFIX   = "02:00"
```

Image Repository configuration

The Image Repository is used to maintain an organized catalog of disk images. Users can create, clone, and delete disk images, which can contain operative systems or data. Each image can be used by several VMs simultaneously, and also be shared with other users.

- `DEFAULT_IMAGE_TYPE`: This is the default data type for virtual disks managed in the repository. The values accepted are `OS`, `CDROM`, and `DATABLOCK`. A single VM can use only one OS image and many `DATABLOCK` and `CDROM` devices.

- `DEFAULT_DEVICE_PREFIX`: This is the default device type for virtual disks managed in the repository and represents what type of emulated hardware disk controllers will be attached to the device. The values accepted are as follows:

    - `hd`: The IDE interface
    - `sd`: The SCSI interface
    - `xvd`: The Xen disk
    - `vd`: The Virtio KVM disk

A working example is as follows:

```
DEFAULT_IMAGE_TYPE    = "OS"
DEFAULT_DEVICE_PREFIX = "hd"
```

Please note that `hd` and `sd` are standards supported by every hypervisor, while `xvd` and `vd` are Xen- and KVM-specific. Hence, it should be a good idea to use them as default, only if you use hosts with Xen or KVM hypervisors.

> These are the default values used when you omit them in a specific new disk configuration. You can always reconfigure them as needed.

Information Manager driver configuration

The Information Manager drivers are used to gather information from the hosts, and they depend on the hypervisor that is currently in use. Actually, the frontend will `rsync` a few scripts through `ssh/rsync` and execute them on the remote host.

As an example, the default IM scripts executed for a KVM host are found in `/var/lib/one/remotes/im/kvm.d`, for system-wide installs, or `$ONE_LOCATION/var/remotes/im/kvm.d`, for self-contained installs. They are as follows:

- `architecture.sh`: A bash script to retrieve the host CPU architecture
- `cpu.sh`: A bash script to retrieve the host CPU model
- `kvm.rb`: A ruby script that asks through Libvirt CPU, RAM, and network usage on the current host, for all the running VMs
- `name.sh`: A bash script to retrieve the hostname of the host

You can define more than one Information Manager, if your cluster hosts have heterogeneous hypervisors in use.

Required values for each Information Manager driver are as follows:

- `name`: The name of the driver
- `executable`: The path to the Information Manager driver executable/script
- `arguments`: Passed to the executable, usually a configuration file

You will notice that, on your `oned.conf`, the KVM information driver is already enabled with the following values:

```
IM_MAD = [
    name        = "im_kvm",
    executable  = "one_im_ssh",
    arguments   = "-r 0 -t 15 kvm" ]
```

If you plan to use Xen or VMware, you should enable the corresponding Information driver, de-commenting the relative section as follows:

```
IM_MAD = [
  name        = "im_xen",
  executable  = "one_im_ssh",
  arguments   = "xen" ]
```

For VMware, it should be done as follows:

```
IM_MAD = [
  name = "im_vmware",
  executable = "one_im_sh",
  arguments   = "-t 15 -r 0 vmware" ]
```

The arguments passed are:

- -r: The number of retries when a monitored host does not respond
- -t: The number of threads, for example, the number of hosts monitored at the same time

Virtualization Manager driver configuration

Virtualization drivers are used to create, manage, and monitor VMs on the hosts. As earlier, you can enable multiple Virtualization Manager drivers, if your cluster hosts have heterogeneous hypervisors in use.

For example, the default VMM scripts executed for a KVM host are found in /var/lib/one/remotes/vmm/kvm, for system-wide installs, or in $ONE_LOCATION/var/remotes/vmm/kvm, for self-contained installs. They are as follows:

- cancel: Used to stop an already running instance
- deploy: Used to start a new instance
- migrate: Used to start a live migration between hosts
- poll: Used to retrieve stats about a single VM instance
- poll_ganglia: Used to retrieve stats from the ganglia instance
- restore: Used to resume a stopped instance
- save: Used to save a snapshot of a running instance and stop it
- shutdown: Used to initiate an instance shutdown

The required parameters for a Virtualization Manager driver are:

- `name`: The name of the driver
- `executable`: The path to the virtualization driver executable/script
- `arguments`: Passed to the executable, usually a configuration file
- `type`: The driver type; supported drivers — Xen, KVM, or XML
- `default`: The default values and configuration parameters for the driver can be an absolute path or relative to `/etc/one/`

The already enabled KVM Virtualization driver should be configured as:

```
VM_MAD = [
name = "vmm_kvm",
executable = "one_vmm_exec",
arguments = "-t 15 -r 0 kvm",
default = "vmm_exec/vmm_exec_kvm.conf",
type = "kvm" ]
```

For any other hypervisor, such as, Xen, you need to de-comment:

```
VM_MAD = [
name = "vmm_xen",
executable = "one_vmm_exec",
arguments = "-t 15 -r 0 xen",
default = "vmm_exec/vmm_exec_xen.conf",
type = "xen" ]
```

In order to support vmware hosts use the following code:

```
VM_MAD = [
name = "vmm_vmware",
executable = "one_vmm_sh",
arguments = "-t 15 -r 0 vmware",
default = "vmm_sh/vmm_sh_vmware.conf",
type = "vmware" ]
```

Arguments passed are:

- `-r`: The number of retries when a monitored host does not respond
- `-t`: The number of threads, for example, the number of hosts monitored at the same time

More details on the configuration of a hypervisor on the hosts will be discussed in the next chapter.

Transfer Manager driver configuration

Transfer Manager drivers are used to transfer, create, remove, and clone VM images. It is possible to use more than one Transfer Manager in your infrastructure, but it is usually preferred to use the same driver for every host, even on shared or non-shared storage environments.

For example, the scripts for the Transfer Manager on a shared storage environment are found in `/usr/lib/one/tm_commands/shared`, for system-wide installs, or in `$ONE_LOCATION/lib/tm_commands/shared`, for self-contained installs. The scripts used are as follows:

- `tm_clone.sh`: Used to clone an existing image when launching a new VM instance
- `tm_delete.sh`: Used to delete an image, for example, when deleting a VM instance
- `tm_ln.sh`: Used to create a `symlink` of a file, for example, when deploying a VM with a persistent disk image
- `tm_mkimage.sh`: Used to create a new disk image, for example, when initializing an empty disk as additional space during the deployment of a new VM
- `tm_mkswap.sh`: Used to create a swap disk
- `tm_mv.sh`: Used to move a file or a folder, for example, when a cloned image is saved back on the Image Repository after a shutdown

Required parameters for a Transfer Manager driver are as follows:

- `name`: The name of the driver
- `executable`: The path to the transfer driver `executable/script`
- `arguments`: Passed to the executable, usually a configuration file

The already enabled Transfer Manager for shared storage is:

```
# SHARED Transfer Manager Driver Configuration
TM_MAD = [
  name        = "tm_shared",
  executable  = "one_tm",
  arguments   = "tm_shared/tm_shared.conf" ]
```

For a non-shared storage you can enable the SSH Transfer Manager:

```
# SSH Transfer Manager Driver Configuration
TM_MAD = [
  name        = "tm_ssh",
  executable = "one_tm",
  arguments  = "tm_ssh/tm_ssh.conf" ]
```

More details on shared and non-shared storage solutions will be discussed in the following chapters.

Finally, there is a specific driver for VMware hosts, which can be configured using the following code:

```
TM_MAD = [
  name = "tm_vmware",
  executable = "one_tm",
  arguments = "tm_vmware/tm_vmware.conf" ]
```

Image Manager driver configuration

The Image Manager driver is used to manage the Image Repository storage backend. With the current release of OpenNebula, the unique driver available is a file backed repository.

For example, the scripts used to manage the Image Repository are found in `/var/lib/one/remotes/image/fs`, for system-wide installs, or in `$ONE_LOCATION/var/remotes/image/fs`, for self-contained installs. The scripts are as follows:

- `cp`: In order to copy a file or directory
- `mkfs`: In order to create a new filesystem
- `mv`: In order to move a file or directory
- `rm`: In order to remove a file or directory

Required parameters for an Image manager driver are:

- `executable`: The path to the Image Manager driver executable/script
- `arguments`: Passed to the `executable`, usually a configuration file

The already enabled and unique Image Manager driver is configured with:

```
# FS based Image Manager Driver Configuration
IMAGE_MAD = [
  executable = "one_image",
  arguments = "fs -t 15" ]
```

The argument passed is -t, which is the number of threads, for example, number of concurrent operations on the repository.

Hook system configuration

The Hook Manager is used to trigger custom scripts when a change in state in a particular resource occurs for either host or virtual machine. OpenNebula includes a bunch of useful scripts that can easily be enabled for a simple and effective fault-tolerance feature.

The main driver is already enabled with:

```
HM_MAD = [ executable = "one_hm" ]
```

The first host hook that can be enabled will automatically restart the running VM instances on a host that is no longer responding, for whatever reason.

Un-comment the HOST_HOOK you find in oned.conf, as follows:

```
HOST_HOOK = [
  name = "error",
  on = "ERROR",
  command = "ft/host_error.rb",
  arguments = "$HID -r n",
  remote = "no" ]
```

Now if a host stops responding, every VM running on it will automatically be restarted on a new host.

Another manageable situation is when the host is working correctly but, for whatever reason, a particular VM instance has crashed. You can enable the VM_HOOK de-commenting as follows:

```
VM_HOOK = [
  name = "on_failure_resubmit",
  on = "FAILED",
  command = "/usr/bin/env onevm resubmit",
  arguments = "$VMID" ]
```

Now, if a VM reaches the FAILED state, it will automatically be restarted.

Further discussion about hooks and monitoring tasks will take place in *Chapter 7, Health and Monitoring*.

Managing users and groups

Now that you have achieved a correctly running OpenNebula instance, you may need to configure multiple users, besides oneadmin.

The two commands that you use for managing OpenNebula users and groups are:

```
$ oneuser <command> [<args>] [<options>]
```
```
$ onegroup <command> [<args>] [<options>]
```

In order to see the current user list, use the following command:

```
$ oneuser list
```

In order to see the current group lists, use the following command:

```
$ onegroup list
```

You will see that the default OpenNebula groups include two main groups — oneadmin and users.

As you may have imagined, users in the oneadmin group will have full administrative privileges, while users in the users group will have access only to objects (for example, VM, images, and networks) created by themselves or to public ones.

Let us try to create a new regular user that will authenticate to OpenNebula through a password:

```
$ oneuser create john thepassword
```

The command will output the ID with which the user has been created. Now, check the user details you have just created by using the following command:

```
$ oneuser show 1
```

The following command can also be used:

```
$ oneuser show john
```

You will see relevant user data, for example, the password hash, the group to which the user belongs and the current enable/disable user status.

Local and remote user login

Please note that you do not need to create a new Unix account in the frontend for each OpenNebula user, as OpenNebula does not rely on them.

Actually, the entire log-in/log-out session is handled directly by OpenNebula through the XML-RPC interface. Thus, you can interact with OpenNebula both from another local UNIX account on the frontend and from any other remote machine with OpenNebula CLI programs available.

Enterprise users may be interested in the LDAP authentication module (`http://opennebula.org/documentation:rel3.2:ldap`) to integrate an already existing LDAP infrastructure in OpenNebula.

There are two environment variables involved in OpenNebula login that you need to configure for your active shell session — `$ONE_XMLRPC` and `$ONE_AUTH`.

In order to connect to a remote OpenNebula frontend, use the following command:

```
$ echo export ONE_XMLRPC=http://hostname:2633/RPC2 >> ~/.profile
```

It defaults to `http://localhost:2633/RPC2`, so you do not need to configure it if you are connecting from a local host.

The login credentials are searched by default in `~/.one/one_auth`, a file which contains the username and password separated by a colon:

```
$ mkdir ~/.one
$ echo john:thepassword > ~/.one/one_auth
```

You can configure a different `one_auth` file path location with:

```
$ echo export ONE_AUTH=/path/to/one_auth
```

Remember that, if you are using a self-contained install, you will need to configure `$ONE_LOCATION` and `$PATH`, as described previously in the *Self-contained installations* section.

Now, you should be able to connect with your own credentials to a running OpenNebula instance from a different UNIX account on the frontend, or from a remote host.

Creating custom groups with custom ACLs

In your environment, you may need to create more groups besides the default `oneadmin` and `users`.

In order to create a new group and assign our previously created account to it, use the following commands:

```
$ onegroup create developers
$ oneuser chgrp john developers
```

The new group has ID `100`, to differentiate the system groups from the user-defined ones.

Whenever a new group is created, two ACL rules are also created to provide a default behavior.

You can list the current ACLs with the following command:

```
$ oneacl list
```

After you execute the command a list appears like that in the following screenshot:

ID	USER	RES_VHNIUTG	RID	OPE_CDUMIPpTWY
0	@1	V - NI - T -	*	C - - - - - p - - -
1	@1	- H - - - - -	*	- - U - - - - - - -
2	@100	V - NI - T -	*	C - - - - - p - - -
3	@100	- H - - - - -	*	- - U - - - - - - -

The first column is `ID`, and it identifies each rule `ID`.

The next column is `USER`, which can be an individual user (#), group ID (@), or all users (*).

The `RES_VHNIUTG` (resources) column lists the existing resource types, as follows:

- `V`: Virtual machine instance
- `H`: Host
- `N`: Virtual Network
- `I`: Image
- `U`: User
- `T`: Template
- `G`: Group

The `RID` column stands for resource ID; it can be an individual object (#), group ID (@), or all (*) objects.

The last `OPE_CDUMIPpTWY` (operations) column lists the allowed operations, as follows:

- `C`: `CREATE` (in order to create a new resources)
- `D`: `DELETE` (in order to delete an existing resources)
- `U`: `USE` (in order to use a particular resources)

- M: MANAGE (in order to start and stop resources)
- I: INFO (in order to show commands for a resources)
- P: INFO_POOL (in order to list commands for every owner)
- p: INFO_POOL_MINE (in order to list commands for only our resources)
- T: INSTANTIATE (in order to instantiate a new resource from a template)
- W: CHOWN (in order to change an owner)
- Y: DEPLOY (in order to start an instance, migrate a virtual machine, and so on)

For example, the existing default ACL states are as follows:

- **ID 0**: The users in the group 1 (users) can create and ask pool information only for their resources (for example, VM, networks, images, and templates).
- **ID 1**: The users in the group 1 (users) can use any available host.
- **ID 2**: The users in the group 100 (developers) can create and ask pool information only for their resources (for example, VM, networks, images, and templates).
- **ID 3**: The users in the group 100 (developers) can use any available host.

There exists a set of predefined ACLs, not listed by the oneacl list, that cannot be altered but are evaluated before any other user-configured ACL. They are as follows:

- The oneadmin user or users in the oneadmin group are authorized to perform any operation.
- The owner of a resource can DELETE, USE, MANAGE, INFO, and INSTANTIATE any ACL.
- Any user can perform USE, INSTANTIATE, or INFO over a NET, IMAGE, or TEMPLATE, if the object is public and belongs to the same group as the user.

For example, imagine we want to limit users in the group developers to a particular development host machine (with 4 as ID to be replaced); delete the last ACL, using the following command:

```
$ oneacl delete 3
```

Create a new ACL, as follows:

```
oneacl create <user|rulestr> [<resource>] [<rights>]
$ oneacl create "@100 HOST/#4 USE"
```

Rights management is rather straightforward, but if you encounter problems, do not hesitate to take a look at the online API (http://opennebula.org/documentation:rel3.0:api), which includes detailed tables of the permissions that are required to run a specific command.

If you feel that managing ACL in that way is too complicated, do not worry. Later, you will see how it is simpler using the Sunstone web interface.

Quota

OpenNebula includes a basic per-user quota support, which is used to limit the resources available to every user. It is possible to define the following:

- **Default quotas**: These are applicable to every created user.
- **Per-user quotas**: These are applicable to a specific user and could be used to increase or decrease resource limits from the default quota.

Available quotas are of four types:

Quota	Unit	Meaning
cpu	Float	Total amount of CPU allowed (the exact meaning for this will be discussed in the next chapter, when describing VM templates)
memory	Megabytes	Total amount of allocated RAM
num_vms	Integer	Total number of running VMs
storage	Megabytes	Total amount of storage used

Default quotas are defined in a single text file in `etc/auth/quota.conf` and by default do not limit anything. The quotas are represented as follows:

```
:defaults:
  :cpu:
  :memory:
  :num_vms:
  :storage:
```

For example, a `quota.conf` file could be configured as follows:

```
:defaults:
  :cpu: 2
  :memory: 1024
  :num_vms: 4
  :storage: 20480
```

With those values every single user can allocate at most four virtual machines using 2.0 GHz CPU, 1 GB of memory, and 20 GB of storage space.

Instead, for per-user quotas, we can use the the `onequota` utility:

```
$ onequota set john num_vms 8
```

Now, `john` can execute twice the number of VMs as any other user.

You can check for existing per-user quotas with the following command:

```
$ onequota list
 uid  num_vms    memory      cpu  storage
   1       8           0           0         0
```

In order to see the actual usage and quota for a specific user, use:

```
$ onequota show john -f
 uid     num_vms      memory       cpu      storage
   1       0/8          0/0         0/0        0/0
```

The `-f` flag is useful if you want to see the real-time quota usage for the specified user, otherwise you will get the latest cached value, which may be out of date.

The final step for enabling quota is to enable the Auth Manager driver module, as it is disabled by default in `oned.conf`:

```
# Auth Manager Configuration
AUTH_MAD = [
    executable = "one_auth_mad",
    arguments  = "--authz quota" ]
```

> OpenNebula support for group quotas is not available yet, but it is on the roadmap for future releases.

Summary

After taking a look at the typical hardware configurations that could be used, we started to configure our basic system with networking. We created a dedicated user for OpenNebula and finally carried out our first OpenNebula installation.

Now that you have a working and well-configured OpenNebula frontend node, you should start working on the hosts by installing the base operating system and configuring hypervisors on them.

The next chapter will be about the required configuration steps for every hypervisor supported by OpenNebula.

3
Hypervisors

Now that we are done with the frontend configuration, we should take care of preparing the hosts that will run on our VMs.

A host is a server that has the ability to run virtual machines using a special software component called a hypervisor that is managed by the OpenNebula frontend.

All the hosts do not need to have homogeneous configurations, but it is possible to use different hypervisors on different GNU/Linux distributions on a single OpenNebula cluster.

Using different hypervisors in your infrastructure is not just a technical exercise but assures you greater flexibility and reliability. A few examples where having multiple hypervisors would prove to be beneficial are as follows:

- A bug in the current release of A hypervisor does not permit the installation of a virtual machine with a particular legacy OS (let's say, for example, Windows 2000 Service Pack 4), but you can execute it with B hypervisor without any problem.

- You have a production infrastructure that is running a closed source free-to-use hypervisor, and during the next year the software house developing that hypervisor will request a license payment or declare bankruptcy due to economic crisis.

The current version of OpenNebula will give you great flexibility regarding hypervisor usage since it natively supports KVM/Xen (which are open source) and VMware ESXi. In the future it will probably support both VirtualBox (Oracle) and Hyper-V (Microsoft).

Configuring hosts

The first thing to do before starting with the installation of a particular hypervisor on a host is to perform some general configuration steps. They are as follows:

1. Create a dedicated oneadmin UNIX account (which should have sudo privileges for executing particular tasks, for example, iptables/ebtables, and network hooks that we configured in the last chapter).
2. The frontend and host's hostname should be resolved by a local DNS or a shared/etc/hosts file.
3. The oneadmin on the frontend should be able to connect remotely through SSH to the oneadmin on the hosts without a password.
4. Configure the shared network bridge that will be used by VM to get the physical network.

The oneadmin account and passwordless login

Every host should have a oneadmin UNIX account that will be used by the OpenNebula frontend to connect and execute commands.

If during the operating system install you did not create it, create a oneadmin user on the host by using the following command:

```
youruser@host1 $ sudo adduser oneadmin
```

You can configure any password you like (even blank) because we are going to set up a passwordless login from the frontend:

```
oneadmin@front-end $ ssh-copy-id oneadmin@host1
```

Now if you connect from the oneadmin account on the frontend to the oneadmin account of the host, you should get the shell prompt without entering any password by using the following command:

```
oneadmin@front-end $ ssh oneadmin@host1
```

> **Uniformity of oneadmin UID number**
>
> Later, we will learn about the possible storage solutions available with OpenNebula. However, keep in mind that if we are going to set up a shared storage, we need to make sure that the UID number of the oneadmin user is homogeneous between the frontend and every other host. In other words, check that with the id command the oneadmin UID is the same both on the frontend and the hosts.

Verifying the SSH host fingerprints

The first time you connect to a remote SSH server from a particular host, the SSH client will provide you the fingerprint of the remote server and ask for your permission to continue with the following message:

```
The authenticity of host 'host01 (192.168.254.2)' can't be established.
RSA key fingerprint is 5a:65:0f:6f:21:bb:fd:6a:4a:68:cd:72:58:5c:fb:9f.
Are you sure you want to continue connecting (yes/no)?
```

Knowing the fingerprint of the remote SSH key and saving it to the local SSH client fingerprint cache (saved in ~/.ssh/known_hosts) should be good enough to prevent man-in-the-middle attacks.

For this reason, you need to connect from the oneadmin user on the frontend to every host in order to save the fingerprints of the remote hosts in the oneadmin known_hosts for the first time. Not doing this will prevent OpenNebula from connecting to the remote hosts.

In large environments, this requirement may be a slow-down when configuring new hosts. However, it is possible to bypass this operation by instructing the remote client used by OpenNebula to connect to remote hosts and not check the remote SSH key in ~/.ssh/config. The command prompt will show the following content when the operation is bypassed:

```
Host*

StrictHostKeyChecking no.
```

If you do not have a local DNS (or you cannot/do not want to set it up), you can manually manage the /etc/hosts file in every host, using the following IP addresses:

```
127.0.0.1       localhost
192.168.66.90   on-front
192.168.66.97   kvm01
192.168.66.98   xen01
192.168.66.99   esx01
```

Now you should be able to remotely connect from a node to another with your hostname using the following command:

```
$ ssh oneadmin@kvm01
```

Configuring a simple DNS with dnsmasq

If you do not have a local DNS and manually managing the plain host's file on every host does not excite you, you can try to install and configure **dnsmasq**. It is a lightweight, easy-to-configure DNS forwarder (optionally DHCP and TFTP can be provided within it) that services well to a small-scale network.

The OpenNebula frontend may be a good place to install it.

For an Ubuntu/Debian installation use the following command:

```
$ sudo apt-get install dnsmasq
```

The default configuration should be fine. You just need to make sure that /etc/resolv.conf configuration details look similar to the following:

```
# dnsmasq
nameserver 127.0.0.1
# another local DNS
nameserver 192.168.0.1
# ISP or public DNS
nameserver 208.67.220.220
nameserver 208.67.222.222
```

The /etc/hosts configuration details will look similar to the following:

```
127.0.0.1        localhost
192.168.66.90    on-front
192.168.66.97    kvm01
192.168.66.98    xen01
192.168.66.99    esx01
```

Configure any other hostname here in the hosts file on the frontend by running dnsmasq. Configure /etc/resolv.conf configuration details on the other hosts using the following code:

```
# ip where dnsmasq is installed
nameserver 192.168.0.2
```

Now you should be able to remotely connect from a node to another with your plain hostname using the following command:

```
$ ssh oneadmin@kvm01
```

When you add new hosts, simply add them at /etc/hosts on the frontend and they will automatically work on every other host, thanks to dnsmasq.

Configuring sudo

To give administrative privileges to the oneadmin account on the hosts, add it to the sudo or admin group depending on your /etc/sudoers configuration using the following code:

```
# /etc/sudoers
Defaults env_reset
root ALL=(ALL) ALL
%sudo ALL=NOPASSWD: ALL
```

With this simple sudo configuration, every user in the sudo group can execute any command with root privileges, without requiring to enter the user password before each command.

Now add the oneadmin user to the sudo group with the following command:

```
$ sudo adduser oneadmin sudo
```

> Giving full administrative privileges to the oneadmin account might be considered inappropriate for most security-focused people. However, I can assure you that if you are taking the first step with OpenNebula now, having full administrative privileges could save some headaches. This is a suggested configuration but it is not required to run OpenNebula.

Configuring network bridges

Every host should have its bridges configured with the same name. Check the following /etc/network/interfaces code as an example:

```
# The loopback network interface

auto lo
iface lo inet loopback

# The primary network interface

iface eth0 inet manual
auto lan0
iface lan0 inet static
  bridge_ports eth0
  bridge_stp off
  bridge_fd 0
  address 192.168.66.97
  netmask 255.255.255.0
  gateway 192.168.66.1
  dns-nameservers 192.168.66.1
```

You can have as many bridges as you need, bound or not bound to a physical network. By eliminating the bridge_ports parameter you get a pure virtual network for your VMs but remember that without a physical network different VMs on different hosts cannot communicate with each other.

Managing hosts in OpenNebula

For each hypervisor supported by OpenNebula, we will describe the necessary steps to install and configure it. Knowledge about them is highly recommended but it is not needed to achieve a working virtualization host. Having experience with at least one hypervisor helps a lot for better understanding of how things work (and how they don't). The suggested hypervisor for newcomers is KVM as will be outlined later, because it is easier to set up.

To use a particular host on our OpenNebula cluster, it is required to register that host in OpenNebula using the following onehost command:

```
onehost command [args] [options]
```

The command with relevant available options is as follows:

```
$ onehost create hostname im_mad vmm_mad tm_mad vnm_mad
```

The hostname is the name of the remote host, which should be managed by the current OpenNebula frontend. It should be a correctly configured domain name (try to connect to it through ssh oneadmin@hostname). The parameters present in the command are used to specify the names of the scripts that will be used to retrieve information, manage virtual machines, and transfer images to a particular host. They also depend on the hypervisor running on the host or on our configuration needs. The last parameter is used to specify a network driver to enforce traffic management (for example, iptables, ebtables, and vlan). You will learn which script should be used depending on the hypervisor, later in this chapter.

In order to delete a previously created host we use the following command:

```
$ onehost delete range|hostid_list
```

The command should be used only when you are dismissing a host. A hostid_list is a comma separated list of IDs or names of hosts, and a range is a ranged list of IDs such as 1..8.

In order to `enable` or `disable` a registered host, we bypass the monitoring and prevent the launch of new instances on the host. This could be used when you need to perform maintenance work on a host and you are migrating machines off it. The commands are as follows:

```
$ onehost enable range|hostid_list
$ onehost disable range|hostid_list
```

In order to launch an editor for changing properties of an already existing host, we use the following command. It can also be used to change an incorrect hostname.

```
$ onehost update hostid
```

We can also re-synchronize monitoring scripts on the remote hosts. This should be used if you have modified something at `/var/lib/one/remotes` or `$ONE_LOCATION/var/remotes`, or if after a `onehost create` the connection to the remote host fails for whatever reason (for example, you forgot to do the `ssh-copy-id oneadmin@host` and `ssh oneadmin@host`). The command for re-synchronization is as follows:

```
$ onehost sync
```

In order to list all the registered hosts on this frontend, use the following command:

```
$ onehost list
```

In order to show the configuration details and latest errors of a particular host, use the following command:

```
$ onehost show hostid
```

In order to show the list of registered hosts in a top-style way that is refreshed automatically every `-d` seconds, use the following command:

```
$ onehost top -d 3
```

Networking drivers

The last parameter while creating a new host is used to configure a particular network driver that will be used when launching every new VM.

The available network drivers are as follows:

- **dummy**: This is the default driver that does not enforce any particular network policy. Every VM connected on the same physical bridge will be able to freely talk to the others.

- **fw**: This automatically creates iptable rules on the host executing the VM. This driver can be used to filter different TCP/UDP ports and ICMP for every VM.

- **ebtables**: This automatically creates ebtable rules on the host to enable network isolation between different VMs running on the same bridge, but only on different /24 networks.

- **802.1Q**: This is used to enable network isolation provided through host-managed VLANs with the 802.1Q standard. A bridge will be automatically created for each OpenNebula virtual network, and a VLAN tag will be attached to all the bridge traffic. Indeed, 802.1Q-compliant network switches must be used.

- **ovswitch**: This is a complete network switching solution (for example, the VMwares vNetwork distributed vswitch). It supports VLANs, traffic filtering, QoS, and monitoring through standard interfaces (for example, NetFlow, sFlow, SPAN, and RSPAN).

- **vmware**: This is the the specific VMware driver that can be used to achieve network isolation between VMs and 802.1Q VLAN support when using ESXi hosts.

We are going to take a look only at the fw and ebtables network drivers as they are the simplest to configure and do not need any special networking hardware to use them.

Configuring the fw support

In order to use the fw networking driver, the hosts need to have the `iptables` package installed. Install it using the following command:

```
$ sudo apt-get install iptables
```

The `iptables` command is made available to the `oneadmin` user through `sudo` using the following command:

```
$ sudo visudo

oneadmin    ALL = NOPASSWD: /sbin/ifconfig
```

Adding the new sudo rule is not needed if we have configured full sudo privileges to `oneadmin` as suggested earlier.

In order to enable fw support for a particular host, we should add it using the following command:

```
$ onehost create host01 im_kvm vmm_kvm tm_shared fw
```

Configuring the ebtables support

In order to use the ebtables networking driver, we need to install the `ebtables` package on every host using the following command:

```
$ sudo apt-get install ebtables
```

In order to enable `sudo` access to `oneadmin`, if needed, use the following command:

```
$ sudo visudo
oneadmin    ALL = NOPASSWD: /sbin/ebtables
```

Although it is the most easily usable driver, as it does not require any special hardware configuration, it lacks the ability to share IPs on the same subnet amongst different VNETs (for example, if a VNET is using some leases of 192.168.0.0/24 another VNET cannot be using any available IPs in the same subnet).

In order to enable ebtables support for a particular host, we should add it using the following command:

```
$ onehost create host01 im_kvm vmm_kvm tm_shared ebtables
```

KVM installation

KVM is currently the easiest hypervisor to configure. The core module is included in the mainline Linux kernel and most distributions enable it in the generic kernels. It runs on hosts that support hardware virtualization and can virtualize almost all operating systems (`http://www.linux-kvm.org/page/Guest_Support_Status`). It is the recommended choice if you do not have experience with any other virtualization technologies.

For installing a KVM host for OpenNebula, you need to install and configure a base system plus some packages as follows:

- A kernel with `kvm-intel` or `kvm-amd` module
- A `libvirt` daemon
- A Ruby interpreter
- The `qemu-kvm` package

In order to check that your current kernel has the needed modules available, try to load it using the following command:

```
$ sudo modprobe kvm-intel
```

If you are running an AMD CPU, use the following command:

```
$ sudo modprobe kvm-amd
```

The command should not return any message. To double-check if the module has been correctly loaded, issue the following command:

```
$ lsmod|grep kvm
```

You should see the module loaded.

For the other needed packages on Ubuntu it is sufficient to install the required libvirt, Ruby, and qemu packages. Use the following command:

```
$ sudo apt-get install libvirt-bin qemu-kvm ruby
```

In order to add the oneadmin user to their groups use the following command:

```
$ sudo adduser oneadmin libvirtd
```

In order to enable live migrations, as they are directly managed by libvirt, you should enable the libvirt TCP port in /etc/default/libvirt-bin using the following code:

```
# options passed to libvirtd, add "-l" to listen on tcp
libvirtd_opts="-d -l"
```

For the /etc/libvirt/libvirtd.conf bin, use the following code:

```
# This is disabled by default, uncomment this to enable it.
listen_tcp = 1
```

As a test, add this brand new host to the OpenNebula pool from the frontend using the following command:

```
$ onehost create kvm01 im_kvm vmm_kvm tm_ssh dummy
```

In order to check whether the kvm01 host has been successfully added to OpenNebula pool use the following command:

```
$ onehost list
```

After the first monitoring loop starts, you should see something like:

ID NAME	RVM	TCPU	FCPU	ACPU	TMEM	FMEM	AMEM	STAT
0 kvm01	0	400	400	400	2.9G	2.8G	2.9G	off

If something goes wrong, you will see the string **err** on the **STAT** column. In this case, double-check that you can remotely connect without password from the oneadmin user on the frontend to the oneadmin user of kvm01 with the following command:

```
$ ssh oneadmin@kvm01
```

That is all! As you can see, KVM host configuration is pretty straightforward and does not need any special fine-tuning. The following paragraphs dealing with KVM are optional but they will improve your KVM experience.

Enabling kernel samepage merging

KSM is a Linux feature used to de-duplicate identical pages in memory. It is very useful when on the same host are running a bunch of homogeneous virtual machines with similar software versions running on them. This not only maximizes the available memory on the host but actually permits the over-committing of memory without performance penalties for swapping.

In order to check if KSM is enabled by default on the host, use the following command:

```
$ cat /sys/kernel/mm/ksm/run
```

If the resulting output of the command is 0, KSM is currently disabled. If No such file or directory is printed, the current kernel does not support KSM.

In order to enable KSM on boot, you can edit your /etc/rc.local configuration file with the following:

```
#!/bin/sh -e
echo 1 > /sys/kernel/mm/ksm/run
exit 0
```

After some minutes, you can check the effectiveness of the KSM feature by checking the pages_shared value, which should now be greater than zero. Use the following command:

```
$ cat /sys/kernel/mm/ksm/pages_shared
```

Using an updated kernel in Ubuntu Lucid

As the core module of KVM is directly included in the mainline Linux kernel, using a more recent kernel signifies getting a more recent KVM module. This will ensure that you have the latest improvements in terms of features, performance, and stability for your virtual instances. On the other hand, a recent kernel is less tested and your mileage may vary. Do not update if you are happy with the standard Lucid kernel.

However, building a newer kernel is not an easy task for a newbie. Fortunately, both Ubuntu (and Debian) provide special repositories that contain backports of recent software, namely recompiled packages from newer releases that were not originally included in the current version.

You can see the currently available backported kernel for Ubuntu Lucid at the following link, `http://packages.ubuntu.com/search?keywords=linux-image-server-lts-backport`.

In order to install a backported kernel in Ubuntu Lucid, append the following line to your `/etc/apt/sources.list` file:

```
deb http://de.archive.ubuntu.com/ubuntu/ lucid-backports main
restricted universe multiverse
```

In order to update the indexes and search for a package, use the following commands respectively:

```
$ sudo apt-get update
$ sudo apt-cache search linux-image-server-lts-backport
```

As an example, install the backported natty kernel with the following command:

```
$ sudo apt-get install linux-image-server-lts-backport-natty
```

On reboot, GRUB will automatically start the most recent kernel available.

The Xen installation

Xen has been the first open source hypervisor available on Linux. Nowadays, it is probably the most used hypervisor by many IT businesses with tons of guides and howtos available on the Web.

It supports **full virtualization** using the native CPU extensions like KVM with very similar performances (Xen uses a patched QEMU as well). It also supports the plain old **paravirtualization**, which works only on supported OS (Linux, NetBSD, FreeBSD, OpenSolaris, and Novell Netware), but the virtualization overhead is lower providing more raw performance and scalability than full virtualization.

Unfortunately Ubuntu 10.04 does not include any pre-built binary packages for Xen, but Debian 6.0 does. So our first approach to Xen will be a fast and easy installation on a Debian Squeeze using Debian packages.

Installing on Debian Squeeze through standard repositories

You should make a clean Debian Squeeze install using the same partitioning advice as stated in the previous chapter.

> **Make a stripped down installation**
>
> During the setup process, the Debian installer will ask you about the packages that should get installed along with "Standard base system". If you de-select them, you will get a working base system with size less than 200 MB occupied space!

After the base system installation, login as `root` is completed; install your required packages using the following command:

```
# apt-get install sudo openssh-server ruby xen-hypervisor-4.0-amd64
linux-image-xen-amd64 xen-qemu-dm-4.0
```

Remember that you need to create `oneadmin` user, configure sudo, DNS, and network as described earlier in this chapter.

Let us take a look inside the Debian Xen packages. They are as follows:

- **Xen-hypervisor-4.0-amd64**: This is the core of Xen. It is the kernel that will execute Dom0 and DomU instances, and boot up by GRUB before anything else. It controls the CPU and memory sharing between running instances.

- **Linux-image-xen-amd64**: This is a Linux kernel with support for Dom0 (the instance used for managing the entire Xen system) and DomU (the kernel for virtual machines).

- **Xen-qemu-dm-4.0**: This is a QEMU patch for specific Xen support. With this you can run a fully virtual machine using CPU virtualization support.

To boot the Xen system, you need to reboot your system using the newly installed Xen-enabled Linux kernel.

However, the default GRUB configuration for the first kernel is the new `linux-image-xen-amd64` without Xen hypervisor enabled. To make it the default kernel that will start the hypervisor too, you can change the priority of the first GRUB script that can autodetect the standard local kernel with the following commands:

```
$ sudo mv /etc/grub.d/10_linux /etc/grub.d/50_linux
$ sudo update-grub
```

Let's take a look at our new `/boot/grub/grub.cfg` auto-generated configuration. The code is as follows:

```
### BEGIN /etc/grub.d/20_linux_xen ###

menuentry 'Debian GNU/Linux, with Linux 2.6.32-5-xen-amd64 and XEN
4.0-amd64' --class debian --class gnu-linux --class gnu --class os
--class xen {
  insmod part_msdos
  insmod ext2
  set root='(hd0,msdos2)'
  search --no-floppy --fs-uuid --set bf1132b4-0727-4c4b-a91f-
    617913a2ad48
  echo 'Loading Linux 2.6.32-5-xen-amd64 ...'

multiboot        /boot/xen-4.0-amd64.gz placeholder
```

The parameter `multiboot` is used to load the Xen core component:

```
module  /boot/vmlinuz-2.6.32-5-xen-amd64 placeholder
  root=UUID=bf1132b4-0727-4c4b-a91f-617913a2ad48 ro  quiet
```

The first `module` parameter is used to define the kernel that will be the kernel used to boot the `Dom0` instance, where we will manage an entire Xen environment.

```
  echo 'Loading initial ramdisk ...'
  module  /boot/initrd.img-2.6.32-5-xen-amd64
```

The second `module` parameter is used to define the usage of a standard initrd image.

```
}
### END /etc/grub.d/20_linux_xen ###
```

After this section, you will actually find the standard kernel entries that can boot for an environment without a Xen instance running. It is useful for maintenance purposes or if something goes really wrong with the Xen enabled instance. The code to be used is as follows:

```
### BEGIN /etc/grub.d/25_linux ###
menuentry 'Debian GNU/Linux, with Linux 2.6.32-5-xen-amd64' --class
  debian --class gnu-linux --class gnu --class os {
```

```
insmod part_msdos
insmod ext2
set root='(hd0,msdos2)'
search --no-floppy --fs-uuid --set bf1132b4-0727-4c4b-a91f-
   617913a2ad48
echo 'Loading Linux 2.6.32-5-xen-amd64 ...'
linux   /boot/vmlinuz-2.6.32-5-xen-amd64 root=UUID=bf1132b4-0727-
   4c4b-a91f-617913a2ad48 ro  quiet
```

As you can see the Xen-enabled kernel is used but it is run standalone without the Xen core.

```
echo     'Loading initial ramdisk ...'
initrd   /boot/initrd.img-2.6.32-5-xen-amd64
}
### END /etc/grub.d/25_linux ###
```

Now if you reboot, you should get a default kernel as follows:

```
Debian GNU/Linux, with Linux 2.6.32-5-xen-amd64 and XEN 4.0-amd64
```

You should also be able to execute from `root` using the following command:

$ sudo xm dmesg

If you get a screen message as follows:

WARNING! Can't find hypervisor information in sysfs!

Error: Unable to connect to xend: No such file or directory. Is xend running?

Then you are probably running the Xen-enabled kernel, but without using Xen. Make sure that the GRUB entry you boot is the one that contains the multiboot command with `xen*.gz`.

Installing Xen through sources

If Xen is not available on your distribution or it is quite outdated, you can compile it from the upstream source **Tarball** downloadable from `http://xen.org/`.

Download it from **Products | Xen Hypervisor | Download the latest stable release** and unpack it using the following command:

$ wget http://bits.xensource.com/oss-xen/release/4.1.2/xen-4.1.2.tar.gz

tar xvf xen-*.tar.gz

On Ubuntu and Debian systems, you need to install build-essential tools and some libraries. It can be done by using the following command:

```
$ sudo apt-get install build-essential bcc bin86 gawk bridge-utils
iproute libcurl3 libcurl4-openssl-dev bzip2 module-init-tools transfig
tgif texinfo texlive-latex-base texlive-latex-recommended texlive-
fonts-extra texlive-fonts-recommended pciutils-dev mercurial build-
essential make gcc libc6-dev zlib1g-dev python python-dev python-twisted
libncurses5-dev patch libvncserver-dev libsdl-dev libjpeg62-dev iasl
libbz2-dev e2fslibs-dev git-core uuid-dev ocaml ocaml-findlib libx11-dev
bison flex xz-utils
```

If you are running an `amd64` distribution, you need gcc-multiarch support. The command is as follows:

```
$ sudo apt-get install gcc-multilib
```

If you have trouble installing Xen dependencies, always take a look at the release notes on the official Xen Wiki for the version you are trying to install (`http://wiki.xen.org/xenwiki/Xen4.1`).

While you proceed with the Xen compilation, please note that an active Internet connection is required to download the following specific patches:

```
$ cd xen-*
$ make xen
$ make tools
$ make stubdom
$ sudo make install-xen
$ sudo make install-tools PYTHON_PREFIX_ARG=
$ sudo make install-stubdom
```

Please note that specifying an empty `PYTHON_PREFIX_ARG` is currently required for a Ubuntu/Debian system; check release notes for additional information.

> **Speed up compilation**
>
> In order to speed up the compilation process, add `-j5` or the value of the running CPU cores of your system plus one.

Now enable the automatic start up of Xen services on system boot with the following commands:

```
$ sudo update-rc.d xencommons defaults 19 18

$ sudo update-rc.d xend defaults 20 21

$ sudo update-rc.d xendomains defaults 21 20

$ sudo update-rc.d xen-watchdog defaults 22 23
```

A suitable kernel with dom0 support – Debian Squeeze

Now that you have installed the Xen core and utilities, you need a Linux kernel with support for the `dom0` instance.

On Ubuntu 10.04, the most straightforward way to get a stable kernel with `dom0` support is to use the Debian Squeeze kernel (yes, it will work!).

Type the following URL into your browser: `http://packages.debian.org/ squeeze/linux-image-xen-amd64`. This is the main page of the main meta-package for Linux with Xen support. At the center of the page, you can find the latest available binary package that is:

dep: linux-image-2.6.32-5-xen-amd64

On this new page, scroll down to the **Download linux-image-2.6.32-5-xen-amd64** section.

Click on **amd64**, pick a mirror from the ones listed, and download using the following command:

```
$ wget http://ftp.de.debian.org/debian/pool/main/l/linux-2.6/linux-image-
2.6.32-5-xen-amd64_2.6.32-38_amd64.deb
```

Now download the Linux-base package (`http://packages.debian.org/squeeze/ linux-base`) that is a dependency of the Linux-image package:

```
$ wget http://ftp.de.debian.org/debian/pool/main/l/linux-2.6/linux-
base_2.6.32-38_all.deb
```

In order to fix the dependencies, install the packages through `dpkg` using the following commands:

```
$ sudo dpkg -i linux-image-*-xen-*.deb linux-base*.deb

$ sudo apt-get install -f
```

Now configure GRUB as in Debian Squeeze with the following command:

```
$ sudo mv /etc/grub.d/10_linux /etc/grub.d/50_linux
```

Append the following code to /etc/grub.d/40_custom:

```
menuentry "Xen" {
  insmod ext2
  set root='(hd0,1)'
  multiboot (hd0,1)/boot/xen.gz dummy=dummy
  module (hd0,1)/boot/vmlinuz-2.6.32-5-xen-amd64 dummy=dummy
    root=/dev/sda1 ro
  module (hd0,1)/boot/initrd.img-2.6.32-5-xen-amd64
}
```

> Carefully check the device definition (hd0,1) and the root parameter passed to vmlinuz. Also go through the already existing GRUB entries in /boot/grub/grub.cfg, otherwise the system will not boot.

You can find all the currently available options of a kernel with dom0 support for main distributions at http://wiki.xen.org/xenwiki/XenDom0Kernels.

A suitable Kernel with dom0 support – Oneiric backport

The Ubuntu 11.10 Oneiric contains a kernel with support for dom0. Even if it is for a different distribution, it is advisable to use the Debian Squeeze kernel rather than the Ubuntu Oneiric kernel on Ubuntu Lucid for stability purposes.

However, you might prefer the backported kernel as it is more recent than the Debian kernel, and it is directly installable and upgradeable through the standard Ubuntu backports repository.

In order to enable the backports repository in your /etc/apt/sources.list configuration file, use the following line:

```
deb http://de.archive.ubuntu.com/ubuntu/ lucid-backports main
restricted universe multiverse
```

In order to install the backport package of the Oneiric kernel on Lucid, use the following commands:

```
$ sudo apt-get update
$ sudo apt-get install linux-image-server-lts-backport-oneiric
```

If `apt` complains about `Package not found`, maybe the package is still in the proposed repository for testing purposes. If you want to use it, enable it in the `/etc/apt/sources.list` configuration file using the following line:

```
deb http://de.archive.ubuntu.com/ubuntu/ lucid-proposed main
restricted universe multiverse
```

> Please note that `lucid-backports` and `lucid-proposed` contain many packages. Revert back to your `/etc/apt/sources.list` file if you do not have any intention to install or upgrade the installed packages to recent (and possibly buggy) releases.

Now configure GRUB using the following command:

```
$ sudo mv /etc/grub.d/10_linux /etc/grub.d/50_linux
```

Append the following code to `/etc/grub.d/40_custom`:

```
menuentry "Xen 4 with Linux 3.x" {
  insmod ext2
  set root='(hd0,1)'
  multiboot (hd0,1)/boot/xen.gz dummy=dummy
  module (hd0,1)/boot/vmlinuz-3.0.0-13-server  dummy=dummy
    root=/dev/sda1 ro
  module (hd0,1)/boot/initrd.img-3.0.0-13-server
}
```

Checking if your current kernel has Xen support

For every kernel installed on Ubuntu and Debian distribution Xen support is available under `/boot` in a file named `config-*`, which is the configuration file used to build the kernel.

Alternatively, you can get the kernel configuration of a running kernel through `/proc/config.gz`.

The kernel options required for domU support are as follows:

```
CONFIG_PARAVIRT_GUEST
CONFIG_XEN
CONFIG_HVC_DRIVER and CONFIG_HVC_XEN
CONFIG_XEN_BLKDEV_FRONTEND
CONFIG_XEN_NETDEV_FRONTEND
CONFIG_XEN_PCIDEV_FRONTEND
CONFIG_INPUT_XEN_KBDDEV_FRONTEND
CONFIG_XEN_FBDEV_FRONTEND
CONFIG_XEN_XENBUS_FRONTEND
CONFIG_XEN_GRANT_DEV_ALLOC
CONFIG_XEN_TMEM
```

The kernel options required for dom0 support in addition to domU kernel options are as follows:

```
CONFIG_X86_IO_APIC
CONFIG_ACPI
CONFIG_PCI_XEN
CONFIG_XEN_DEV_EVTCHN
CONFIG_XENFS
CONFIG_XEN_SYS_HYPERVISOR
CONFIG_XEN_GNTDEV
CONFIG_XEN_BACKEND
CONFIG_XEN_NETDEV_BACKEND
CONFIG_XEN_BLKDEV_BACKEND
CONFIG_XEN_PCIDEV_BACKEND
```

You can check if the CONFIG options mentioned earlier are available with the following command:

```
grep CONFIG_XEN /boot/config-2.6.32-5-xen-amd64
```

Alternatively, you can also use the following command:

```
zgrep CONFIG_XEN /boot/config.gz
```

In the output from the previous command, =y means available, =m means available as a module, is not set means not available for dom0 support.

Building a custom kernel with dom0 and domU support

For v2.x Linux kernels, you should download kernel sources with Xen support from the following Git repository link:

`http://git.kernel.org/?p=linux/kernel/git/jeremy/xen.git;a=summary`

Scroll down and click on **tags | xen-2.6.32.* | snapshot**; download, unpack, and enter the following commands into the newly created directory:

```
$ tar xvf xen-*.tar.gz
$ cd xen-*
```

Now copy your actual kernel configuration file here as `.config` and run the kernel utility `oldconfig` to update the Ubuntu standard kernel configuration to the new kernel with the following commands:

```
$ cp /boot/config-2.6.32-34-server .config
$ make oldconfig
```

> You can use the `-generic` configuration file without problems too, but if you use `-server` most options are already configured as is best for server equipment.

You will be prompted about enabling some new features that were not present in the default Ubuntu kernel especially the Xen-specific ones. You should reply y if you need to include support for a particular feature, m to include it as a module, or n to exclude it.

In this situation it is okay to enable all the Xen related features except debugging ones. It can be done using the following code:

```
Paravirtualized guest support (PARAVIRT_GUEST) [Y/n/?] y
  Xen guest support (XEN) [Y/n/?] y
    Enable Xen debug and tuning parameters in debugfs (XEN_DEBUG_FS)
[N/y/?] n
    Enable Xen privileged domain support (XEN_DOM0) [N/y/?] (NEW) y
    Enable support for Xen PCI passthrough devices (XEN_PCI_PASSTHROUGH)
[N/y/?] (NEW) y
Xen PCI Frontend (XEN_PCIDEV_FRONTEND) [Y/n/m/?] (NEW) y
  Xen Watchdog support (XEN_WDT) [N/m/y/?] (NEW) y
  Xen virtual frame buffer support (XEN_FBDEV_FRONTEND) [M/n/y/?] m
Xen memory balloon driver (XEN_BALLOON) [Y/n/?] y
  Scrub pages before returning them to system (XEN_SCRUB_PAGES)
```

```
[Y/n/?] y
Xen /dev/xen/evtchn device (XEN_DEV_EVTCHN) [M/n/y/?] m
Backend driver support (XEN_BACKEND) [Y/n/?] (NEW) y
  Xen backend network device (XEN_NETDEV_BACKEND) [N/m/y/?] (NEW) y
  Block-device backend driver (XEN_BLKDEV_BACKEND) [N/m/y/?] (NEW) y
  Block-device tap backend driver (XEN_BLKDEV_TAP) [N/m/y/?] (NEW) y
  PCI-device backend driver (XEN_PCIDEV_BACKEND) [Y/n/m/?] (NEW) y
    PCI Backend Mode
    > 1. Virtual PCI (XEN_PCIDEV_BACKEND_VPCI) (NEW)
      2. Passthrough (XEN_PCIDEV_BACKEND_PASS) (NEW)
      3. Slot (XEN_PCIDEV_BACKEND_SLOT) (NEW)
    choice[1-3]: 1
    PCI Backend Debugging (XEN_PCIDEV_BE_DEBUG) [N/y] (NEW) n
Xen filesystem (XENFS) [M/n/y/?] m
Create compatibility mount point /proc/xen (XEN_COMPAT_XENFS) [Y/n/?]
y
Create xen entries under /sys/hypervisor (XEN_SYS_HYPERVISOR) [Y/n/?]
y
userspace grant access device driver (XEN_GNTDEV) [N/m/y/?] (NEW) y
xen platform pci device driver (XEN_PLATFORM_PCI) [M/n/y/?] (NEW)  m
```

Now you could start building the new kernel with default options, but maybe we can easily fine-tune other settings as well.

In order to run the kernel configuration utility, use the following command:

$ make menuconfig

After this a text-based menu will appear and we will be able to change the kernel configuration interactively.

```
.config - Linux Kernel v2.6.32.46 Configuration

                    Linux Kernel Configuration
 Arrow keys navigate the menu.  <Enter> selects submenus --->.
 Highlighted letters are hotkeys.  Pressing <Y> includes, <N>
 excludes, <M> modularizes features.  Press <Esc><Esc> to exit, <?>
 for Help, </> for Search.  Legend: [*] built-in  [ ] excluded

       General setup  --->
   [*] Enable loadable module support  --->
   -*- Enable the block layer  --->
       Processor type and features  --->
       Power management and ACPI options  --->
       Bus options (PCI etc.)  --->
       Executable file formats / Emulations  --->
   -*- Networking support  --->
       Device Drivers  --->
       Firmware Drivers  --->
       File systems  --->
       Kernel hacking  --->
       Security options  --->
   -*- Cryptographic API  --->
   [*] Virtualization  --->
       Library routines  --->

            <Select>    < Exit >    < Help >
```

A first simple but effective change is to tune our new kernel to our specific CPU model. It can be done as follows:

Click on the **Processor Type and Features | Processor Family** and change from **Generic-x86-64** to your specific CPU model (probably, Core 2/Newer Xeon or Opteron/Athelon64).

In virtualization, disable the Kernel-based Virtual Machine (KVM). As we are building for Xen we will certainly not use KVM.

1. Once you enter the **Device drivers** section you will see a lot of specific hardware drivers for which support can be disabled. This is done in order to optimize speed and save space by not building the drivers that will not be used at all.

2. If it is the first time that you recompile a kernel, or if you do not want to waste some hours figuring out why your new kernel would not boot, directly move to compilation without touching anything else.

We will use the native Debian/Ubuntu tools and use the following commands to generate a new kernel DEB package:

```
$ sudo apt-get install kernel-package fakeroot
$ make-kpkg clean
$ CONCURRENCY_LEVEL=5 fakeroot make-kpkg --initrd --append-to-version=-myversion kernel-image kernel-headers
```

> The make-kpkg command with CONCURRENCY_LEVEL=5 gives the same results as that of the make-j5 command.

If anything goes wrong, you should install our shiny new kernel package from where you have downloaded the original source package and use the following commands:

```
$ sudo dpkg -i ../linux-image-2.6.*-myxen_2.6.*-myxen-10.00.Custom_amd64.deb
$ sudo update-initramfs -c -k 2.6.32.46-myxen
```

On systems different than Debian and Ubuntu, you need to use the standard way to install the kernel, which can be done by using the following commands:

```
$ make bzImage
$ make modules
$ sudo make modules_install
$ sudo cp -a .config /boot/config-2.6.32.46-myxen
$ sudo cp -a System.map /boot/System.map-2.6.32.46-myxen
$ sudo cp -a arch/x86/boot/bzImage /boot/vmlinuz-2.6.32.46-myxen
$ sudo mkinitrd -f /boot/initrd.img-2.6.32.46-myxen version
```

> Please consult your distribution manual about kernel compilation for more information.

Now you can configure GRUB as usual by using the following command:

```
$ sudo mv /etc/grub.d/10_linux /etc/grub.d/50_linux
```

Append the following code to `/etc/grub.d/40_custom` file:

```
menuentry "Xen 4 with custom Linux 2.6.32" {
  insmod ext2
  set root='(hd0,1)'
  multiboot (hd0,1)/boot/xen.gz dummy=dummy
  module (hd0,1)/boot/vmlinuz-2.6.32.46-myxen  dummy=dummy
    root=/dev/sda1 ro
  module (hd0,1)/boot/initrd.img-2.6.32.46-myxen
}
```

Autoloading necessary modules

Depending on your kernel it may be necessary to manually add to the `/etc/modules` configuration file a reference to a bunch of Xen modules, one per line, so the kernel will auto-load them on system start up. The Xen Dom0 modules are as follows:

* xen-evtchn
* xen-gntdev
* xen-netback
* xen-blkback
* xenfs
* blktap

Now you should be able to install Xen in every environment that you face.

Onehost create for Xen hosts

After we have finished configuring our Xen host, we should let it join the OpenNebula host pool in a similar way as we did with KVM. Use the following command:

```
onehost create xen01 im_xen vmm_xen tm_ssh dummy
```

> The last parameter depends on the storage system used in OpenNebula and will be discussed in the next chapter.

Installing VMware ESXi

The third hypervisor choice on our OpenNebula environment could be one of the VMware virtualization products such as VMware ESXi. It is a lightweight bare-metal hypervisor given for free (but it is not open source like KVM and Xen, thus requiring a free registration to obtain a serial number).

Although the current VMware driver supports VMware ESX and VMware Server products, here we will cover only ESXi as it is simpler to configure and because the other two are becoming legacy software. VMware itself advices its customers to migrate existing deployments to VMware ESXi.

The installation on the host is really simple, you just need to download and burn the ISO available from the link `https://www.vmware.com/tryvmware/?p=free-esxi5&lp=default&ext=1`, boot from your CD/DVD, and follow the Easy Wizard for the installation.

During the installation, your hardware is checked to make sure it meets the minimum requirements for ESXi, which are as follows:

- A 64 bit CPU with VT-X or AMD-V available
- A memory space of 2 GB
- A supported RAID or AHCI/SATA Controller

> Before buying your hardware, please remember to check the VMware Certified Compatibility Guides at `https://www.vmware.com/go/hcl` or the Community-Supported Hardware and Software at `http://communities.vmware.com/community/vmtn/general/cshwsw`.

If you are performing a fresh install, your local storage will be automatically wiped and repartitioned. Hence, make a backup of your existing data, if any.

Required software on the frontend

To be able to manage VMware hypervisors, you need the following software components on the frontend:

- A libvirt built with the `with-esx` flag used by the OpenNebula VMware drivers
- The VMware driver add-ons available as a separate download from the OpenNebula site

Installing Libvirt with ESX support

Most distributions do not include the support for VMware hypervisor in the Libvirt package, so we should probably recompile it.

Browse to `http://libvirt.org/` and click on **Downloads | Official Releases | HTTP Server** and download the latest `libvirt-x.x.x.tar.gz` package. Unpack it on your frontend and install some required build-dependencies using the following command:

```
$ sudo apt-get install build-essential gnutls-dev libdevmapper-dev
python-dev libcurl4-gnutls-dev libnl-dev
```

In order to configure, build, and install use the following commands:

```
$ ./configure –with-esx
$ make
$ sudo make install
$ sudo ldconfig
```

> Libvirt should not be started as a daemon but it will be called directly by the VMware management scripts.

Adding a oneadmin user with privileges

A new user with administration privileges needs to be created in ESXi with the same UID and username as the `oneadmin` user of the OpenNebula frontend. A matching UID is required because of the storage limitations in ESXi that will be detailed in the next chapter.

For creating the new user, you need to download the VMware VI client on a Windows machine: type-in into your browser the IP address of your ESXi node and click on **Download vSphere client**.

After the download and install, connect to your ESXi node:

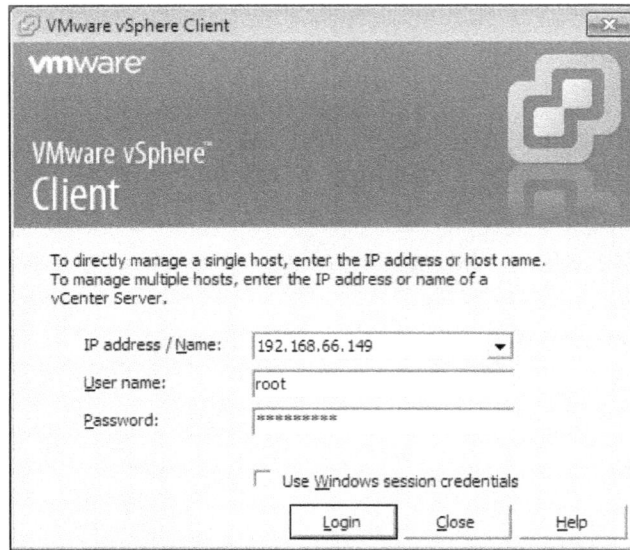

1. Click on the **Local Users & Groups** tab.

2. Right-click on the list and click on **Add**.

3. Insert new user information for the following tabs, **User**: oneadmin, **UID**: 1000 (check the ID of oneadmin with the command id on the frontend), and **group membership**: root.

4. Switch to the **Permission** tab and right-click on **Add Permission**.

5. Add the oneadmin user with **Assigned Role** as **Administrator** and confirm by clicking on **OK**.

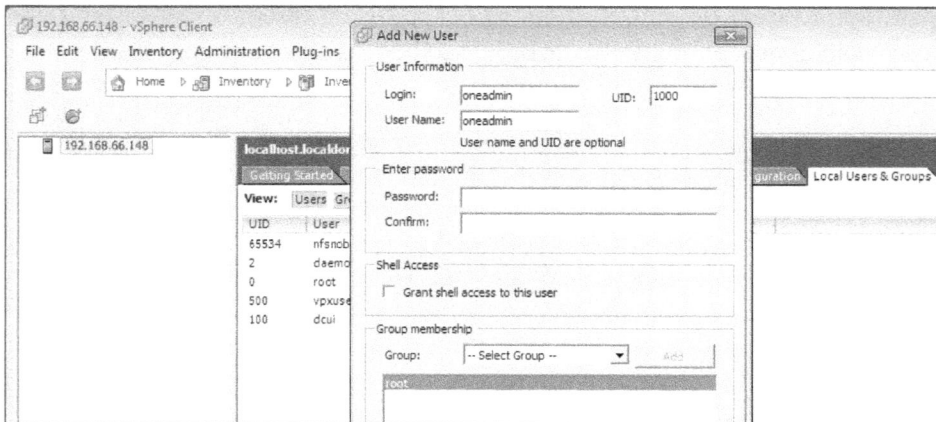

Now you need to configure the user credentials in the `vmware` configuration files inside the OpenNebula `/etc` folder:

```
# Libvirt configuration
:libvirt_uri: "'esx://@HOST@/?no_verify=1&auto_answer=1'"
# Username and password of the VMware hypervisor
:username: "oneadmin"
:password:
```

Now you can register your ESXi host on your OpenNebula frontend with the following command:

```
$ onehost create esx01 im_vmware vmm_vmware tm_vmware dummy
```

The dummy driver for networking is the simplest choice with VMware. Through the vSphere Client, you must manually configure at least one vSphere standard switch through the **Configuration** tab after clicking on the **Networking** tab.

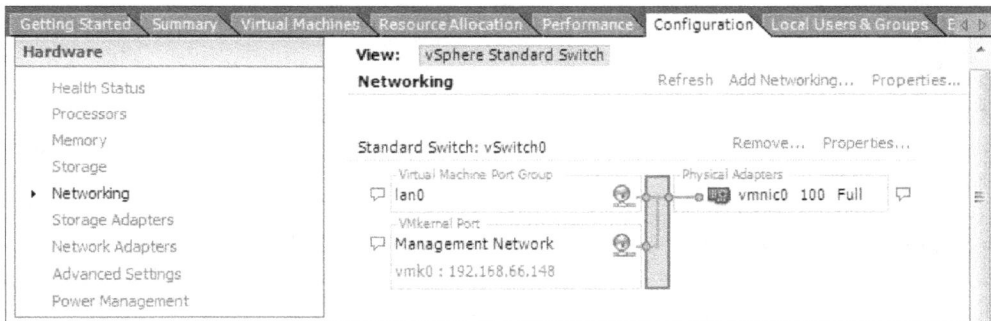

The name of the network should be used in the same way as we will use the standard KVM/Xen host bridge name (for example, `lan0`) when we see how to configure virtual networks. Remember to update it by clicking on the **Properties** on the right of **Standard Switch: vSwitch0**, selecting the default **Virtual Machine Port Group**, clicking on the **Edit** button and finally updating the **Network Label**.

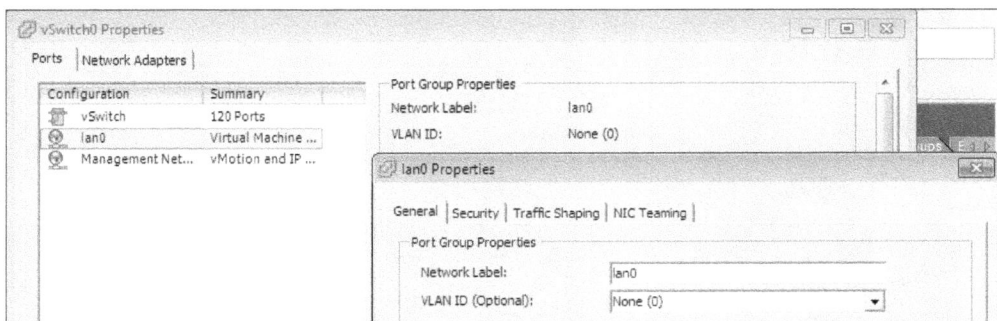

An alternative, for advanced network setups including VLAN support, is available since the OpenNebula 3.2 release. The `vmware` network driver can dynamically allocate vSphere standard switches and group each VM in different VLANs. However, network switches with IEEE 802.1Q support are needed and will not be covered in this chapter. For additional information, please refer to the documentation page at the link, `http://opennebula.org/documentation:rel3.2:evmwareg`.

Wait for the next monitoring cycle to start and afterwards check the correctness of the procedure with the following command:

```
$ onehost list
```

If for whatever reason the first probe is unsuccessful and host resources are not reported correctly, try to connect from the frontend to the `esx` host with the following command:

```
$ virsh -c esx://esx01/?no_verify=1
```

Summary

In this chapter, we have learned how to install and configure all the available hypervisors supported by OpenNebula on our host machines, and seen how much is ready to be used by every hypervisor. KVM is a lot easier to set up than Xen as it is integrated in the mainline Linux kernel. However, Xen may be a good choice for a skilled system integrator who is already accustomed to it. ESXi hosts are easier to set up too, but the lack of freedom can be a problem when working on a heterogeneous environment. In the next chapter, we will discuss in detail the storage solutions available with OpenNebula and how we can integrate third-party storage solutions in our infrastructure.

4
Choosing Your Storage Carefully

After having introduced and carefully described every hypervisor supported by OpenNebula, in this chapter, we will discuss another key component of your cloud infrastructure, The Storage.

Besides the database used by the OpenNebula daemon, separate storage is required for running virtual machines and to maintain an Image Repository that is used to bootstrap the newly created virtual machines.

The default folder used for storage is /var/lib/one or $ONE_LOCATION/var. A separate folder will be created for each configured virtual machine. The folder name is an incremental ID, which will contain the automatically generated configuration files for the current hypervisor and images that belong to the current virtual machine.

The images of the Image Repository are saved in a separate folder, named images.

Along with raw CPU power and available memory, the type and quality of your storage will affect the speed of deployment, migration, and day-to-day operations of your virtual instances.

The two main types of storage can be classified into:

- Non-shared storage
- Shared storage

Non-shared storage is the simplest configuration as it does not require any additional hardware or software requirements. The unique bottleneck will be because of single disk or array performance in every host. On the other hand, the first deployments will be slower as images will be copied entirely from one host to another through a file transfer protocol before launch (for example, from the frontend to a KVM host through a secure copy command in Linux). This applies to migration and shutdown procedures too.

Shared storage is a way to enable direct access from every host to the Image Repository. It also gives you the ability for near-instant deployment, migration, and shutdown procedures for every virtual instance. A unique drawback is that the storage can easily become a bottleneck if virtual instances perform disk-intensive operations or require low-latency responses, for example, high-traffic databases. The most common choice for having shared storage is using NFS (through NAS or SAN). Later in this chapter we will discuss the usage of distributed network filesystems too.

OpenNebula bundles two simple but effective transfer managers, which are as follows:

- `tm_ssh`: The transfer manager for non-shared storage
- `tm_shared`: The transfer manager for shared storage

How a transfer manager works

A transfer manager is composed of a set of scripts, which get executed for a particular action by the frontend using two parameters, SRC and DST. These two parameters have the form `host:path`.

In the following diagram, you will see how OpenNebula requests the required storage operations during a VM launch, how the transfer manager handles them and acts on the Image Repository and host's storage accordingly.

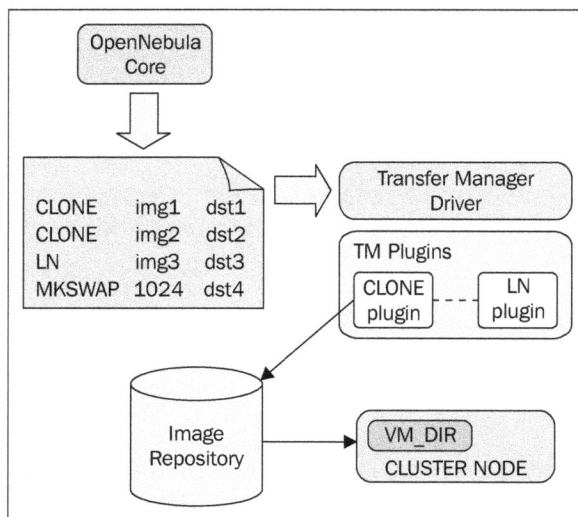

The available actions of a transfer manager are as follows:

- **CLONE**: This is used to create a copy of the image from SRC to DST when deploying a virtual machine without persistent storage from an Image Repository.

- **LN**: This is used to create a symbolic link in DST that points to SRC when deploying a virtual machine with persistent storage from an Image Repository.

- **MKSWAP**: This is used to generate a swap image in DST; its size is specified in SRC in MBs.

- **MKIMAGE**: This is used to create a disk image in DST and populate it with the files inside the SRC directory.

- **DELETE**: This is used to delete the SRC file or directory.

- **MV**: This is used to move the SRC file to the DST file or directory.

Each action script should exit with code 0 on success and any other value on failure, as the frontend needs to know the result of each submitted command. Anything echoed on STDOUT in the script will get logged in the virtual machine logfile.

Each transfer manager can rely on a small helper script named tm_common.sh, which provides some functions that are useful in every transfer manager script. The functions available are as follows:

- get_vmdir: Used to check and export the shared directory from $VMDIR for running a VM as declared inside oned.conf

- fix_paths: Used to check and remove any useless slashes from the pathnames and return a local or remote path depending on the shared or non-shared configuration for the variables SRC_PATH and DST_PATH (containing the dirname value of SRC and DST)

- log_debug: Used to print a message in the logs during the transfer manager script execution

- log_error: Used to used to print an error message in the logs during the transfer manager script execution

- exec_and_log: Used to execute a command and log the output

- timeout_exec_and_log: Used to execute a command, log the output, and eventually kill it after the expiration period that is specified in seconds

Now we can start analyzing the two different transfer managers available in OpenNebula.

Non-shared storage through SSH/CP

Without shared storage between frontend and hosts when a VM is deployed OpenNebula copies the image files from the Image Repository to the folder specified as VM_DIR in the oned.conf on the remote host.

For this reason, make sure that you can connect remotely through SSH without providing any password from the frontend to every host (instructions on how to set up passwordless SSH login was given in the previous chapter).

When creating a new host, you should use the onehost command with tm_ssh as the third parameter, as shown in the following command:

```
onehost create host01 im_hypervisor vmm_hypervisor tm_ssh dummy
```

> **Non-shared storage: common use cases**
>
> Without a shared filesystem you cannot achieve real high availability. If a node goes down because of a physical failure (for example, power supply or disk controller) the virtual instances that were running on it cannot be directly restarted on another host. It requires a fresh redeployment from the original disk images saved in the frontend Image Repository.
>
> For this reason, never deploy stateful virtual instances (for example, a database) on a host with non-shared storage. Instead, use them for stateless virtual instances, such as for Java application servers, HTTP load balancers, or proxy servers that can be instantly redeployed elsewhere with the original disk image.

Non-shared storage scripts

For better understanding, and if you need to extend or implement a new non-shared transfer manager, for example the tm_clone script uses the following code:

```
#!/bin/bash
SRC=$1
DST=$2
```

The two variables contain the source and destination files in the form host:path (for example, frontend:/srv/vms/images/vm.img and kvm01:/srv/vms/deploy/100/images/vm.img).

```
if [ -z "${ONE_LOCATION}" ]; then
  TMCOMMON=/usr/lib/one/mads/tm_common.sh
```

```
    else
        TMCOMMON=$ONE_LOCATION/lib/mads/tm_common.sh
    fi
    . $TMCOMMON
```

This is present in every transfer manager action script and is used to import the common function script.

```
SRC_PATH=`arg_path $SRC`
DST_PATH=`arg_path $DST`
SRC_HOST=`arg_host $SRC`
DST_HOST=`arg_host $DST`
```

The $SRC and $DST variables get split into their respective host and path parts.

```
log_debug "$1 $2"
log_debug "DST: $DST_PATH"
DST_DIR=`dirname $DST_PATH`
log "Creating directory $DST_DIR"

exec_and_log "$SSH $DST_HOST mkdir -p $DST_DIR" \
    "Error creating directory $DST_DIR"
```

In order to connect to the remote host through SSH and to create the directory that will contain the cloned image, use the following code:

```
case $SRC in
http://*)
    log "Downloading $SRC"

    exec_and_log "$SSH $DST_HOST $WGET -O $DST_PATH $SRC" \
        "Error downloading $SRC"
```

If $SRC is a HTTP URI, download it through wget on the remote destination.

```
*)
    log "Cloning $SRC"
    exec_and_log "$SCP $SRC $DST" \
        "Error copying $SRC to $DST"
esac
```

If it is a standard file, copy it through SCP from $SRC to the $DST file or directory.

```
exec_and_log "$SSH $DST_HOST chmod a+rw $DST_PATH"
```

Make sure that the transferred file is readable and writable.

Shared storage through NFS on the frontend

A typical and simple setup consists of installing and configuring an NFS server on the frontend. After this, mount a common directory on every host as configured by the VM_DIR parameter in oned.conf, or directly at /var/lib/one or $ONE_LOCATION/var (which is the default location of VM_DIR).

In order to install the NFS server on the frontend use the following command:

```
$ sudo apt-get install nfs-kernel-server
```

Also configure the /etc/exports file using the following code:

```
/var/lib/one
    192.168.66.0/24(rw,async,no_subtree_check,no_root_squash)
```

Now take a look at the options that are used. They are as follows:

- rw: This is used by the clients to read and write on the storage.

- async: This is used to yield better performance at the cost of possible data corruption if the server reboots while keeping unwritten data and/ or metadata in its caches. As our files will be disk images that probably contain a journaled filesystem, we should not worry too much. Use sync if performance is sufficient for you or if you are paranoid (but you need to make backups anyway).

- no_subtree_check: This is used to slightly speed things up by removing additional checks that file exists made while running. Use a subtree_check if you do not trust your network clients.

- no_root_squash: This is required in order to let clients operate with root privileges on the storage. This is required as many hypervisors need to change owners or permissions on disk images before starting to use them.

Remember to reload the NFS service when you finish configuring exports with the following command:

```
$ sudo /etc/init.d/nfs-kernel-server reload
```

Then on the hosts, install the NFS client with the following command:

```
sudo apt-get install nfs-common
```

In order to configure the /etc/fstab for auto-mounting on boot, use the following command:

```
on-front:/var/lib/one /var/lib/one nfs udp,_netdev 0 0
```

The parameters of the command and a description of them are as follows:

- _netdev: This is used to prevent the system from attempting to mount the filesystem until the network is available at boot time.
- udp: Using user datagram protocol as a transport protocol provides better throughput in stable local networks. Consider using tcp in high-load environments or if you get poor performances with udp.

After this, mount it using the following commands:

```
sudo mkdir -p /var/lib/one
sudo mount /var/lib/one
```

If everything is OK on every host you should see content similar to the /var/lib/one folder of the host on the frontend.

In order to create a new host, you should use the onehost command with tm_shared as the third parameter. This is shown in the following command:

```
onehost create host01 im_hypervisor vmm_hypervisor tm_shared dummy
```

Shared storage through NFS using NAS/SAN

In larger environments, you may prefer to use dedicated **Network Attached Storage (NAS)** or a **Storage Area Network (SAN)** to host virtual images

A reasonable requirement is a Gigabit network between the storage, frontend, and hosts.

Most network storages support NFS that need to be configured both on the frontend and the hosts.

Please be aware that if you are using a 10/100 or even a gigabit Ethernet network, you may be interested in Ethernet bonding that can be used to aggregate multiple Ethernet channels together, to form a single channel. This can be used to provide increased network performance or high availability. Check for the ifenslave system utility and the support of your network switches for the different available bonding modes.

In order to install the NFS client use the following command:

```
$ sudo apt-get install nfs-common
```

In order to configure the `/etc/fstab` file for auto-mounting use the following command:

```
nas:/mnt/whatever /var/lib/one nfs _netdev 0 0
```

Before mounting on the frontend, we need to transfer all the local content present at `/var/lib/one` to the NFS share.

Make sure that the `oned` daemon is stopped by using the following command:

```
$ one stop
```

Move the existing folder away and create the new empty mountpoint by using the following commands:

```
$ sudo mv /var/lib/one /var/lib/one_old
$ sudomkdir /var/lib/one
$ sudo chown oneadmin: /var/lib/one
```

In order to mount the NFS share use the following command:

```
$ sudo mount nas:/mnt/whatever /var/lib/one
```

In order to copy everything from the local directory to the NAS, use the following command:

```
$ sudo rsync -a /var/lib/one_old/ /var/lib/one/
```

In order to start `one` again use the following command:

```
$ one start
```

Now mount the NFS share on all the remaining hosts using the following command:

```
$ sudo mount /var/lib/one
```

If everything is OK, on every host you should see content similar to that of the `/var/lib/one` folder on both the frontend and host.

When creating a new host, you should use the `onehost` command with `tm_shared` as the third parameter using the following command:

```
onehost create host01 im_hypervisor vmm_hypervisor tm_shared dummy
```

Shared storage scripts

Take an example of the `tm_clone` script for the shared storage transfer manager:

```
#!/bin/bash
SRC=$1
```

```
DST=$2
if [ -z "${ONE_LOCATION}" ]; then
  TMCOMMON=/usr/lib/one/mads/tm_common.sh
  else
    TMCOMMON=$ONE_LOCATION/lib/mads/tm_common.sh
fi
. $TMCOMMON
get_vmdir
```

As we are on a shared storage environment now, we need to acquire the correct
VMDIR parameter as specified in the main configuration file that will be used later
by fix_paths.

```
SRC_PATH=`arg_path $SRC`
DST_PATH=`arg_path $DST`
fix_paths
```

This time, we do not need to prepare source and destination hostnames but only the
two paths.

```
log_debug "$1 $2"
log_debug "DST: $DST_PATH"
DST_DIR=`dirname $DST_PATH`
log "Creating directory $DST_DIR"
exec_and_log "mkdir -p $DST_DIR"
exec_and_log "chmod a+w $DST_DIR"
```

In order to create the new directory and use the chmod command, which is used to
change permissions on files and folder.

```
case $SRC in
http://*)
    log "Downloading $SRC"
    exec_and_log "$WGET -O $DST_PATH $SRC" \
        "Error downloading $SRC"
    ;;
*)
    log "Cloning $SRC_PATH"
    exec_and_log "cp -r $SRC_PATH $DST_PATH" \
        "Error copying $SRC to $DST"
    ;;
esac
exec_and_log "chmod a+rw $DST_PATH"
```

Copy the disk image using the standard cp utility from source to destination directory.

Shared storage through distributed file systems

A distributed file system allows clients to access files present on multiple hosts through the network. As with NFS, the clients do not have direct access to the underlying block storage but interact with folders and files over the network using a protocol depending on the distributed filesystem in use.

The main advantages of using distributed file systems are as follows:

- Fault-tolerance: The data is accessible to clients even after a specific number of host crashes. This is achieved by transparently replicating data across different nodes, as defined during their configuration phase. More copies mean more fault-tolerance.
- Scalability: It is usually easy to hot-add new nodes to an active distributed filesystem, enabling you to increase tolerance or available storage space.
- Avoiding vendor lock-in: It uses open standards so that you do not have to place your precious data on third-party storage solutions.
- Affordability: It uses commodity hardware, which is easily replaceable when needed.

However, a few drawbacks are present as well. They are as follows:

- Increased complexity: Distributed file systems introduce an additional layer to your infrastructure (more software components mean more possible bugs you can face).
- Performance: Owing to the manner in which distributed file systems work, high loads and network latency actually kill performance especially when dealing with random writes (so, do not expect miracles from them).
- Clients: Many distributed file systems require the usage of a native FUSE-based client that is available only on the supported platform (usually Linux, sometimes *BSD, rarely Windows). However, some of these provide a fall-back client access with NFS, usually limiting high-availability and performance but permitting data access from legacy environments.

In this chapter we will cover the installation and configuration of two different open source distributed filesystems, GlusterFS and MooseFS. Each has its strengths and weaknesses, which we will analyze later.

From the OpenNebula point of view, using a distributed file system is very similar to using NFS and so it does not have any additional requirement than using `tm_shared`.

Shared storage through GlusterFS

GlusterFS is an open source distributed file system developed by Gluster Inc in 2005 (http://www.gluster.com) and it has been recently acquired by Red Hat in late 2011 (http://www.redhat.com/promo/storage/press-release.html).

GlusterFS features a completely decentralized architecture meaning that there is not a single point of failure and this is great for a cloud infrastructure.

In small and medium infrastructures, the GlusterFS server components could be installed directly on the OpenNebula hosts along with the hypervisor. Instead, for large deployments, it is advisable to install GlusterFS on dedicated machines and perhaps arrange them in a SAN.

GlusterFS hardware requirements

Before installing the GlusterFS, verify that your system matches the following minimum requirements:

- CPU: An AMD 64 CPU (because i686 is not tested by Gluster developers)
- Storage: The storage can be either local or shared as follows:
    - Direct attached storage, such as SATA, SAS, or Fibre Channel disks
    - SAN storage, such as fibre channel, Infiniband, iSCSI
- Memory: A minimum of 1 GB memory is required, however, 4 GB memory space is recommended
- Network: A minimum of 1 Gigabit data rate, 10 Gigabit, or InfiniBand is recommended
- Operating System: Any of the recent x86_64 GNU/Linux distribution systems
- File system: Any POSIX filesystem EXT4 or XFS filesystems that are recommended

GlusterFS server installation

From the main website, you can download the latest available GlusterFS package for your distribution http://download.gluster.com/pub/gluster/glusterfs/LATEST/.

On an Ubuntu/Debian installation, you can install the available DEBs with the following command:

```
$ sudo dpkg -i glusterfs_*_amd64.deb
```

> GlusterFS with InfiniBand support is available as a separate package named `glusterfs_*_with_rdma_amd64.deb`.

In order to fix the required dependencies, use the following command:

```
$ sudo apt-get install -f
```

In order to make sure that the basic Python interpreter is installed, use the following command:

```
$ sudo apt-get install python
```

In order to start the main `glusterd` process that is used to communicate with the other GlusterFS nodes, use the following command:

```
$ sudo /etc/init.d/glusterd start
```

In order to configure autostart on boot for `glusterd`, use the following command:

```
$ sudo update-rc.d glusterd defaults
```

Repeat this procedure on every host that uses the GlusterFS server.

Now that Gluster is installed on a bunch of nodes, you need to add every node to the same trusted pool. Each node will talk only with nodes in its trusted pool, and only a node that is already in a trusted pool can grant access to an external node.

So, assuming you have two nodes, `stor01` (192.168.66.81) and `stor02` (192.168.66.82) ask node `stor01` to probe node `stor02` with the following command:

```
$ sudo gluster peer probe 192.168.66.82
```

After a few seconds, the command should return a message of `Probe successful`. Double-check that the two nodes now know each other by using the following command:

```
$ sudo gluster peer status
```

```
libersoft@stor01:~$ sudo gluster peer probe 192.168.66.82
Probe successful
libersoft@stor01:~$ sudo gluster peer status
Number of Peers: 1

Hostname: 192.168.66.82
Uuid: 6c98e65d-547b-473d-8aa5-5f76f48578df
State: Peer in Cluster (Connected)
libersoft@stor01:~$
```

It is possible to use hostname instead of IP address as nodes will recognize each other using the auto-generated UUID.

Setting up a GlusterFS volume

As GlusterFS does not manage the backend storage directly, you need to predispose a folder where GlusterFS will store data on each node. Eventually, creating a separate partition or using dedicated disks is highly advisable.

As an example, imagine that we have two nodes that will be used for storage, each one with an already configured hardware RAID volume of 1 TB, containing the following:

- /dev/sda1: Mounted as / containing the OS
- /dev/sda2: Used as the swap partition
- /dev/sda3: Used as a large ext4 filesystem, mounted at /srv/local folder

A volume is a logical collection of bricks identified as a pair host:path and you can create as many volumes as you want on the same trusted pool.

Each volume can be created with a particular behavior, which can be as follows:

- **Distributed**: Each file in the volume is distributed across the pool but maintains its integrity on the filesystem (used for scaling storage space).

- **Replicated**: Each file is replicated across the pool and each replica should stay on bricks on different nodes (used to provide fault-tolerance to the volume).

- **Striped**: Each file in the volume is chunked and distributed across the volume (used for increasing performances by parallelizing read and write requests).

Each of these behaviors can be combined with the others to achieve additional behaviors as follows:

- Distributed replicated
- Distributed striped
- Distributed striped replicated
- Striped replicated

As a practical example, you can create a simple replicated volume with the following command:

```
$ sudo gluster volume create volume-name replica 2 192.168.66.81:/srv/
local 192.168.66.82:/srv/local
```

In this case, each /srv/local contains a copy of every file available on the volume. If a server crashes, the client will continue to access the entire volume. The total available space is the size of a brick.

If you add two more bricks by adding a new disk to the two nodes, we can configure a distributed replicated volume with the following command:

```
$ sudo gluster volume create volume-name replica 2 192.168.66.81:/
srv/local1 192.168.66.82:/srv/local1 192.168.66.81:/srv/local2
192.168.66.21:/srv/local2
```

> Brick orders matter! With replica, the first copy goes on the first brick, the second copy on the second brick, and so on.

In this case, two copies for each file will be distributed among the four bricks. A node can crash without a client losing access to the volume and the total available space is twice that of a single brick. This is the suggested configuration when operating with OpenNebula.

You can improve performance but lose the ability to easily recover files from the disk in case of failures (with RAID 0). However, you can enable striping in RAID, which actually splits each file into chunks on different bricks with the following command:

```
$ sudo gluster volume create volume-name stripe 2 replica 2
192.168.66.81:/srv/local1 192.168.66.82:/srv/local1 192.168.66.81:/srv/
local2 192.168.66.21:/srv/local2
```

As in the previous example, a node can crash without the client losing access to the volume. The total available space is the double of a single brick and also read and write requests are speeded up as they are served by two different bricks at a time.

Starting a GlusterFS volume

Before being able to mount a volume from a client, you need to start it by using the following command:

```
$ sudo gluster volume start volume-name
```

After this command, the main `glusterd` process should have started a `glusterfsd` process on each host with active bricks.

Check it out with the following command:

```
$ ps aux|grep glusterfsd
```

The output for the command will be as follows:

```
root      1713  0.0  2.9  83452 14692 ?         Ssl  16:35   0:00 /usr/sbin/glus
terfsd --xlator-option vms-server.listen-port=24009 -s localhost --volfile-id v
ms.192.168.66.81.srv-local -p /etc/glusterd/vols/vms/run/192.168.66.81-srv-loca
l.pid -S /tmp/e72cce03d67f54a8265ec0e9aa131f8a.socket --brick-name /srv/local -
-brick-port 24009 -l /var/log/glusterfs/bricks/srv-local.log
```

Accessing GlusterFS data

For accessing an active GlusterFS volume, you have three choices:

- Native GlusterFS client: It provides high concurrency, performance, and transparent fail-over but runs only on supported GNU/Linux distributions; it is the recommended way for frontend, KVM, and Xen hosts.

- NFS client: It is compatible with most NFS implementations (including FreeBSD and Mac OS X) but does not provide transparent fail-over; it is the only viable option for using GlusterFS with VMware hypervisors in OpenNebula.

- CIFS client: It has the same limitations as those of NFS; it is useful only to access files from Windows clients.

In order to mount the volume, it is sufficient to instruct the client to query any of the active GlusterFS servers in the pool, and use the `volume-name` as a requested resource using the following commands.

```
$ sudo mount -t glusterfs 192.168.66.81:/volume-name /var/lib/one
$ sudo mount -t nfs 192.168.66.81:/volume-name /var/lib/one
$ sudo mount -t cifs 192.168.66.81:/volume-name /var/lib/one
```

If you are mounting the client on the same host running the GlusterFS server, it is advisable to mount it with `localhost` as the hostname using the following command:

```
$ sudo mount -t glusterfs localhost:/volume-name /var/lib/one
```

You can configure automount at `/etc/`fstab` using the following code:

```
192.168.66.81:/volume-name /var/lib/one glusterfs _netdev 0 0
```

> **FUSE module requirement**
>
> As the native GlusterFS client uses the **Filesystem in Userspace** (**FUSE**) library, you may need to load the `fuse` kernel module with `sudo modprobe fuse` or add it at `/etc/modules` in order to autoload on start up.

Tuning volume options

After the initial volume creation, there is a bunch of options that can be configured at run time to fine-tune the GlusterFS behavior.

In order to change a volume option use the following command:

```
$ sudo gluster volume set <volume-name> <option-name> <value>
```

The following is a list of the most commonly used options to tune your GlusterFS volume:

- `auth.allow`: This is a comma-separated list of IP address (use * as wildcard) authorized to mount the volume (for example, 192.168.66.*).

- `auth.reject`: This is a comma-separated list of IP address, which should be denied permission to mount the volume.

- `cluster.min-free-disk`: This is the percentage of the size of a brick that should be left empty (useful when you have non-uniform bricks).

- `nfs.disable`: This is set to `on` in order to disable NFS exporting of the volume (defaults to `off`).
- `performance.flush-behind`: This is set to `off` to prevent the returning of success to applications writing to the volume before data is flushed to disk (similar to the behavior of setting the `sync` option with NFS).
- `performance.cache-size`: This is the size of the client in-memory read cache in bytes (defaults to 32 MB).

Operations on volume

It is possible to expand or shrink a running volume without downtime.

For expanding a volume, you first need to insert the new host into the trusted pool issuing the following command:

```
$ sudo gluster peer probe <ip>
```

In order to add it to the volume use the following command:

```
$ sudo gluster volume add-brick <volume-name> stor03:/srv/local
```

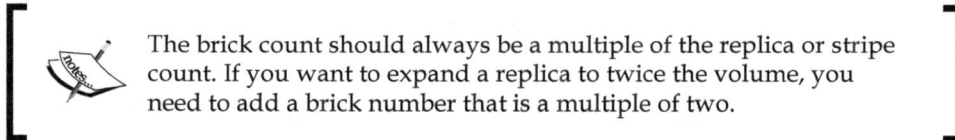

> The brick count should always be a multiple of the replica or stripe count. If you want to expand a replica to twice the volume, you need to add a brick number that is a multiple of two.

It is possible to remove broken or unavailable bricks in a similar way with the following command:

```
$ sudo gluster volume remove-brick <volume-name> stor03:/srv/local
```

Remember that the data present on the removed bricks is not automatically transferred to other bricks, so you will probably need to move it manually to another active peer, using the `rsync` command from `stor03:/srv/localfolder`.

After an `add-brick` or `remove-brick` operation, you will probably want to get your data automatically rebalanced among the existing bricks with the following command:

```
$ sudo gluster volume rebalance <volume-name> start
```

It is even possible to replace an existing brick with a new one, for example, if you want to migrate your volume to new servers use the following command:

```
$ sudo gluster volume replace-brick <volume-name> stor02:/srv/local
stor03:/srv/local start
```

In this case, data will be transferred from the old brick to the new brick and you can check migration status using the `status` command (in place of `start`), `pause` to temporarily pause migration, and `abort` to stop it.

After the data migration has completed, `commit` the replacement with the following command:

```
$ sudo gluster volume replace-brick <volume-name> stor02:/srv/local
stor03:/srv/local commit
```

Self-heal on replicated volumes

The maintenance of data integrity on a replicated GlusterFS volume is performed automatically when a client requires read or write access to a particular file. For this reason if you have data that gets rarely accessed on your volume it is a good idea to schedule a Cron job, on a GlusterFS client with the following command:

```
find /var/lib/one -noleaf -print0 | xargs --null stat >/dev/null
```

Overview of GlusterFS integration with OpenNebula

GlusterFS is great in conjunction with OpenNebula for its completely decentralized and clustered architecture that does not expose any single point of failure. In other words, it continues to work even when multiple hardware failures occur, depending on its initial layout configuration.

Another drawback, besides the difference in performance when compared to a dedicated NAS/SAN is that GlusterFS requires the brick count to be a multiple of the replica and stripe count (for example, with replica 4 you must have 4, 8, 12, and so on bricks). It would be better to keep bricks of the same size otherwise file distribution among them will obviously not be optimally balanced.

The complete GlusterFS manual is available both online and in PDF version; you can download it from the following link,

```
http://gluster.com/community/documentation/.
```

Shared Storage through MooseFS

MooseFS is an open source distributed file system actively developed and maintained by Gemius SA (http://www.gemius.com), a Poland-based online research agency.

Apart from the common features of distributed file systems, the usage of MooseFS with OpenNebula is encouraged due to some particular features, which are as follows:

- **Snapshots**: It is possible to make real-time snapshots of directories and files.

- **Expandability**: Redundancy is not defined by volume layout during creation like that of GlusterFS, but on a directory or file level. Every storage server that gets added to the cluster is automatically introduced and its space is immediately made available.

- **Automatic re-balancing**: As soon as something bad happens to a storage server, missing copies are immediately replaced by new copies on remaining storage servers. If a storage server comes back online, it will get resynchronized automatically and the file copies that are in excess will be discarded.

- **Modularity**: The MooseFS server software is split into three independent software components and a client that can be installed on different nodes as follows:

    - master: This is a single daemon per cluster that manages the whole filesystem storing metadata for every file saved on the volume (considering size, position, and attributes).

    - chunkserver: This stores the file data and they communicate directly with each other while replicating files.

    - metalogger: This receives metadata changelogs from the master server, keeping a real-time backup of them.

    - client: This communicates with the master for availability of files and on what chunkservers it can retrieve them.

The metadata is kept entirely in the memory of the master server while active. It is saved on a disk as a single binary file every 24 hrs and immediately as incremental logs. Having one or more metaloggers is highly advisable for backup purposes (a server that is running a metalogger can be made to act as a master server).

File data is divided into fragments (called chunks) with a maximum size of 64 MiB each.

High availability is achieved by configuring a goal value (number of copies to be kept) for a given file or directory at runtime. Thanks to this, you can set a higher goal value for important files and a lower value for irrelevant data (for example, temporary data, old data logs, and so on).

MooseFS hardware requirements

Before installing MooseFS, verify that your system matches the following minimum requirements:

- **Master**:
    - High-stability machine: As the master is a crucial component, the master should have RAID storage, redundant power supply, and ECC memory.
    - Memory: The most important factor is RAM as the entire metadata is kept in memory when the master is active for performance purposes. Around 300 MiB of RAM is required for every 1 million files on the chunkserver. As we are keeping mainly big disk images it should not be too much.
    - Disk space: The required space is 1 GB for every 1 million files in order to store the metadata changelogs.

- **Metalogger**:
    - Memory: It requires memory but it should be ready to be switched to act as a master server if a crash occurs.
    - Disk space: Around 1 GB for every 1 million files for storing the metadata changelogs.

- **Chunkserver**:
    - Memory: It requires a memory of 1 GB.
    - Disk space: As needed (you may need 8 GB for each virtual machine you plan to run multiplied by the number of copies you want to keep, at least two).

MooseFS server installation through sources

Unfortunately, there are no binary packages that are ready for Ubuntu or Debian in the main repositories, but the upstream source **Tarball** released by MooseFS (http://www.moosefs.org/download.html) is a DEB-ready package.

In order to download the latest version and unpack it, use the following commands:

```
$ tar xvf mfs-*.tar.gz
$ cd mfs-*/
```

In order to install the toolchain and Debian package scripts, use the following command:

```
$ sudo apt-get install build-essential devscripts debhelper pkg-config
```

In order to install the required dependencies, use the following command:

```
$ sudo apt-get install autotools-dev libfuse-dev zlib1g-dev
```

In order to launch the .deb build process, use the following command:

```
$ debuild -us -uc -b
```

If everything goes successfully, you can find the MooseFS binary DEB package on the top directory using the following command:

```
$ ls ../mfs-*.deb
```

In order to install them using dpkg, use the following command:

```
$ sudo dpkg -i ../mfs-*.deb
```

If you are running on a non-DEB distribution, you can go with the plain old ./configure && make && make install option using the following commands:

```
$ ./configure -prefix=/usr
$ make
$ sudo make install
```

Even with the plain ./configure && make && make install it is possible to modularize the components that are going to be installed on the system. For the configure scripts the following switches are available:

- --disable-mfsmaster: Do not build mfsmaster
- --disable-mfschunkserver: Do not build mfschunkserver
- --disable-mfsmount: Do not build mfsmount
- --disable-mfscgi: Do not install the CGI scripts
- --disable-mfscgiserv: Do not install the CGI server

MooseFS server installation through PPA

For Ubuntu Lucid, you can find binary packages for MooseFS prepared by me on the following **Personal Package Archive (PPA)**:

```
https://launchpad.net/~libersoft/+archive/moosefs.
```

In order to add the PPA to your /etc/apt/sources.list and retrieve the GNU Privacy Guard (GPG) key that is used to sign off the package, use the following commands:

```
$ echo deb http://ppa.launchpad.net/libersoft/moosefs/ubuntu lucid main |
sudo tee -a /etc/apt/sources.list.d/moosefs.list

$ sudo apt-key adv --keyserver keyserver.ubuntu.com --recv-keys
28EFF7957119F175
```

We can use the apt-add-repository utility with the following command:

```
$ sudo apt-get install python-software-properties

$ sudo apt-add-repository ppa:libersoft/moosefs
```

In order to install the MooseFS components use the following command:

```
$ sudo apt-get update

$ sudo apt-get install mfs-master mfs-chunkserver mfs-metalogger mfs-
client mfs-cgi
```

MooseFS master configuration

The master server must be running on one machine only, as it is used to orchestrate the volume. It requires the configuration of two files mfsmaster.cfg and mfsexports. cfg. By default MooseFS provides example configuration files within the source package, and you can find them already copied to your /etc directory with a .dist extension. Copy them and start editing with the following commands:

```
$ sudo cp /etc/mfsmaster.cfg.dist /etc/mfsmaster.cfg

$ sudo cp /etc/mfsexports.cfg.dist /etc/mfsexports.cfg
```

The mfsmaster.cfg file contains the main configuration parameters used by a master, such as IP address, port binding, and chunkserver management options.

```
# mfsmaster.cfg
WORKING_USER = mfs
WORKING_GROUP = mfs
# SYSLOG_IDENT = mfsmaster
# LOCK_MEMORY = 0
# NICE_LEVEL = -19
```

```
# EXPORTS_FILENAME = /etc/mfsexports.cfg
# DATA_PATH = /var/lib/mfs
# BACK_LOGS = 50
REPLICATIONS_DELAY_INIT = 300
REPLICATIONS_DELAY_DISCONNECT = 3600
# MATOML_LISTEN_HOST = *
# MATOML_LISTEN_PORT = 9419
# MATOCS_LISTEN_HOST = *
# MATOCS_LISTEN_PORT = 9420
# MATOCU_LISTEN_HOST = *
# MATOCU_LISTEN_PORT = 9421
CHUNKS_LOOP_TIME = 300
CHUNKS_DEL_LIMIT = 100
CHUNKS_WRITE_REP_LIMIT = 1
CHUNKS_READ_REP_LIMIT = 5
# REJECT_OLD_CLIENTS = 0
# deprecated, to be removed in MooseFS 1.7
# LOCK_FILE = /var/run/mfs/mfsmaster.lock
```

Interesting configuration options are highlighted and the following is an explanation of these options:

- WORKING_USER and WORKING_GROUP: For security reasons each daemon should be running with a dedicated system user. Check for existence with ID mfs. If a dedicated user has not been created by MooseFS install script, create one yourself with adduser --system mfs.

- REPLICATIONS_DELAY_INIT: When a chunkserver goes online, the master waits for this delay before starting to replicate chunks on this server (to be sure that the server is going to stay online).

- REPLICATIONS_DELAY_DISCONNECT: When a chunkserver goes offline and comes back after a few minutes, the master waits for this delay before restarting to save chunks on this server (in order to be sure to not rely too much on faulty machines).

- CHUNKS_LOOP_TIME: The timed operations of the master are repeated with a fixed interval in seconds. Each operation is controlled by the following directives:

  ○ CHUNKS_DEL_LIMIT: It is the max number of chunk deletions on each loop (used so that the chunkserver does not get flooded when mass deletions occur).

  ○ CHUNKS_READ_REP_LIMIT and CHUNKS_WRITE_REP_LIMIT: When replication for some chunks is below the goal, chunkserver will perform only a limited number of operations (used so that cluster performances do not degrade too much when replication is running).

Instead, the `mfsexports.cfg` configuration file is used to list and configure the available volumes on the cluster, like `/etc/exports` does for NFS. The syntax is as follows:

```
ADDRESS DIRECTORY [OPTIONS]
```

A simple example for the configuration of the `mfsexports.cfg` file is as follows:

```
192.168.66.0/24/rw,alldirs,maproot=0
```

This allows access from 192.168.66.0/24 clients to a unique read/write volume. Some of the interesting options that are available are as follows:

- **alldirs**: The client can mount every subdirectory of the main volume not only the main one.
- **maproot**: This maps access of `root` user with a specified `user:group` (to provide the same behavior as the NFS `no_root_squash` option).
- **password**: A password could be configured to provide minimal security for client mounting.

When done, you should enable the automatic start up of `master` modifying the `/etc/default/mfs-master` file by altering the default configuration line to:

```
MFSMASTER_ENABLE=true
```

In order to start the `master` use the following command:

```
$ sudo /etc/init.d/mfs-master start
```

If you get a message as follows:

```
Can't create lockfile in working directory: EACCES (Permission denied)
```

make sure that the user on which master is running (as specified with `WORKING_USER` and `WORKING_GROUP`) has permission on `/var/lib/mfs` (or the folder specified with `DATA_PATH`) using the following commands:

```
sudo chown mfs:mfs /var/lib/mfs
sudo chmod 770 /var/lib/mfs
```

MooseFS chunkserver configuration

You can (and should) have multiple chunkservers to store and replicate your cluster data, providing fault-tolerance and high-availability.

A chunkserver needs atleast two configuration files; they are as follows:

- `mfschunkserver.cfg`: This contains the main configurations, such as where to find the master server, timeouts, IP address, and port binding.

- `mfshdd.cfg`: This contains a list of the mountpoints that the chunkserver can use to store data that should be already formatted (Ext4 or XFS filesystems recommended) and mounted.

As done earlier, copy the `.dist` configuration files to the right path with the following commands:

```
$ sudo cp /etc/mfschunkserver.cfg.dist /etc/mfschunkserver.cfg
$ sudo cp /etc/mfshdd.cfg.dist /etc/mfshdd.cfg
```

In order to edit the `mfschunkserver.cfg` configuration file, use the following code:

```
WORKING_USER = mfs
WORKING_GROUP = mfs
# SYSLOG_IDENT = mfschunkserver
# LOCK_MEMORY = 0
# NICE_LEVEL = -19
# DATA_PATH = /var/lib/mfs
# MASTER_RECONNECTION_DELAY = 5
# BIND_HOST = *
MASTER_HOST = 192.168.66.81
# MASTER_PORT = 9420
# MASTER_TIMEOUT = 60
# CSSERV_LISTEN_HOST = *
# CSSERV_LISTEN_PORT = 9422
# HDD_CONF_FILENAME = /etc/mfshdd.cfg

HDD_TEST_FREQ = 10
# deprecated, to be removed in MooseFS 1.7
# LOCK_FILE = /var/run/mfs/mfschunkserver.lock
# BACK_LOGS = 50
# CSSERV_TIMEOUT = 5
```

Interesting configuration options and their explanation are as follows:

- `WORKING_USER` and `WORKING_GROUP`: Apply the same considerations as for `master`.

- `MASTER_HOST`: This is the IP address or the hostname where chunkserver can reach the master server. On start up, if a chunkserver does not find its master, it will shut down immediately.

- HDD_TEST_FREQ: Each chunkserver checks continuously every *x* seconds that a chunk is correctly readable and that its checksum value is correct. If storage degradation occurs, master will be notified and the chunk will be immediately replicated somewhere else.

The mfshdd.cfg configuration file contains a list of available mountpoints for storing MooseFS chunks. The following code is used to mount points for the HDD drives:

```
# mount points of HDD drives
#/srv/vol1
/srv/vol2
```

Now, you should enable the automatic startup of each chunkserver, modifying the /etc/default/mfs-chunkserver configuration file by altering the default line to:

```
MFSCHUNKSERVER_ENABLE=true
```

In order to start it, use the following command:

```
$ sudo /etc/init.d/mfs-chunkserver start
```

If you get a message as follows:

```
Can't create lockfile in working directory: EACCES (Permission denied)
```

make sure that the user on which the chunkserver is running (as specified with WORKING_USER and WORKING_GROUP) has permission on the mountpoints specified in the mfshdd.cfg configuration file:

```
sudo chown mfs:mfs /srv/vol1 /srv/vol2
sudo chmod 770 /srv/vol1 /srv/vol2
```

After the first chunkserver starts, take a look inside any one of the mountpoints used by the chunkserver:

```
libersoft@stor01:/srv/local/mfs$ ls
00  0F  1E  2D  3C  4B  5A  69  78  87  96  A5  B4  C3  D2  E1  F0  FF
01  10  1F  2E  3D  4C  5B  6A  79  88  97  A6  B5  C4  D3  E2  F1
02  11  20  2F  3E  4D  5C  6B  7A  89  98  A7  B6  C5  D4  E3  F2
03  12  21  30  3F  4E  5D  6C  7B  8A  99  A8  B7  C6  D5  E4  F3
04  13  22  31  40  4F  5E  6D  7C  8B  9A  A9  B8  C7  D6  E5  F4
05  14  23  32  41  50  5F  6E  7D  BC  9B  AA  B9  C8  D7  E6  F5
06  15  24  33  42  51  60  6F  7E  8D  9C  AB  BA  C9  D8  E7  F6
07  16  25  34  43  52  61  70  7F  8E  9D  AC  BB  CA  D9  E8  F7
08  17  26  35  44  53  62  71  80  8F  9E  AD  BC  CB  DA  E9  F8
09  18  27  36  45  54  63  72  81  90  9F  AE  BD  CC  DB  EA  F9
0A  19  28  37  46  55  64  73  82  91  A0  AF  BE  CD  DC  EB  FA
0B  1A  29  38  47  56  65  74  83  92  A1  B0  BF  CE  DD  EC  FB
0C  1B  2A  39  48  57  66  75  84  93  A2  B1  C0  CF  DE  ED  FC
0D  1C  2B  3A  49  58  67  76  85  94  A3  B2  C1  D0  DF  EE  FD
0E  1D  2C  3B  4A  59  68  77  86  95  A4  B3  C2  D1  E0  EF  FE
```

A chunkserver will create a hashed-like directory structure where it will store chunks in a position based on their own checksum value (for example, all chunks with checksum starting with BB will be saved in the subfolder BB).

Please be aware that if something goes wrong with the master server that holds the metadata database, and you do not have metalogger or metadata backups, all the data will be lost. It is quite impossible to correctly reassemble each chunk and obtain the original data.

MooseFS metalogger configuration

Metaloggers are crucial components of a MooseFS cluster. Without an active metalogger after a master crash all your data will no longer be accessible.

A metalogger simply receives updated metadata information from the active master server in the form of binary logs. A complete database copy is downloaded from the master server every 24 hrs (by default).

A configuration file is needed, which can be created using the following command:

```
sudo cp /etc/mfsmetalogger.cfg.dist /etc/mfsmetalogger.cfg
```

Edit the /etc/mfsmetalogger.cfg configuration file accordingly:

```
WORKING_USER = mfs
WORKING_GROUP = mfs
# SYSLOG_IDENT = mfsmetalogger
# LOCK_MEMORY = 0
# NICE_LEVEL = -19

# DATA_PATH = /var/lib/mfs
# BACK_LOGS = 50
# META_DOWNLOAD_FREQ = 24
# MASTER_RECONNECTION_DELAY = 5
MASTER_HOST = 192.168.66.81
# MASTER_PORT = 9419
# MASTER_TIMEOUT = 60
# deprecated, to be removed in MooseFS 1.7
# LOCK_FILE = /var/run/mfs/mfsmetalogger.lock
```

Now you should enable the automatic startup of each metalogger modifying the /etc/default/mfs-metalogger configuration file by altering the default line to:

```
MFSMETALOGGER_ENABLE=true
```

In order to start it use the following command:

```
$ sudo /etc/init.d/mfs-metalogger start
```

If you get a message as follows:

```
Can't create lockfile in working directory: EACCES (Permission denied)
```

make sure that the user on which the metalogger is running (as specified with `WORKING_USER` and `WORKING_GROUP`) has permission on the `/var/lib/mfs` (or the folder specified with `DATA_PATH`) using the following commands:

```
sudo chown mfs:mfs /var/lib/mfs
sudo chmod 770 /var/lib/mfs
```

Master takeover with metalogger data

If something goes wrong with the master server, you can start up a new master server (that should have the same IP address as that of the old one if you do not want to manually reconnect every client and chunkserver) with the data acquired through an active metalogger. The following is the recovery procedure:

1. Once you are sure that the main master server is dead, connect to a metalogger machine and stop the metalogger service using the following command:

   ```
   sudo /etc/init.d/mfs-metalogger stop
   ```

2. In order to merge recently downloaded changelogs in the main database file, use the following command:

   ```
   sudo mfsmetarestore -a
   ```

3. In order to start the `master` process, use the following command:

   ```
   sudo /etc/init.d/mfs-master start
   ```

> You need to have already copied the original `mfsmaster.cfg` and `mfsexports.cfg` configuration files from the master server to the metalogger server. For this reason, it is advisable to copy those files through a `rsync` command those files to every server running a metalogger after the initial configuration of the `master` and after each change.

MooseFS client mounting

MooseFS provides only a FUSE-based client for accessing files on the cluster.

You can mount a MooseFS cluster with the `mfsmount` command available in the `mfs-client` package using the following syntax:

```
mfsmount <mountpoint> -H <master_host> -S <volume-path> -p <password>
```

As an example, use the following command:

```
$ sudo mfsmount /srv/mfs -H 192.168.66.81
```

Do a brief write and read test with the following commands:

```
$ sudo dd if=/dev/zero of=/srv/mfs/test1.dat bs=8096 count=100k
$ sudo dd if=/srv/mfs/test1.dat of=/dev/null bs=8096
```

These commands will create an 800 MB zero-filled file and read it back. After the execution of each `dd` command, the speed of each operation will be printed on the standard output. It could be something similar to the following line:

```
829030400 bytes (829 MB) copied, 9.5509 s, 86.8 MB/s.
```

NFS fallback mount through unfs3

Although MooseFS does not include native NFS support like GlusterFS, you can use a standalone user space NFS server to re-export a MooseFS mountpoint. You cannot use the standard `nfs-kernel-server` as it will not work because of the usage of FUSE in the MooseFS client.

On Ubuntu, you can install a user space NFS server on the frontend (or on any other machine running an `mfs-client`) with the following command:

```
$ sudo apt-get install unfs3
```

And then configure the `/etc/exports` configuration file (please note that it does not have the same exports syntax as that of the standard Linux NFS server). An example of the configuration line is as follows:

```
/var/lib/one 192.168.66.0/24(rw,no_root_squash)
```

In order to restart it, use the following command:

```
$ sudo /etc/init.d/unfs3 restart
```

Now you can access MooseFS files on every platform with NFS support.

MooseFS web interface

MooseFS includes a tiny web interface called `mfscgi` that when executed spawns a Python-based web server responding on the 9425/TCP port.

In order to start it on the master server, use the following command:

```
$ sudo mfscgiserv
```

Type in the following URL address in your browser, `http://192.168.66.81:9425`.

A page will be displayed as follows:

The first page will show a matrix containing the number of chunks with correct (green), under (red) or over (blue) goal copy numbers. From this you can have a rapid look through the MooseFS health status in addition to the space and file information.

MFS | Info + | Servers − | Disks − | Exports − | Mounts − | Operations + | Master Charts + | Server Charts + | W3C c

Chunk Servers

#	host	ip	port	version	'regular' hdd space				'marked for removal' hdd space			
					chunks	used	total	% used	chunks	used	total	% used
1	stor01.local	192.168.66.81	9422	1.6.20	26	3.2 GiB	24 GiB	13.37	0	0 B	0 B	-
2	stor02.local	192.168.66.82	9422	1.6.20	26	3.2 GiB	24 GiB	13.37	0	0 B	0 B	-

Metadata Backup Loggers

#	host	ip	version
1	stor02.local	192.168.66.82	1.6.20

Disks

#	Info				I/O stats last day (switch to min,hour)								space		
					transfer		avg time (switch to max)			# of ops					
	IP path (switch to name)	chunks	last error	status	read	write	read	write	fsync	read	write	fsync	used	total	used (%)
1	192.168.66.81:9422:/srv/local/	26	no errors	ok	219 MiB/s	25 MiB/s	285 us	175 us	93544 us	37279	6731	159	3.2 GiB	24 GiB	13.37
2	192.168.66.82:9422:/srv/local/	26	no errors	ok	33 MiB/s	16 MiB/s	1877 us	117 us	54423 us	31981	30560	1990	3.2 GiB	24 GiB	13.37

Exports

#	ip range		path	minversion	alldirs	password	ro/rw	restricted ip	ignore gid	root uid:gid	all users uid:gid
1	0.0.0.0	255.255.255.255	(META)	0.0.0	-	no	rw	yes	-	-	-
2	0.0.0.0	255.255.255.255	/	0.0.0	yes	no	rw	yes	no	0	0	-	-

Active mounts (parameters)

#	session id	host	ip	mount point	version	root dir	ro/rw	restricted ip	ignore gid	root uid:gid	all users uid:gid
1	3	localhost	127.0.0.1	/mnt	1.6.20	(META)	rw	yes	-	-	-
2	5	stor01.local	192.168.66.81	/srv/mfs	1.6.20	/	rw	yes	no	0	0	-	-
3	1	stor02.local	192.168.66.82	/srv/mfs	1.6.20	/	rw	yes	no	0	0	-	-

Subsequent tabs will show up information about the disk usage, the currently connected chunkserver, metalogger and clients, and the configured exports.

In particular, you can monitor performance and the status of a single chunkserver disk from which you can easily notice performance degradations or a disk failure.

The last tabs show RRD-like graphs with performances over time for master, chunkservers, and clients.

Setting goals and fault tolerance

Unlike many other distributed file systems, with MooseFS it is possible to define the redundancy level at the directory or file level. The number of copies for each chunk that gets stored on different chunkservers is called a **goal**.

With the utility mfssetgoal, it is possible to see and adjust the goal values for each directory or file on a mounted client.

The complete command syntax is:

```
mfssetgoal [-r] GOAL[-|+] filename [filename|...]
```

It is possible to increase the goal of our entire volume by two with the following command:

```
$ sudo mfssetgoal -r 2 /srv/mfs
```

When using the -r parameter, the goal is set recursively from the specified folder.

In order to check the goal modification use the following command:

```
$ sudo mfsgetgoal -r /srv/mfs
```

You should get a summary of the number of files for each configured goal.

Obviously the goal for particular files could be changed at runtime and MooseFS will automatically replicate or remove chunks in excess as needed.

Setting trash time and access to the trash bin

Another interesting feature of MooseFS is the availability of a global trash bin for each deleted file on the volume. This feature exists mainly to avoid mass deletions that would impact the performance of a running volume. For this reason, every deleted file is not removed immediately but remains on the chunkserver and is removed on each loop as configured on the master. Under these conditions, it is easy to consider a trash time configurable similar to the goal in order to decide how much time must pass before starting to definitively remove the chunks.

You can use the mfsgettrashtime and mfssettrashtime commands to see and adjust the time after which a removed file will be physically removed from the chunkserver:

```
$ sudo mfsgettrashtime -r /srv/mfs
```

By default, a file is kept in the trash bin for 24 hours.

For example, you can increase the trash time to one week with the following command:

```
$ sudo mfssettrashtime -r 604800 /srv/mfs/
```

The removed files may be accessed through a separate mounted meta filesystem. You need to add a line on the master mfsexports.cfg configuration file as follows:

```
127.0.0.1 .... rw
```

It can be mounted only by the master server with the following command:

```
$ sudo mfsmount -o mfsmeta -H localhost /srv/mfsmeta
```

In particular, it contains a trash directory listing the deleted files available for recovery and an undel directory. Every file you move from the trash directory to the undel directory will be restored at the original position on the volume becoming newly accessible to the clients.

Making snapshots

MooseFS includes a snapshot feature that permits making a consistent copy of a file in zero time. This feature is good for an OpenNebula cluster as it reduces the virtual instance deployment timings and eases the backup procedures of active virtual machines.

You can make directory and file snapshots on a mounted MooseFS volume through the `mfsmakesnapshot` utility with the following syntax:

```
mfsmakesnapshot [-o] src [src ...] dst
```

MooseFS OpenNebula integration

MooseFS is a shared file system like NFS, so you could simply use the `tm_shared` transfer manager. However, we can take advantage of the MooseFS snapshot feature to speed up the deployment, and undeployment operations.

You can download the optimized shared transfer manager for MooseFS from the following link: `https://github.com/libersoft/opennebula-tm-moosefs`.

In order to edit our `oned.conf` accordingly, use the following code:

```
VM_DIR=/srv/mfs/deploy
IMAGE_REPOSITORY_PATH = /srv/mfs/images
TM_MAD = [ name = "tm_moosefs",
  executable = "one_tm",
  arguments = "tm_moosefs/tm_moosefs.conf" ]
```

Now copy the directory `tm_moosefs` at `/etc/one` or `$ONE-LOCATION/etc`.

Also copy `tm_commands/moosefs` at `/usr/lib/one/tm_commands` or `$ONE_LOCATION/lib/tm_commands`.

In order to stop and start the process `oned` as usual, use the following command:

```
$ one stop
```

```
$ one start
```

In order to configure every Nebula host to use the new transfer manager instead of the default `tm_shared`, use the following command:

```
$ onehost create host01 im_kvm vmm_kvm tm_moosefs dummy
```

Summary

In this chapter we explored most of the available storage options when using OpenNebula, detailing the pros and cons of each one of them. Besides the usage of mainstream storage solutions, such as NFS and NAS/SAN, we explored the ability to use open source distributed file systems to provide better flexibility and scalability to our infrastructure.

In the next chapter, we finally start to use our cloud resources and learn to launch and manage our virtual instances, networks, and the Image Repository.

5
Being Operational— Everything Starts Here!

Once the basic infrastructure configuration of OpenNebula is complete, we can really start using it for our needs.

In the first section of this chapter, we will go straight down to launch a ttylinux test virtual machine, provided by the OpenNebula guys. Later, we will dig into the configuration procedures for virtual networks, virtual images, and virtual machines. Lastly, we will learn how to create our own images, ready to be used with OpenNebula.

But first, I want to make a clarification regarding a peculiar feature of cloud computing solutions. Unlike standard virtualization tools, you must understand that the operating system installation should not be carried out after the creation of a new virtual machine. We need to prepare a template image that will contain a basic system installation (of your favourite Linux distribution, *BSD, and so on) plus a configuration script to configure the basic functionalities (for example, network) and eventually a provisioning with customized software (which will be explained later in the *Contextualization* section).

This prerequisite that may appear as a slowdown for newcomers will permit you to easily launch new instances and to rationalize your Image Repository. You will see in the following paragraphs how straightforward it is to launch a new virtual machine with an existing image template.

Launch a test instance—ttylinux

For the hungriest among us, let us start a test instance without delay (do not try it if you are using VMware; it will not work, as it does not use VMDK as disk image format, sorry).

In order to download the VM sample package on the frontend, use the following link:

`http://dev.opennebula.org/attachments/download/355/ttylinux.tar.gz`.

In order to create a new temporary folder, unpack the archive and move the sample package into it using the following commands:

```
$ mkdir /tmp/ttylinux
$ tar xvf ttylinux.tar.gz -C ttylinux/
$ cd /tmp/ttylinux
```

Briefly examine `small_network.net` and configure your host network bridge, as follows:

```
NAME = "Small network"
TYPE = FIXED
#Now we will use the cluster private network (physical)
BRIDGE = lan0
LEASES = [ IP="192.168.66.5"]
```

In order to adjust the path in `image.one`, use the following code:

```
NAME = ttylinux
PATH = "/tmp/ttylinux/ttylinux.img"
TYPE = OS
```

In order to submit the templates to the OpenNebula frontend, use the following commands:

```
$ onevnet create small_network.net
$ oneimage create image.one
```

We have just inserted, into our OpenNebula database, a new virtual network configuration and the disk image of our test VM.

Now adapt the VM configuration template, `ttylinux.one`. For now, just check that the IDs `IMAGE_ID` and `NETWORK_ID` match the ID returned by the two previous commands as in the following code:

```
NAME    = ttylinux
CPU     = 0.1
MEMORY = 64
DISK    = [ IMAGE_ID = 0 ]
NIC     = [ NETWORK_ID = 0 ]
FEATURES=[ acpi="no" ]
```

Now cross your fingers and execute the following command:

```
$ onevm create ttylinux.one
```

In order to monitor the launch of the `ttylinux` instance, execute the `onevm list` or `onevm top` command.

If the machine is stuck in `pending` status or gets a `failed` status (depending on how we configured the host hooks), we probably missed something.

It is very important that you check the logfiles for errors when something goes wrong, as missing any of the configuration steps may lead to unsuccessful deployment.

The first place to check is `oned.log` at `$ONE_LOCATION/var` or `/var/log/one`. You can further find the following files to analyze, at `$ONE_LOCATION/var/VM_ID`:

- `deployment.*`: This contains the hypervisor-specific configuration for the virtual machine.
- `transfer.*`: This contains the commands issued by the transfer manager.
- `vm.log`: This contains all the relevant frontend operations for the currently running VM.

Most deployment failures are caused by:

- Wrong host configurations: It includes configurations, such as missing library dependencies, wrong hypervisor configurations, and `oneadmin` not belonging to libvirt or KVM users group
- Wrong storage configurations: It includes folders not writable by the `oneadmin` user or some hosts that did not mount the shared volume correctly

Instead, if everything is fine and the instance status is `running`, retrieve the IP address that the frontend has assigned to this instance and try to connect to it through SSH, with the user `root` and the password `password`.

In order to retrieve the IP address, use the following command:

```
$ onevm show 3|grep IP
```

That is great, is it not?

Now calm down and explore all the configuration options for network, image, and VM templates.

Managing the virtual networks

Each host is connected to one or more physical networks. These can be made accessible to virtual instances through the relative bridges we configured before.

Bridges can be created even without any physical devices attached to them, meaning that they will be accessible only from virtual instances running on the same host. If you need to have an isolated network that is shared in between hosts, you can place an isolated switch between your hosts.

A virtual machine can be connected to one or more physical networks, either a LAN or a DMZ, depending on your needs.

A DHCP server is not needed in OpenNebula, as the network auto-configuration will be completely carried out by the contextualization script.

To create a new virtual network, you need to use the onevnet utility from the OpenNebula frontend.

Template for ranged networks

A ranged network needs only two parameters for its configuration: NETWORK_SIZE and NETWORK_ADDRESS.

In order to create a file containing a basic network template for a new virtual network, use the following code:

```
NAME = "Green"
TYPE = RANGED
PUBLIC = YES
BRIDGE = lan0
NETWORK_SIZE = 24
NETWORK_ADDRESS = 192.168.66.0
# Custom Attributes
GATEWAY = 192.168.66.1
DNS = 192.168.66.1
```

Let us focus on the important parameters. They are as follows:

- **NAME**: This is the name you assign to this network and should be something that will let you remember the purpose of this network (for example, lan, dmz, and public_network).

- **PUBLIC**: This is a virtual public network that can be used by every OpenNebula user. A non-public (private) virtual network can be used only by the user who created it.

- **BRIDGE**: This is the name of the bridge we already created on the physical hosts to which the virtual network will be attached. For VMware, you need to use the name defined in the vSwitch configuration. The default name is VM Network (but you can change it to integrate it with KVM and Xen through the vSphere interface).

Custom attributes will not be used by OpenNebula frontend but will be passed to the VMs contextualization script during VM start up. We will learn to use them later in this chapter.

Template for fixed networks

A fixed virtual network is useful when you need to make available only certain IP addresses, such as a public IP on the Red interface.

In this case, you need to change the TYPE value, remove the NETWORK_SIZE and NETWORK_ADDRESS attributes, and add the different LEASES definitions. Sample code that can be used is as follows:

```
NAME    = "Red"
TYPE    = FIXED
BRIDGE  = red0
LEASES  = [IP=130.10.0.1]
LEASES  = [IP=130.10.0.2, MAC=50:20:20:20:20:21]
LEASES  = [IP=130.10.0.3]
LEASES  = [IP=130.10.0.4]
# Custom Attributes
GATEWAY = 130.10.0.1
DNS     = 130.10.0.1
```

You can even assign a particular MAC address to the machine that will get a particular IP address to circumvent pre-existing firewalls or ISP rules on MAC addresses.

Submitting and managing a network template

In order to instruct the OpenNebula frontend to create a virtual network using the template we have just created, use the following command:

```
$ onevnet create <filename>
```

Unless any error is displayed, we have created a new virtual network successfully!

Use the `list` and `show` commands, as in the following screenshot.

```
oneadmin@odin:~$ onevnet list
  ID USER      GROUP     NAME              TYPE BRIDGE PUB  LEASES
   1 oneadmin oneadmin Green                R    lan0 Yes       0
oneadmin@odin:~$ onevnet show Green
VIRTUAL NETWORK 1 INFORMATION
ID              : 1
USER            : oneadmin
GROUP           : oneadmin
PUBLIC          : Yes
USED LEASES     : 0

VIRTUAL NETWORK TEMPLATE
DNS=192.168.66.1
GATEWAY=192.168.66.1
NETWORK_ADDRESS=192.168.66.0
NETWORK_SIZE=24
```

The `show` command will be particularly useful when we need to know which IP addresses are used and which are available.

Managing the disk images

OpenNebula includes an Image Repository component to ease the management of multiple disk images. Each disk image can contain an operating system or application data.

Even in this case, you need to prepare a template file to be submitted to OpenNebula frontend, in order to create a new disk image.

Template for operating system images

Let us see a simple OS disk image using the following code:

```
NAME = "Ubuntu Server"
PATH = /tmp/ubuntu.img
TYPE = OS
PUBLIC = YES
DESCRIPTION = "Ubuntu server basic installation"
```

Please understand that you need to submit an existing disk image (with the operating system already installed). You can prepare a disk image using standard virtualization tools, such as virt-manager, VirtualBox, or the VMware vSphere for ESXi, on your desktop PC.

Be aware that the disk image should be in the proper format to be recognized and used by the hypervisor:

Hypervisor	Disk image format
KVM	`.raw`, `.qcow2`, `.vmdk`
Xen	`.raw`, `.vmdk`
VMware	`.vmdk`

It is even possible to convert between disk image formats using various utilities, such as `qemu-img` (available in the `qemu-utils` package) or `VboxManage converthd` (available in the main VirtualBox distribution).

Again, be aware that OpenNebula requires a particular script to be configured at bootup, for proper virtual machine configuration. Do not skip the *Contextualization* section.

Template for datablock images

For application data, you can define an empty disk that will automatically be formatted on instance start up:

```
NAME = "Data for application X"
TYPE = DATABLOCK
# No PATH set, this image will start as a new empty disk
SIZE = 20480
FSTYPE = ext3
PUBLIC = no
PERSISTENT = yes
DESCRIPTION = "Storage for my application X"
```

We set `persistent` to `yes`, so that data is maintained across instance creation and deletion, and `public` to `no` to hide this image from other users.

In `fstype`, you can set every filesystem for which the `mkfs` utility is available on the host, using the following command:

```
$ ls /sbin/mkfs.*
```

You may want to install, on hosts, the packages `dosfstools` and `ntfsprogs`, in order to format disk images with native Windows filesystems. As you can imagine, you can also format disks at the first instance boot up without problems.

> **The mkfs.* - command not found**
>
> Some GNU/Linux distributions, such as Debian, do not include in the PATH environment variable the /sbin and /usr/sbind directories for non-root users. This results in Command not found errors when deploying a new virtual machine with datablock storage. To solve this, add to oneadmin accounts ~/.profile file the following environmental variable PATH="/sbin:/usr/sbin:$PATH".

Template for CDROMs

It is possible to create a read-only resource (for example, a .iso file) in the Image Repository. The code for the template is as follows:

```
NAME         = "MATLAB install CD"
TYPE         = CDROM
PATH         = /tmp/matlab.iso
DESCRIPTION  = "Contains the MATLAB installation files. Mount it to
install MATLAB on new OS images."
```

Specific image handling for VMware

When you are using VMware as a hypervisor, the driver requires that the PATH attribute be used as follows:

```
PATH=vmware:///absolute/path/to/disk/folder
```

The mentioned folder should contain a disk.vmdk file (this is a mandatory requirement; rename it if necessary) that is a text-readable file linking to flat .vmdk files in the same folder. You do not need to rename the flat .vmdk too; if you do so, edit the main disk.vmdk accordingly.

Submitting a new disk image

Once you are satisfied with the template definitions, submit them to OpenNebula with the oneimage utility, using the following command:

```
$ oneimage create <template.one>
```

In order to check for importing errors, use the `list` and `show` commands:

```
oneadmin@odin:/var/cloud$ oneimage list
    ID USER    GROUP     NAME          SIZE TYPE        REGTIME PUB PER STAT  RVMS
     5 oneadmin oneadmin ttylinux1      40M  OS   12/08 12:41:15  No  No used     1
oneadmin@odin:/var/cloud$ oneimage show 5
IMAGE 5 INFORMATION
ID             : 5
NAME           : ttylinux1
USER           : oneadmin
GROUP          : oneadmin
TYPE           : OS
REGISTER TIME  : 12/08 12:41:15
PUBLIC         : No
PERSISTENT     : No
SOURCE         : /var/cloud//one/var/images/19146fb4163f075137ddccd1721845ce
PATH           : /var/cloud/ttylinux/ttylinux.img
SIZE           : 40
STATE          : used
RUNNING_VMS    : 1

IMAGE TEMPLATE
DEV_PREFIX=hd
```

Later, if you decide to remove this image template, you can use `oneadmin delete` to remove it or `oneadmin update` to directly make changes to the template attributes.

Changing attributes of submitted templates

The utility `oneimage` includes a bunch of commands to easily alter every attribute of the already submitted templates. The following is a list of attributes available in the utility:

- `persistent <id>`: This makes the image persistent and saves the changes made to the images (for example, if after shutdown, a non-shared filesystem is used). Persistent images can be attached to only one VM instance at a time.

- `nonpersistent <id>`: This makes the image non-persistent. Changes will be lost if VM is shutdown and `SAVE=yes` is not used.

- `disable <id>`: This disables the given image so no one can use it.

- `enable <id>`: This enables a disabled image.

- `chtype <id> <type>`: This changes the type of the image (for example, OS, DATABLOCK, or CD-ROM).

- `unpublish <id>`: This unpublishes the image; private images can only be used by those who created them.

- `publish <id>`: This publishes the image; a public image can be used by every user.

- `chown <id> <userid> [<groupid>]`: This changes the image owner and group.

- `chgrp <id> <groupid>`: This changes the group for a particular image.

Managing virtual machines

A virtual machine template can be very complex due to the high number of sections and attributes available, but fortunately, most defaults are fine, so we will start with another simple example.

Each virtual machine template needs to contain information about the required CPU and memory, and about which disk images should be available and to which networks the VM should be attached.

Most machines you need will probably be configured correctly, as follows:

```
NAME    = web001
CPU = 0.25
VCPU = 4
```

The first is a dedicated host CPU portion (where 1.0 is a core at full power), and the second is the number of virtual CPUs attached to the virtual machine.

A swap partition would be practically useless if submitted into the Image Repository, so it is defined directly here in the machine template. The code is as follows:

```
MEMORY = 512
DISK = [ image_id = 2 ]
DISK = [ type = swap,
  size  = 1024 ]
```

This datablock is kept even after the VM shut down. Otherwise, it will be automatically removed on shut down, which is good for caches but not for your precious data. The code is as follows:

```
DISK = [ type = fs,
  size = 10240,
  save = yes,
  format = ext3 ]
```

It is very useful to troubleshoot a running VM with a VNC session on the main screen of the virtual machine (and to enable no VNC in the Sunstone web interface). The code is as follows:

```
NIC = [ NETWORK_ID = 0 ]
FEATURES = [ acpi="yes" ]
GRAPHICS = [ type = "vnc", passwd = "vncpassword", listen = "0.0.0.0",
KEYMAP = "it"]
```

By default, instances are of the i686 processor; if you need to run an x86_64 machine, you need the architecture configuration specification, which is as follows:

```
OS = [ ARCH ="x86_64"  ]
```

The Rank attribute is used by the OpenNebula Scheduler to decide on which host it should start the VM. In this case, the machine will be started on the active host with greater available memory than any other.

```
RANK = FREEMEMORY
```

Here you are!

We need to know about the various states (and their meanings) that a virtual instance can get into, before proceeding further.

Virtual machine life-cycle

The life-cycle of a virtual instance in OpenNebula includes the following stages (the first word is the full name of the state, and following between brackets is the string that will appear on the onevm list output):

- **Pending** (pend): By default a VM starts in the pending state, waiting for a host to run on. It will stay in this state until the scheduler decides to deploy it, or the user deploys it using the deploy command.
- **Hold** (hold): The user holds the VM, and it will not be scheduled until it is released or it can be deployed manually.
- **Prolog** (prol): The transfer manager is transferring the VM files' disk images to the host in which the virtual machine will run.
- **Running** (runn): The VM is running correctly.
- **Migrate** (migr): The VM is migrating from one host to another.
- **Epilog** (epil): The system cleans up the host used to virtualize the VM, and additionally, the disk images to be saved are copied back to the frontend.

- **Stopped** (`stop`): The VM is stopped. The VM state has been saved and it has been transferred back along with the disk images to the frontend.

- **Suspended** (`susp`): The VM is paused and the files are left in the host to later restart the VM there.

- **Failed** (`fail`): The VM startup has failed. In this case, check the logfiles; there is probably a frontend misconfiguration.

- **Unknown** (`unknown`): The VM cannot not be reached anymore; it is in an unknown state (it may have crashed or its host may have rebooted).

- **Done** (`done`): The VM instance has finished running; it will not be displayed anymore by `onevm list`.

Managing the instances

Besides `create`, `onevm` provides a lot of commands to manage a virtual instance. Every command can be executed only when the machine is in a particular state; if you try to execute a command with a VM in an incorrect state, you will be warned with a message.

Here is a list of the available `onevm` commands:

- `deploy <vm-id> <host-id>`: This starts an existing VM in a specific host.

- `shutdown <vm-id>`: This gracefully shuts down a running VM, sending the ACPI signal (for a Linux VM, it must be running `acpid`).

- `livemigrate <vm-id> <hostid>`: The VM is transferred between hosts with no noticeable downtime. This action requires a shared file system storage (and for a KVM host, a libvirt running with `listen_tcp` enabled).

- `migrate <vm-id> <hostid>`: The VM gets stopped and resumed in the target host.

- `hold <vm-id>`: This sets the VM to a hold state, so the scheduler will not deploy it.

- `release <vm-id>`: This releases a VM from the hold state, setting it to pending.

- `stop <vm-id>`: The VM state is transferred back to the frontend for a possible reschedule.

- `cancel <vm-id>`: The VM is immediately destroyed. Use this action instead of `shutdown`, when the VM does not have ACPI support or when it has become unresponsive. The difference with the `delete` action is that the persistent images are saved back to the repository.

- `suspend <vm-id>`: This is the same as `stop`, but the VM state is left in the host for resuming.

- `resume <vm-id>`: This resumes the execution of a saved VM.

- `saveas <vm-id> <disk-id> <img-name>`: This sets the specified VM disk to be saved in a new image.

- `delete <mv-id>`: The VM is immediately destroyed. Using this action instead of `cancel` will set the images meant to be saved in the error state.

- `restart <vm-id>`: This forces the hypervisor to reboot a VM stuck in the UNKNOWN or BOOT state.

- `resubmit <vm-id>`: This resubmits a VM to a PENDING state. This is intended for VMs stuck in a transient state. In order to redeploy a fresh copy of the same VM, create a template and instantiate it.

The following diagram shows all the possible transitions between each VM state.

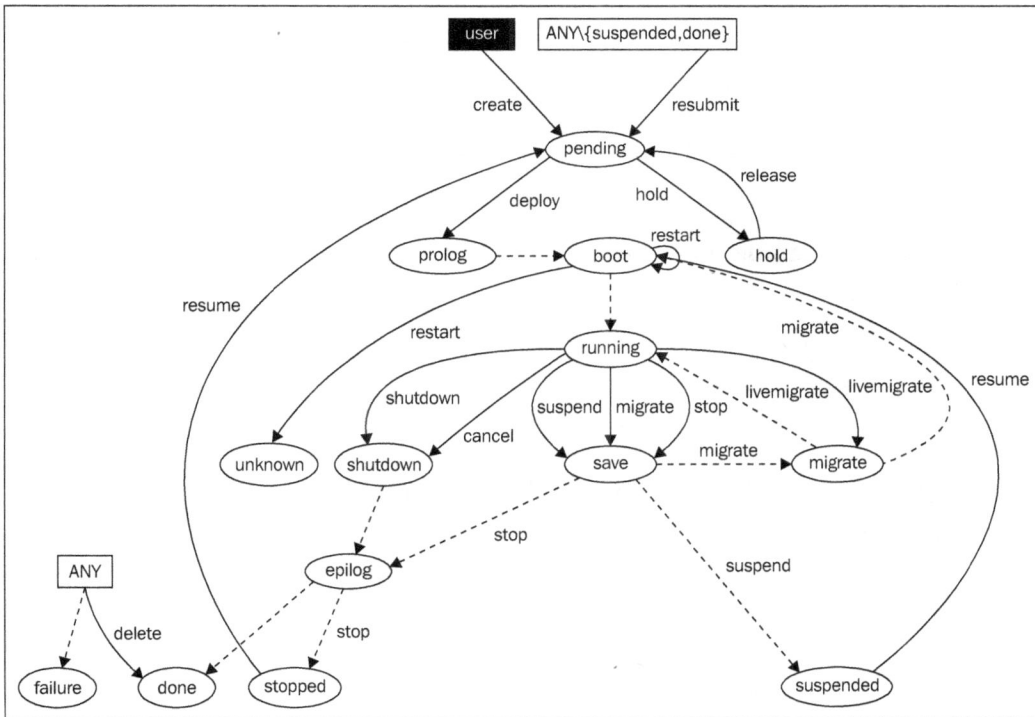

The virtual machine template

In the following paragraphs, we will analyze every section and its relative attributes that can be used to configure a VM.

The capacity section

The first section of a VM template is used to configure the resources allocated to it. The following table provides information about the various capacity attributes and their descriptions:

Attribute	Description	Default
NAME	Name assigned to the VM.	one-id
MEMORY	Amount of RAM required for the VM, in MB.	Must be set.
CPU	Percentage of CPU divided by 100 assigned to the VM.	1.0
VCPU	Number of virtual CPUs attached to VM.	1

An updated reference is available at the following link:

`http://opennebula.org/documentation:rel3.2:template#capacity_section`

An example for assigning the values to the capacity section parameters is as follows:

```
NAME    = test-vm
MEMORY = 1024
CPU     = 0.5
VCPU = 4
```

The OS and boot options section

This section is used to specify boot options, such as kernel, initrd, and bootloader. Every attribute is included inside the OS array. The following table provides information about the various attributes for the OS, the boot section, and their descriptions:

Attribute	Description	XEN default	KVM default	VMWare default
ARCH	CPU architecture to virtualize	N/A	i686/x86_64	i686/x86_64
KERNEL	Path to kernel	Must be set	Optional	N/A
INITRD	Path to the initrd image	Optional (for kernel)	Optional (for kernel)	N/A
ROOT	Device to be mounted as root	Optional (for kernel)	Optional (for kernel)	N/A
KERNEL_CMD	Arguments for the booting kernel	Optional (for kernel)	Optional (for kernel)	N/A
BOOTLOADER	Path to the bootloader executable	Must be set	Optional	N/A
BOOT	The options available are hd, cdrom, network, and fd	N/A	hd	N/A

An updated reference is available at the following link:

```
http://opennebula.org/documentation:rel3.2:template#os_and_boot_
options_section
```

An example for Xen with the `pygrub` bootloader is as follows:

```
OS = [ bootloader = /usr/lib/xen-default/bin/pygrub, root = sda1]
```

An example of Xen with `kernel` and `initrd` is as follows:

```
OS = [ kernel = "/vmlinuz", initrd = "/initrd.img", root = sda1,
KERNEL_CMD = "ro xencons=tty console=tty1"]
```

An example for configuring KVM and VMware is as follows:

```
OS = [ boot = hd,  arch = x86_64]
```

The disks section

Every disk is defined inside its own disk array. To use an image present on the Image Repository, you can use the following attributes:

Attribute	Description	Default
IMAGE_ID	ID of the image to use	Must be set
BUS	Type of disk device to emulate (IDE, SCSI, and Virtio)	IDE
TARGET	Used to alter the order of the disk rather than configuration order (sda, sdb, and sdc)	Automatically chosen
DRIVER	Specific disk image format (for KVM: .raw and .qcow files; for Xen: tap:aio file)	Depends on hypervisor

You can use an image without registering in the repository first, and you can use a dynamic image with the following attributes.

Attribute	Description	Default
TYPE	Disk type: floppy, disk, cdrom, swap, fs, and block	Depends on hypervisor
SOURCE	Path or HTTP URL to file	
SIZE	Used for swap, fs block TYPE, in MB	
FORMAT	Used for fs TYPE, filesystem type (those for which the frontend has mkfs utility, such as ext2, ext3, ext4, vfat, and ntfs)	
TARGET	Device to map disk (sda, sdb, and sdc)	Must be set
CLONE	If yes, it will make a copy of SOURCE; if no, it will directly use it	yes
SAVE	After VM shutdown, whether to keep the image or delete it	no
READONLY	Useful for .iso	no
BUS	Type of disk device to emulate (IDE, SCSI, Virtio)	IDE
DRIVER	Specific disk image format (KVM: .raw, and .qcow; Xen: tap:aio file:)	Depends on hypervisor

When each disk target is not defined, OpenNebula will expose the configured disks of the virtual machine, as follows:

- **sda**: For OS images
- **sdb**: For contextualization CD-ROM
- **sdc**: For CD-ROM images
- **sdd**: For swap partition
- **sd[e,f,g…]**: For datablocks and remaining images

An updated reference is available at the following link:

```
http://opennebula.org/documentation:rel3.2:template#disks_section
```

A simple definition for an image in the repository (the omitted attributes are inherited from the original image template) is as follows:

```
DISK = [ IMAGE_ID = 2 ]
```

A simple definition for a swap device is as follows:

```
DISK = [ TYPE = swap, SIZE = 1024    ]
```

An empty disk for VM data that is not removed after VM shut down, mounted on the seventh controller port:

```
DISK = [ TYPE = fs, SIZE = 4096, FORMAT = ext3, SAVE = yes,
  TARGET = sdg ]
```

When using KVM, it is highly recommended to use the Virtio bus to reduce overhead on I/O operations. Linux support for Virtio is available from v2.6.25. For Windows OS, there are drivers, which will be required during an OS installation. They are available at, `http://wiki.libvirt.org/page/Virtio`.

A definition for a disk will be as follows:

```
DISK = [ IMAGE_ID = 3, BUS = virtio ]
```

For the same reason, it is advisable to use `tap:aio:` (ending colon is not a typo) when using Xen, thus:

```
DISK = [ IMAGE_ID = 3, BUS = "tap:aio:" ]
```

The SCSI bus controller is also available, besides the standard IDE, to overcome its limitation of four concurrent disk devices, but it is usually less supported by OS than IDE.

The network section

Each network device is specified with **Network Interface Card** (**NIC**) arrays. You can define as many NIC arrays as you need. The following attributes are available for a network:

Attribute	Description	Default
NETWORK_ID	ID of the virtual network to be attached, assigned by onevnet	Must be set, if BRIDGE not present
BRIDGE	Name of the physical bridge to be attached (can be used instead of NETWORK_ID)	Must be set, if NETWORK_ID not present
IP	IP address assigned to the VM	A random available IP from the specified network
MAC	Hardware address assigned to the VM	A particular MAC address containing the encoded IP address, decoded by the Contextualization script
TARGET	Name for the tuning device created for the VM on the Host (useful only for particular needs)	Automatically assigned
SCRIPT	Pathname to a script that will be executed after creating the tun device for the VM	None
MODEL	The hardware that will be emulated	Depends on hypervisor
WHITE_PORTS_TCP	Permits access to the VM only through the specified ports in the TCP protocol	Allow all
BLACK_PORTS_TCP	Doesn't permit access to the VM through the specified ports in the TCP protocol	Deny nothing
WHITE_PORTS_UDP	Permits access to the VM only through the specified ports in the UDP protocol	Allow all
BLACK_PORTS_UDP	Doesn't permit access to the VM through the specified ports in the UDP protocol	Deny nothing
ICMP	Blocks ICMP connections to the VM	Accept

An updated reference is available at the following link:

http://opennebula.org/documentation:rel3.2:template#network_section

A simple NIC definition using the NETWORK_ID attribute is as follows:

```
NIC = [ NETWORK_ID = 1 ]
```

A simple NIC definition using the BRIDGE attribute is as follows:

```
NIC = [ BRIDGE = lan0 ]
```

In order to assign a particular available IP address on the specified network, use the following code:

```
NIC = [ NETWORK_ID = 1, IP = 192.168.66.66 ]
```

In order to enable restricting firewall rules (you should enable firewall on and firewall hooks on in oned.conf), as follows:

```
NIC = [ NETWORK_ID = 1, WHITE_PORTS_TCP="22,80,443,6667:7000",
  ICMP = "drop" ]
```

Network card models available for KVM and QEMU can be retrieved with the following commands.

- For KVM:

  kvm -net nic,model=?

- For a QEMU:

  qemu -net nic,model=?

The default value is rtl8139 (Ethernet 10/100); a common alternative is e1000 (Ethernet 10/100/1000), but you should prefer Virtio for lowering the overhead.

The I/O devices section

Some I/O devices are supported in virtual machines, namely mouse and graphical display, configurable through the INPUT and VNC arrays.

Attribute	Description	Default
TYPE	Type of device attached; mouse or tablet	
BUS	Bus on which the device is attached; usb, ps2, or xen	

The following table provides information on the available attributes for configuring a remote VNC display:

Attribute	Description	Default
TYPE	The graphical device type, vnc or sdl (qemu only, not working with VMware)	
LISTEN	Address to bind to for VNC server	127.0.0.1
PORT	Port for VNC server (KVM uses a real port, Xen 5900, and a port you define)	KVM: 5900 Xen: 0
PASSWD	Password for the VNC server	
KEYMAP	Keyboard configuration locale to use in the VNC display	Server locale

An updated reference is available at the following link:

```
http://opennebula.org/documentation:rel3.2:template#i_o_devices_
section
```

In order to define a VNC server attached to the primary display for your virtual machine, use the following code:

```
GRAPHICS = [ TYPE    = "vnc", LISTEN  = "0.0.0.0", PASSWD = "my
password"]
```

It is advisable to not specify a port but let OpenNebula set an incremental port number depending on the VM ID. To connect to a VM VNC, you need to provide your client the IP address of the host that is running the VM and specify port as 5900 + ID of the VM.

For example, if you wanted to connect to ID 150 through a VNC running on the xen01 host, you would launch it from your desktop using the following command:

```
$ vncviewer xen01 6050
```

The placement section

There are two attributes that let us modify the behavior of the OpenNebula scheduler to choose which host deploys our VM:

Attribute	Description	Default
REQUIREMENTS	Boolean expression to restrict provisioning of particular hosts	Use all available hosts
RANK	An expression that will be used to sort the suitable hosts for this VM	Choose a random available host

The REQUIREMENTS attribute syntax is quite complex. The code is as follows:

```
stmt::= expr';'
expr::= VARIABLE '=' NUMBER
   | VARIABLE '!=' NUMBER
   | VARIABLE '>' NUMBER
   | VARIABLE '<' NUMBER
   | VARIABLE '=' STRING
   | VARIABLE '!=' STRING
   | expr '&' expr
   | expr '|' expr
   | '!' expr
   | '(' expr ')'
```

For the RANK attribute, the code is as follows:

```
stmt::= expr';'
expr::= VARIABLE
   | NUMBER
   | expr '+' expr
   | expr '-' expr
   | expr '*' expr
   | expr '/' expr
   | '-' expr
   | '(' expr ')'
```

Let us clarify both the attributes with some examples.

- An example definition for placing our VM on a host whose name starts with a particular string is as follows:

  ```
  REQUIREMENTS = "NAME = \"thor*\""
  ```

- For a host using the VMware hypervisor specify REQUIREMENTS as:

  ```
  REQUIREMENTS = "HYPERVISOR=\"vmware\""
  ```

- For an host with at least more than two CPU units to be free REQUIREMENTS would be specified as:

  ```
  REQUIREMENTS = FREECPU > 1.9
  ```

As we see the defined template variables can be used as follows:

- `$<template_variable>`: Any single value variable of the VM template
- `$<template_variable>[<attribute>]`: Any single value contained in a multiple-value variable in the VM template
- `$<template_variable>[<attribute>, <attribute2>=<value2>]`: Any single value contained in a multiple value variable in the VM template, setting one attribute to discern between multiple variables named in the same way

Others variables are provided by the Information Manager, and they include: `NAME`, `TOTALCPU`, `TOTALMEMORY`, `FREEMEMORY`, `FREECPU`, `USEDMEMORY`, `USEDCPU`, and `HYPERVISOR`.

It is possible to extend the Information Manager driver to poll and export custom variables, such as the CPU temperature.

An updated reference is available at the following link: `http://opennebula.org/documentation:rel3.2:template#placement_section`

For the attribute `RANK`, a good choice could be to prefer hosts with more spare memory and lower CPU load, thus:

```
RANK = FREEMEMORY - FREECPU * 100
```

The context section

Context information is passed to the Virtual Machine through an ISO mounted as a partition. This information can be defined in the VM template in the optional section called `CONTEXT`, with the following attributes:

An updated reference is available at the following link:

`http://opennebula.org/documentation:rel3.2:template#context_section`.

Attribute	Description	Default
`$VARIABLE`	Any custom variable can be defined.	
`FILES`	Space-separated list of paths to include in context device.	
`TARGET`	Device to attach the context ISO.	sdb

For example, check for the CONTEXT section inside the previous `ttylinux.`
one template:

```
CONTEXT = [
  hostname    = "$NAME",
  ip_public   = "172.17.0.18",
  files       = "init.sh /home/scorp/.ssh/id_rsa.pub",
  target      = "hdc",
  root_pubkey = "id_rsa.pub",
  username    = "user",
  user_pubkey = "id_rsa.pub"
]
```

All the files included in the `files` attribute will be archived inside a dynamically generated ISO image and exported inside the VM. Every other attribute will be placed inside a script file that could be sourced by our `init.sh` file as, follows:

```
if [ -f /mnt/context/context.sh ]
then
  . /mnt/context/context.sh
fi
```

Now `init.sh` can use the variables to achieve some basic machine configuration, using the following code:

```
if [ -n "$HOSTNAME" ]; then
  echo $HOSTNAME > /etc/HOSTNAME
  hostname $HOSTNAME
fi
if [ -n "$IP_PUBLIC" ]; then
  ifconfig eth0 $IP_PUBLIC
fi
```

Any required files can be exported inside the VM (for example, `id_rsa.pub`):

```
if [ -f /mnt/context/$ROOT_PUBKEY ]; then
  cat /mnt/context/$ROOT_PUBKEY >> /root/.ssh/authorized_keys
fi
```

The RAW section

This optional section is used when we need to pass special attributes to the underlying hypervisor. Every parameter specified in the data attribute gets passed straight to the deployment file, unmodified.

Attribute	Description
TYPE	Used to specify when the next parameters need to be sent. Possible values are: kvm, xen.
DATA	Raw data directly passed to the hypervisor

An updated reference is available at the following link:

`http://opennebula.org/documentation:rel3.2:template#raw_section.`

A real use case for a raw attribute in KVM is to attach a serial and console port to a VM:

```
RAW = [ type = "kvm", data = "<devices><serial type=\"pty\"><source
    path=\"/dev/pts/5\"/><target port=\"0\"/></serial><console
    type=\"pty\" tty=\"/dev/pts/5\"><source path=\"/dev/pts/5\"/>
    <target port=\"0\"/></console></devices>" ]
```

For a complete reference, you should take a look at the following wiki page:

`http://libvirt.org/formatdomain.html`

Simple examples

Here follows a VM template working example for every hypervisor.

KVM example

A complete VM definition for a KVM instance is as follows:

```
NAME = kvm-example
MEMORY = 256
CPU = 0.1
DISK = [ IMAGE_ID  = 2 ]
DISK = [
  TYPE = swap,
  SIZE = 1024 ]
NIC = [ NETWORK_ID = 1 ]
GRAPHICS = [
  TYPE    = "vnc",
  LISTEN  = "0.0.0.0" ]
```

Xen HVM example

A complete VM definition for a Xen HVM instance is as follows:

```
NAME    = xen-hvm-example
CPU     = 0.1
MEMORY = 256
OS = [
  BOOTLOADER = "hvmloader",
  BOOT = hd ]
DISK    = [ IMAGE_ID = 1 , target = hda , type = file:]
NIC     = [ NETWORK_ID = 2 , model = rtl8139 ]
FEATURES=[ acpi="yes" ]
GRAPHICS=[
  type ="vnc",
  listen="0.0.0.0",
  port="5900"]
RAW =[type ="xen",data="builder='hvm'"]
RAW =[type="xen",data="device_model='/usr/lib/xen-4.0/bin/qemu-dm'"]
```

In order to use Xen HVM (KVM-like Xen virtualization), you need to specify the bootloader code and pass the two raw parameters to point to the right qemu-dm.

Xen pygrub example

A complete VM definition for a Xen pygrub instance is as follows:

```
NAME = xen-pygrub-example
CPU = 0.1
MEMORY = 256
OS = [
  kernel   = "/vmlinuz",
  initrd   = "/initrd.img",
  root = "xvda1" ]
DISK = [ IMAGE_ID = 1 , target = hda , type = file:]
NIC = [ NETWORK_ID = 2 , model = rtl8139 ]
FEATURES=[ acpi="yes" ]
GRAPHICS = [ type ="vnc", listen="0.0.0.0" ]
```

VMware example

A complete VM definition for a VMware instance is as follows:

```
NAME    = vmware-example
CPU     = 0.1
MEMORY = 256
```

```
OS = [  BOOT = hd ]
DISK=[IMAGE_ID="3"]
NIC=[NETWORK_ID="2"]
```

With a disk image template, the values for NAME and PATH would be as follows:

```
NAME=MyVMwareDisk
PATH=vmware:///home/oneadmin/one/var/vmware-vm
```

Remember that, in that folder, there should be a `disk.vmdk` file.

Contextualization

The main goal of contextualization is to correctly configure network details during a virtual machine boot up without the necessary integration of an external DHCP server.

This is done by inserting a particular script into the virtual machine boot sequence, which in turn will scan the available network interfaces, extract their MAC addresses, compute a MAC-to-IP conversion, and generate a `/etc/network/interfaces` file that will ensure a correct IP assignment to the corresponding interface.

Actually, this function has been extended and you are able to pass an arbitrary number of configuration scripts and custom parameters using a runtime-generated `.iso` file attached to the virtual machine.

You can browse both scripts already customized for the main GNU/Linux distributions at the following link:
`http://dev.opennebula.org/projects/opennebula/repository/revisions/master/show/share/scripts`

For Windows instances, contextualization is not officially supported by OpenNebula, but some hackish examples have appeared on the Internet. A well-documented but very basic implementation is available at the following link:
`http://wiki.ieeta.pt/wiki/index.php/OpenNebula#Using_Windows_Images_for_new_Virtual_Machines`

With a bunch of VBScript/PowerShell scripts, it is possible to dynamically configure the log-in credentials, hostname, and IP addresses.

The basic contextualization

Retrieve the `vmcontext` script for your distribution, and copy it into the `/etc/init.d` folder of your virtual machine image.

On Ubuntu, you should insert the script execution into two network-related startup configuration files, as described at the following page:
`http://dev.opennebula.org/projects/opennebula/repository/revisions/`
`master/entry/share/scripts/ubuntu/net-vmcontext/README`

Open the `/etc/init/networking.conf` configuration file and search for the first occurrence of the code:

```
pre-start exec mkdir -p /var/run/network
```

Replace it to enable basic contextualization during network configuration, using the following code:

```
pre-start script
  /etc/init.d/vmcontext
  mkdir -p /var/run/network
end script
```

Open the `/etc/init/network-interface.conf` configuration file and search for the first occurrence of the code:

```
pre-start script
```

Append the following code, to finish integrating basic contextualization:

```
/etc/init.d/vmcontext
```

The generic contextualization

This method can be used to pass configuration parameters to a newly started virtual machine using an auto-generated ISO image. This method is network-agnostic, so it can be used to configure network interfaces (so, it should be used instead of `vmcontext`).

For example, in the VM template you can define:

```
CONTEXT = [
  hostname   = "$NAME",
  ip_public = "192.168.0.4",
  netmask = "255.255.255.0",
  files = "/home/oneadmin/scripts/ubuntu/init.sh
    /home/oneadmin/scripts/ubuntu/id_rsa.pub",
    root_pubkey = "id_rsa.pub",
    username = "oneadmin",
    user_pubkey = "id_rsa.pub"
]
```

You can use the `init.sh` script available from at following link:

`http://dev.opennebula.org/projects/opennebula/repository/revisions/`
`master/entry/share/scripts/ubuntu/context/init.sh`.

As a starting point for our generic contextualization script, use the following code:

```
#!/bin/bash
if [ -f /mnt/context.sh ]
then
   . /mnt/context.sh
fi
```

The contextualization ISO is present; in order to load the variables from it, use the following code.

```
echo $HOSTNAME > /etc/hostname
hostname $HOSTNAME
sed -i "/127.0.1.1/s/ubuntu/$HOSTNAME/" /etc/hosts
```

In order to reconfigure a virtual machine hostname, use the following code:

```
if [ -n "$IP_PUBLIC" ]; then
  ifconfig eth0 $IP_PUBLIC
fi
if [ -n "$NETMASK" ]; then
  ifconfig eth0 netmask $NETMASK
fi
```

In order to configure the primary network IP and netmask, use the following code:

```
if [ -f /mnt/$ROOT_PUBKEY ]; then
  mkdir -p /root/.ssh
  cat /mnt/$ROOT_PUBKEY >> /root/.ssh/authorized_keys
  chmod -R 600 /root/.ssh/
fi
```

In order to configure passwordless login for the `root` user with your `id_rsa.pub` file, use the following code:

```
if [ -n "$USERNAME" ]; then
  useradd -s /bin/bash -m $USERNAME
  if [ -f /mnt/$USER_PUBKEY ]; then
    mkdir -p /home/$USERNAME/.ssh/
    cat /mnt/$USER_PUBKEY >> /home/$USERNAME/.ssh/authorized_keys
    chown -R $USERNAME:$USERNAME /home/$USERNAME/.ssh
    chmod -R 600 /home/$USERNAME/.ssh/authorized_keys
  fi
fi
```

In order to configure the execution of a contextualization script on the virtual machine adding to your /etc/rc.local, file use the following code:

```
#!/bin/sh -e
mount -t iso9660 /dev/sdc /mnt
if [ -f /mnt/context.sh ]; then
  . /mnt/init.sh
fi
umount /mnt
exit 0
```

The template repository

To ease the VM management, it is possible to register, in the OpenNebula database, every VM template that you plan to use often or that you need to distribute among your users.

The onetemplate utility can be used to register a VM template in the database with the following command:

```
$ onetemplate create <file>
```

In order to list the registered templates, use the following command:

```
$ onetemplate list
```

In order to update it use, the following command:

```
$ onetemplate update <id>
```

Once a template is registered in the template repository, you can easily launch new instances by using the following command:

```
$ onetemplate instantiate <id> -m <number>
```

-m could be used to launch more than one instance at a time.

In order to remove registered templates once they are not needed, use the following command:

```
$ onetemplate delete <id>
```

The onetemplate command supports other common commands, such as chmod, chown, and chgrp.

Let us try with our well-known ttylinux.one template.

In order to register the VM template in the repository, use the following command:

```
$ onetemplate create ttylinux.one
```

In order to examine the template's content, once it is in the repository, use the following command:

```
$ onetemplate show ttylinux
```

In order to update or insert a new attribute in the template, you can automatically open the actual template in a text editor and make changes with the following command:

```
$ onetemplate update ttylinux
```

In order for every user in your OpenNebula installation to be able to use this template, use the following command:

```
$ onetemplate chmod ttylinux 644
```

In order for every user in the group `users` to to be able to use and make changes to this template, use the following commands:

```
$ onetemplate chgrp ttylinux users
$ onetemplate chmod ttylinux 664
```

In order to launch a bunch of new instances from this template, use the following command:

```
$ onetemplate instantiate ttylinux -m 10
```

> The ownership and the permissions of a template do not affect the ownership and the permissions of any instance created from it.

Summary

At this point, you should have basic knowledge, sufficient to configure and run a simple OpenNebula infrastructure from the command line.

In the next chapter, we will see how to simplify our infrastructure management for day-to-day use, using an accessible web interface.

6
Web Management

Despite the fact that the OpenNebula command-line interface is simple and straightforward to use, most users, especially non-technical ones, may prefer to use a more comfortable graphical user interface.

OpenNebula includes, from recent releases, a standalone web interface called Sunstone, which permits cloud administrators to easily manage resources, perform typical operations on them, and keep an eye on what is going on.

Sunstone installation

Sunstone was installed during the main OpenNebula installation and requires some Ruby gems to operate correctly. They are as follows:

- `json`
- `rack`
- `sinatra`
- `thin`

Hopefully, they have already been installed on your system during the execution of the `install_gems` script.

An additional library is required if you want to start a VNC session in an already running VM instance, without having a VNC client installed on your machine.

This is achieved by using a VNC HTML5 web-socket client (that goes by the name **noVNC**; detailed description on the link `http://kanaka.github.com/noVNC/`) on the client side and a VNC proxy translating and redirecting incoming connections on the server side.

The noVNC requirements are as follows:

- **Python 2.5**: Needed by the noVNC proxy
- **Firefox** or **Chrome**: A recent browser with web-socket support works

You need to execute the install_novnc.sh script, in order to download and configure the latest available noVNC release.

For self-contained installations, you will find the script in the $ONE_LOCATION/share folder. The command for the installation is as follows:

```
$ ./install_novnc.sh
```

For system-wide installations use sudo and run the script from the /usr/share/one folder. The commands to be used are as follows:

```
$ cd /usr/share/one
$ ./install_novnc.sh
```

As a final step, check the sunstone-server.conf file in the etc folder. The code for the configuration file is as follows:

```
# OpenNebula sever contact information
:one_xmlrpc: http://localhost:2633/RPC2
# Server Configuration
:host: 0.0.0.0
:port: 9869
:auth: basic
# VNC Configuration
:vnc_proxy_base_port: 29876
:novnc_path: /var/cloud/one/share/noVNC
```

The available configuration parameters are as follows:

- one_xmlrpc: This is the XML-RPC end point used by Sunstone to retrieve OpenNebula data (for example, where the OpenNebula frontend is running).
- host and port: These are the IP address and port to which the Sunstone web interface should be bound.
- auth: We use **basic** for simple authentication or **x509** for using certificate authentication (it requires additional configuration).
- vnc_proxy_base_port: This is the local base port for the VNC proxy. The final port for the proxy is calculated by adding the base port and the VNC port of the host.
- novnc_path: This is the path where the noVNC files will be found (the install_novnc.sh script should have automatically set the right path).

At this point, Sunstone configuration is complete and you just need to launch it with the following command:

```
$ sunstone-server start
```

Deploying Sunstone on a different machine

It is possible to install the Sunstone web interface on a dedicated machine rather than on the frontend. This is useful for deploying multiple Sunstone interfaces for load balancing or fault-tolerance.

You can install the Sunstone components only with the source package by passing the -s parameter to the install.sh script, by using the following commands:

```
$ sudo mkdir /home/oneadmin/sunstone
$ ./install.sh -s -d /home/oneadmin/sunstone
```

For a system-wide install, use the following commands:

```
$ sudo ./install.sh -s
```

Remember that we need both gems and noVNC for self-contained installs.
Use the following commands:

```
$ sudo $ONE_LOCATION/share/install_gems sunstone
$ $ONE_LOCATION/share/install_novnc.sh
```

For system-wide installs, use the following commands:

```
$ sudo /usr/share/one/install_gems sunstone
$ /usr/share/one/install_novnc.sh
```

As Sunstone needs to know how to connect to the OpenNebula frontend, as well as the sunstone-server.conf adjustments, we need to define the same environment variable as required by the OpenNebula frontend. The variable can be configured as: If Sunstone is installed in self-contained mode, this variable must be set to the appropriate path. Otherwise, in the system-wide mode, this variable must be unset.

In order to configure ONE_LOCATION place it in the ~/.profile file as following:

```
export ONE_LOCATION=/home/oneadmin/sunstone
```

Now we need to instruct Sunstone to use the credentials for the special OpenNebula user required for privileged server-side operations, serveradmin.

The `serveradmin` is a special account that gets created automatically during the first run, and its privileges are saved inside a textfile available at `/var/lib/one/.one/sunstone_auth` or `$ONE_LOCATION/var/.one/sunstone_auth`.

This `sunstone_auth` needs to be copied from the frontend to the instance of Sunstone running on a different machine on the right path (depending on the installation type). The available paths are as follows:

```
$ scp /var/lib/one/.one/sunstone_auth oneadmin
@sunstone:/var/lib/one/.one/

$ scp /home/oneadmin/one/var/.one/
sunstone_auth oneadmin@sunstone:~/one/var/.one/
```

In order to double-check that the file is readable only by the user running the Sunstone interface, use the following commands:

```
$ sudo chown oneadmin: /var/lib/one/.one/sunstone_auth
$ sudo chmod 600 /var/lib/one/.one/sunstone_auth
```

In order to check for the `sunstone-server.conf` file in the `etc` folder, use the following code:

```
# OpenNebula sever contact information
:one_xmlrpc: http://front-end:2633/RPC2
# Server Configuration
:host: 0.0.0.0
:port: 9869
:auth: basic
# VNC Configuration
:vnc_proxy_base_port: 29876
:novnc_path: /var/cloud/one/share/noVNC
```

Now you should be able to start Sunstone on the dedicated machine and be able to log in and manage OpenNebula by using the following command:

```
$ sunstone-server start
```

If you get an `OpenNebula is not running` error message check `oned.log` on the frontend for any failures related to this, as this is the generic catch-all error message when something goes wrong (including incorrect `serveradmin` credentials).

> As logs are neither stored in the OpenNebula database nor managed by it, VM logfiles will not be available in Sunstone, if you deploy it outside the frontend.

Configuring an SSL reverse proxy with nginx

As the Sunstone web interface natively supports only clear-text HTTP connections, it may be advisable to configure a reverse proxy with HTTPS support in front of it.

For this purpose, we can use **nginx** (pronounced engine-x), a popular web server and reverse proxy server for HTTP, SMTP, POP3, and IMAP with a strong focus on high concurrency, performance, and low memory usage. Indeed, it is open source and runs on almost every operating system.

On Ubuntu, you can install it using the following command:

```
sudo apt-get install nginx
```

As with the good old Apache, you need to create a new file at `/etc/nginx/sites-available`, using the following code:

```
# host and port for each upstream sunstone server
upstream sunstone {
  server 127.0.0.1:9869;
  }
server {
  listen 443;
  server_namelocalhost;
  ssl on;
# path to private ssl key and certificate
  ssl_certificate server.crt;
  ssl_certificate_keyserver.key;
# Define a custom HTML page to be showed for 50x errors
  error_page    500 502 503 504   /50x.html;
  location = /50x.html {
    root    /var/www/nginx-default;
    }
# Proxy all request to the upstream sunstone servers
  location / {
    proxy_pass http://sunstone;
    }
}
```

The first configuration block, `upstream`, is used to define every available Sunstone web interface to which this proxy will forward its requests. You can define multiple Sunstone interfaces; requests will automatically be balanced in round-robin fashion, and a server will be skipped if repeated connection errors occur.

When multiple Sunstone backends are configured, you may want to fine-tune the nginx upstream configuration by specifying parameters, such as `weight`, `max_fails`, and `fail_timeout`, for each server definition.

For fine-grained upstream server configuration, take a look at the online documentation available at the following link:

```
http://wiki.nginx.org/NginxHttpUpstreamModule#server
```

In order to create your custom 50x HTTP error page use the following commands:

```
$ sudo mkdir -p /var/www/nginx-default
```

```
$ echo "Something is wrong with our Sunstones"  | sudo tee /var/www/
nginx-default/50x.html
```

Now we can activate the new Sunstone virtual host configuration, with the following command:

```
$ sudo ln -s /etc/nginx/sites-available/sunstone /etc/nginx/sites-
enabled/
```

In order to remove the default Sunstone virtual host configuration, use the following command:

```
$ sudo rm /etc/nginx/sites-enabled/default
```

If you are on a multi-core machine, adjust the `worker_processes` parameter with the number of your cores, in the `/etc/nginx/nginx.conf` file.

Before starting nginx, we need to put our server certificate at `/etc/nginx` or generate a self-signed certificate (good for testing).

Generating a self-signed certificate

If you do not want to use a real SSL certificate (because the interface will not be accessible over the public Internet, or you do not have a local certification authority in your infrastructure), you can generate a self-signed certificate using OpenSSL with some commands.

In order to move to the main nginx configuration folder, use the following command:

```
$ cd /etc/nginx
```

In order to generate a new private key and to provide a simple password (it is required now; we will remove it later), use the following code for generating the key:

```
$ sudo openssl genrsa -des3 -out server.key 1024
```

```
Generating RSA private key, 1024 bit long modulus
...++++++
..++++++
e is 65537 (0x10001)
Enter pass phrase for server.key:
Verifying - Enter pass phrase for server.key:
```

In order to generate a certificate signing request for the private key, fill in the information according to your requirements:

```
$ sudo openssl req -new -key server.key -out server.csr
Enter pass phrase for server.key:
You are about to be asked to enter information that will be
incorporated
into your certificate request.
What you are about to enter is what is called a Distinguished Name or
a DN.
There are quite a few fields but you can leave some blank
For some fields there will be a default value,
If you enter '.', the field will be left blank.
-----
Country Name (2 letter code) [AU]:IT
State or Province Name (full name) [Some-State]:Pisa
Locality Name (eg, city) []:Navacchio
Organization Name (eg, company) [Internet Widgits Pty Ltd]:LiberSoft
Organizational Unit Name (eg, section) []:
Common Name (eg, YOUR name) []:sunstone
Email Address []:
Please enter the following 'extra' attributes
to be sent with your certificate request
A challenge password []:
An optional company name []:
```

Now we will strip out the password, as we do not want to provide it for every nginx restart, though security paranoids may disagree. Use the following commands:

```
$ sudo cp server.key server.key.orig
```

```
$ sudo openssl rsa -in server.key.orig -out server.key
Enter pass phrase for server.key.orig:
writing RSA key
```

In order to generate the final certificate, use the following command:

```
$ sudo openssl x509 -req -days 365 -in server.csr -signkey server.key
-out server.crt
    Signature ok
    subject=/C=IT/ST=Pisa/L=Navacchio/O=LiberSoft/CN=sunstone
    Getting Private key
```

You are done with setting a self-signed SSL certificate to be used by nginx.

Starting the nginx SSL proxy-machine

If you copied your SSL certificate to /etc/nginx with the correct name, or successfully generated a self-signed certificate, we can start nginx using the following command:

```
$ sudo /etc/init.d/nginx start
```

Now you should be able to connect with your browser to https://proxy-machine/ and get the Sunstone interface.

With the current implementation, VNC web-socket connections cannot be proxied, and for this reason, they will not work. In the meantime, you can follow the current status of this feature at http://dev.opennebula.org/issues/1209.

First log in

After the Sunstone launch, you can connect with any modern browser to the OpenNebula Web management interface.

Web interfaces use the XML-RPC interface, which is also used by command-line utilities. You can use any of the user credentials that are already working with the command-line utilities.

If you have forgotten the `oneadmin` password, you can retrieve it from the file `~/.one/one_auth`, configured in the early setup stages.

The **Remember me** option, when enabled, will send a persistent cookie to the browser, so you will no longer need to re-enter your credentials every time you come back to the web interface. When the option is unchecked, the web interface will ask for credentials every time you try to access it.

Dashboard

Once you log in successfully, you will be redirected to the dashboard section, which looks like the following screenshot:

At the top-right corner, you will find a few important links to the OpenNebula online resources, such as the following:

- **Documentation**: It can be accessed at:

  `http://opennebula.org/documentation:documentation`

- **Support**: It can be accessed at:

  `http://opennebula.org/support:support`

- **Community**: It can be accessed at:

  `http://opennebula.org/community:community`

Always keep an eye on the documentation section while using the web interface; the various template references, in particular, can help a lot.

Next to those links, you will find a reference to the currently logged-in user, and the link to sign out. Always remember to log out if you are using a shared computer.

At the center of the page, you will find a first box summarizing the current resource usage of the OpenNebula infrastructure.

Summary of resources	
Hosts (total/active)	2 / 2
Groups	2
VM Templates (total/public)	1 / 0
VM Instances (total/running/failed)	11 / 11 / 0
Virtual Networks (total/public)	1 / 0
Images (total/public)	1 / 0
Users	1
ACL Rules	2

After this, there is a handy box that can be used to quickly create new resources. Using this is equivalent to using the **New** button in each resource section that we will see later. The **Quickstart** tab used to create new resources looks as in the following screenshot:

Quickstart	
New:	Host
	VM Instance
	VM Template
	Virtual Network
	Image
	User
	Group
	Acl

Following these two boxes, there is a bigger box containing a few charts about the latest CPU, memory, VM count, and network statistics.

Historical monitoring information

Hosts CPU   cpu_usage   used_cpu   max_cpu

```
1000
 750
 500
 250
   0
     14:20:00 14:28:20 14:36:40 14:45:00 14:53:20 15:01:40 15:10:00 15:18:20
```

Hosts memory   mem_usage   used_mem   max_mem

```
7.2G
4.8G
2.4G
  0K
     14:20:00 14:28:20 14:36:40 14:45:00 14:53:20 15:01:40 15:10:00 15:18:20
```

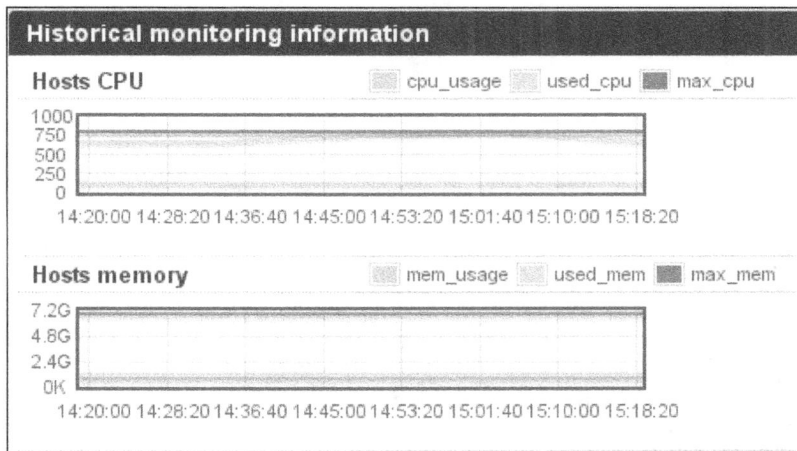

The charts are generated using the data gathered by OpenNebula. The Accounting and Statistics daemon will be presented in the next chapter. For now, it should be sufficient for you to start the service on the frontend, as the `oneadmin` user, with the following command:

```
$ oneacct start
```

Along with the dashboard you will find on the left sidebar, a page for each resource available in OpenNebula, whereby you can see and manage them.

Hosts

On each resource page there are a bunch of action buttons, which are used in order to interact with the currently selected resource. When a button is grayed-down, you should first select at least one row in the following table, using the checkboxes on the left:

```
                          ↻   + New   Update a template   Enable   Disable   Delete host

Show  10  ▼  entries                                     Search:  [            ]
```

You can use the left combobox to select the number of entries showed in each page listing and the **Search** textbox to filter the displayed elements (for example, searching for a particular hostname).

All	ID ⬍	Name ⬍	Running VMs ⬍	CPU Use ⬍	Memory use ⬍	Status ⬍
✔	0	odin	5	13%	18%	ON
☐	1	thor	6	15%	14%	ON

The table will show the currently configured hosts along with their **ID** number, **Name**, count of the **Running VMs**, **CPU Use** and **Memory use**, and **Status**. The information displayed here is not really in real time, but it is in fact the polled data retrieved by the Information Manager driver, so their freshness strictly depends on how you configured the attributes, such as HOST_MONITORING_INTERVAL, and HOST_PER_INTERVAL, in the oned.conf file.

The table can be sorted by a particular column clicking on the corresponding table header.

Showing 1 to 2 of 2 entries

First Previous 1 Next Last

The bottom of the table contains the pager and a summary of the available elements of the particular resource. Use them to know how many resources are available on that particular view and to navigate between the different pages.

Create host

Name:	loki

Drivers

Virtualization Manager:	KVM
Information Manager:	KVM
Virtual Network Manager:	Default (dummy)
Transfer Manager:	Shared

Create Reset

When you press the **New** action button, a pop-up window appears asking for the information needed to add a new host to the OpenNebula database. Please be aware that this procedure will replace the manual creation of a host template file and the subsequent `onehost create` command only. Prior to this, you need to carry out the basic host configuration, including the passwordless SSH login, as described in the earlier chapters.

Once you hit the **Create** button, a new host resource is submitted to the pool, and a small stacked message box will be displayed in the bottom-right corner of the web interface.

The second action button is **Update template**, and it can be used to change attributes of already submitted hosts.

> In this specific case, the majority of the host attributes are dynamically updated by the Information Manager drivers of their respective hypervisors, so it does not make much sense to manually edit them. The only useful attribute that could be meaningfully changed for host is `name`.

A screenshot of the **Update template** looks like this:

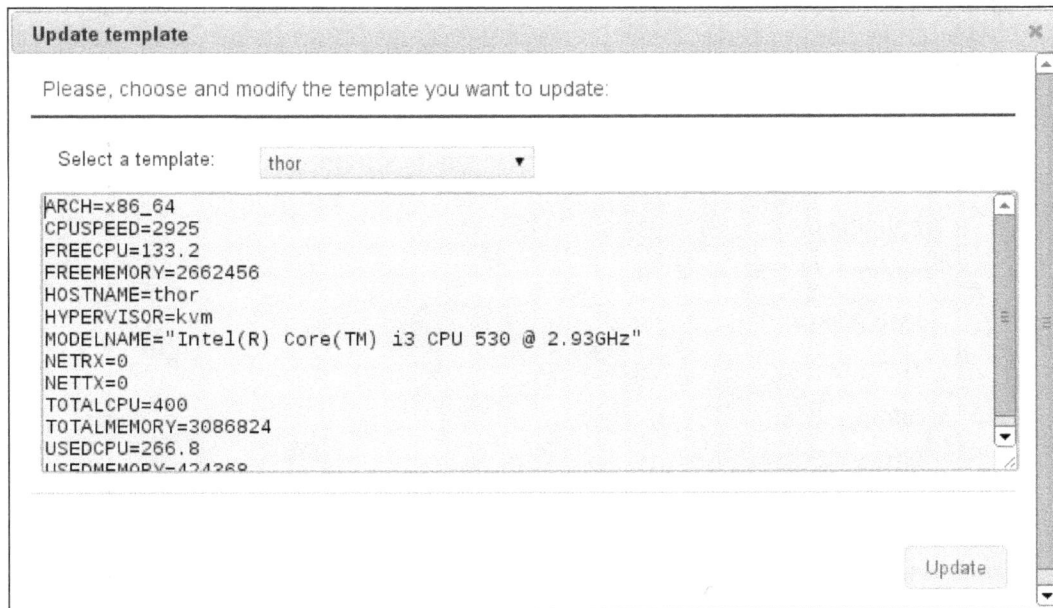

```
Update template                                                    ✕

  Please, choose and modify the template you want to update:
  ───────────────────────────────────────────────────────────────

  Select a template:      thor                          ▼

  ARCH=x86_64
  CPUSPEED=2925
  FREECPU=133.2
  FREEMEMORY=2662456
  HOSTNAME=thor
  HYPERVISOR=kvm
  MODELNAME="Intel(R) Core(TM) i3 CPU 530 @ 2.93GHz"
  NETRX=0
  NETTX=0
  TOTALCPU=400
  TOTALMEMORY=3086824
  USEDCPU=266.8
  USEDMEMORY=424368

                                                        Update
```

The other buttons **Enable, Disable**, and **Delete host**, are the corresponding actions for the `onehost enable`, `onehost disable`, and `onehost delete` commands.

When you click on a table row, a bottom panel will show up, containing detailed information about the resources selected, as shown in the following screenshot:

Host information	Host template	Monitoring information

Host information - thor		Host shares	
ID	1	**Max Mem**	2.9G
State	MONITORED	**Used Mem (real)**	414.3M
IM MAD	im_kvm	**Used Mem (allocated)**	0K
VM MAD	vmm_kvm	**Used CPU (real)**	272
TM MAD	tm_shared	**Used CPU (allocated)**	60
		Running VMs	6

In the **Host information** tab, you will find the driver used to poll and manage a particular host, the physical resource usage, and the allocation to the VM on it.

Host information	Host template	Monitoring information

Host template	
USEDCPU	272.8
CPUSPEED	2925
NETTX	0
HYPERVISOR	kvm
TOTALCPU	400
ARCH	x86_64
NETRX	0
FREEMEMORY	2662628
FREECPU	127.2
TOTALMEMORY	3086824

The second tab, **Host template**, will list the raw attribute values as they are retrieved by the Information Manager.

The last tab in the bottom panel, **Monitoring information**, contains graphs about CPU, memory, network, and disk usage on the currently selected host, giving you a recent overview of the resource usage of the currently selected host for monitoring and troubleshoot needs.

Virtual machines

After the host, you can find a section in Sunstone about virtual machines. This is certainly the most frequently used for day-to-day operations, as it permits you to keep an eye on how the active VMs are performing and also lets you stop and start new instances with a few clicks.

At the top, you can find the action buttons, which can be seen in the following screenshot:

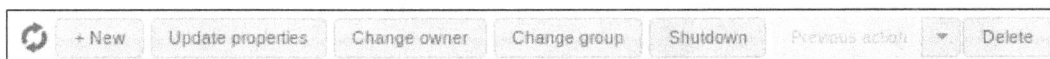

Following them is a list of the currently instantiated virtual machines, which can be seen as follows:

	ID ⇕	Owner ⇕	Group ⇕	Name ⇕	Status ⇕	CPU ⇕	Memory ⇕	Hostname ⇕	Start Time ⇕	VNC Access ⇕
All										
	16	oneadmin	oneadmin	one-16	RUNNING	3	64M	odin	18:05:35 12/17/2011	VNC
	17	oneadmin	oneadmin	one-17	RUNNING	3	64M	odin	18:09:41 12/17/2011	VNC
	18	oneadmin	oneadmin	one-18	RUNNING	3	64M	odin	18:09:42 12/17/2011	VNC
	19	oneadmin	oneadmin	one-19	RUNNING	3	64M	odin	18:09:43 12/17/2011	VNC

For each virtual machine, you are able to see the **Owner** and **Group**, its **Name**, allocated virtual **CPU**, **Memory**, and the **Hostname**. As for the host management page, you can easily change the number of displayed VMs on each page by filtering them, using the search box. If a running VM has been configured with VNC graphics enabled and has started successfully, you will find a colored icon to start a VNC session directly in your browser with web-socket support. If the VNC icon appears to be grayed out, the machine is not yet in a running state or its template does not contain a graphics section with VNC support enabled.

After clicking on the VNC icon, a pop-up window will appear and you can hook into the VM main console to log in and check the network configurations or anything else you may need. There is also a Ctrl+Alt+Del button to send that key combination to the VM.

```
VNC connection                                                              ✕

Connected (unencrypted) to: QEMU (one-16)                       Send CtrlAltDel

mounting local file systems ............................................ [ OK ]
setting up system clock (Tue Dec 27 10:10:07 UTC 2011) ................. [ OK ]
mount: mounting /dev/hdc on /mnt/context failed: No such device or address
umount: can't umount /mnt/context: Invalid argument
initializing random number generator ................................... [ OK ]
startup klogd .......................................................... [ OK ]
startup syslogd ........................................................ [ OK ]
bringing up loopback interface lo ...................................... [ OK ]
bringing up Ethernet interface eth0 .................................... [ OK ]
set up default gateway ................................................. [ OK ]
/etc/rc.d/rc.startup/10.network: line 78: ./ifup-eth0.template: No such file or
directory
startup dropbear ....................................................... [ OK ]
startup inetd .......................................................... [ OK ]


ttylinux  ver 9.0  [RC1]
i486 class Linux kernel 2.6.20  (tty1)
The initial root password is "password".
ttylinux_host login:

ttylinux  ver 9.0  [RC1]
i486 class Linux kernel 2.6.20  (tty1)
The initial root password is "password".
ttylinux_host login: _
```

The unencrypted string that appears means that the connection between you and the VNC server launched by the VM can be intercepted and altered. For this reason, a feature request has been opened and the OpenNebula developers are working on it, you can refer to it at, `http://dev.opennebula.org/issues/1069`.

If you have provided a password in the VM template, in the graphics section, it will automatically be provided by Sunstone to the VNC server; you do not need to type it. The password is required only when connecting with an external VNC client (for example, `vncviewer` or any other desktop VNC client).

Additional information about a particular VM can be retrieved by clicking on its row, after which a bottom panel will appear that looks similar to the following screenshot.

VM information	VM Template	VM log	Monitoring information

Virtual Machine information - one-16		Monitoring information	
ID	16	Net_TX	0
Name	one-16	Net_RX	124184
Owner	oneadmin	Used Memory	64M
Group	oneadmin	Used CPU	3
State	ACTIVE	VNC Session	[VNC]
LCM State	RUNNING		
Hostname	odin		
Start time	18:05:35 12/17/2011		
Deploy ID	one-16		

As with the hosts, the data available here is not in real time, but it is the latest retrieved by the Information Manager driver, as configured in `oned.conf` (for example, the `VM_POLLING_INTERVAL`, and `VM_PER_INTERVAL` attributes).

Besides the **VM Template** tab that contains the raw VM attributes and the graphs in the **Monitoring information** tab for each VM there is a **VM log** tab, where we can find the full VM logfile (available at /var/log/one/VMID/vm.log or at $ONE_LOCATION/var/VMID/vm.log).

```
VM information    VM Template    VM log    Monitoring information
Sat Dec 17 18:05:36 2011 [DiM][I]: New VM state is ACTIVE.
Sat Dec 17 18:05:36 2011 [LCM][I]: New VM state is PROLOG.
Sat Dec 17 18:05:36 2011 [VM][I]: Virtual Machine has no context
Sat Dec 17 18:05:36 2011 [TM][D]: tm_clone.sh: odin:/var/cloud/one/var/images/56c142fba67f483cf54426af642707cc
Sat Dec 17 18:05:36 2011 [TM][D]: tm_clone.sh: DST: /var/cloud/one/var//16/images/disk.0
Sat Dec 17 18:05:36 2011 [TM][I]: tm_clone.sh: Creating directory /var/cloud/one/var//16/images
Sat Dec 17 18:05:36 2011 [TM][I]: tm_clone.sh: Executed "mkdir -p /var/cloud/one/var//16/images".
Sat Dec 17 18:05:36 2011 [TM][I]: tm_clone.sh: Executed "chmod a+w /var/cloud/one/var//16/images".
Sat Dec 17 18:05:36 2011 [TM][I]: tm_clone.sh: Cloning /var/cloud/one/var/images/56c142fba67f483cf542707
Sat Dec 17 18:05:36 2011 [TM][I]: tm_clone.sh: Executed "cp -r /var/cloud/one/var/images/56c142fba67f483cf54426
Sat Dec 17 18:05:36 2011 [TM][I]: tm_clone.sh: Executed "chmod a+rw /var/cloud/one/var//16/images/disk.0".
Sat Dec 17 18:05:36 2011 [TM][I]: ExitCode: 0
Sat Dec 17 18:05:36 2011 [LCM][I]: New VM state is BOOT
Sat Dec 17 18:05:36 2011 [VMM][I]: Generating deployment file: /var/cloud/one/var/16/deployment.0
Sat Dec 17 18:05:36 2011 [VMM][I]: ExitCode: 0
Sat Dec 17 18:05:36 2011 [LCM][I]: New VM state is RUNNING
Sat Dec 17 18:06:36 2011 [VMM][I]: ExitCode: 0
Sat Dec 17 18:06:36 2011 [VMM][D]: Monitor Information:
                CPU   : 98
                Memory: 65536
                Net_TX: 0
                Net_RX: 4614
```

If you need to instantiate a new VM, you can click on the **New** button and a new pop-up window will appear. From the latest OpenNebula release, the new VM action has been greatly simplified, thanks to the integration of the template repository. Now to launch a new VM, it is only essential to specify which template to use and how many instances you want to launch. Easy and fast! While creating a new VM the following screenshot will appear:

```
Create Virtual Machine                                    ✕

    VM Name:          testdeploy

    Select template:  ttylinux                        ▼

    Deploy # VMs:     10



                                      Create    Reset
```

When launching multiple instances, the VM names are automatically generated by appending an incremental ID after the **VM Name** that you specify in the dialog box.

After the **New** action button, you will find two buttons for changing the owner and the group of one or more running VMs. Select a bunch of VMs and click on the **Change Owner** button. A pop-up window will appear, prompting you with the new user that should own the selected VM.

Confirmation of action	✖
Select the new group:	
oneadmin ▾	
OK Cancel	

The other action buttons are reachable through the second-last action button that contains a drop-down box with the `deploy`, `migrate`, `live-migrate`, `hold`, `release`, `suspend`, `resume`, `stop`, `restart`, `resubmit`, `save as`, and `cancel` options. These actions, as you can imagine, are the same commands as available through the command line with the `onevm` utility, so take into account the considerations of the last chapter.

VM Templates

Template management is one of the most complex tasks for day-to-day operations, but fortunately, Sunstone makes life easier for the infrastructure administrators.

When you press the **New** action button, a pop-up window will appear. Depending on the hypervisor you use, you should select the right tab to begin configuring the template. In each wizard, some attributes are simply hidden or available, depending on the hypervisor we are using. The **Create VM Template** window appears as in the following screenshot:

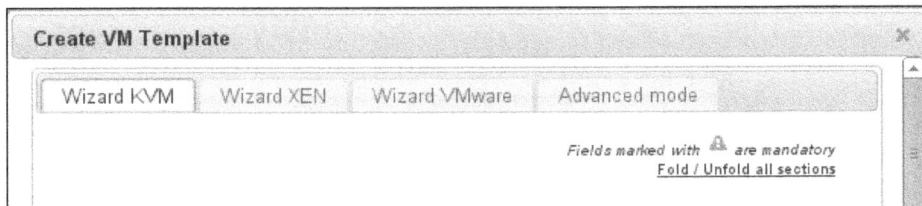

Create VM Template	✖
Wizard KVM	Wizard XEN	Wizard VMware	Advanced mode	
Fields marked with ⚠ are mandatory	
Fold / Unfold all sections	

Each mandatory field is marked with a particular icon and beside each field is a contextual help icon that you can hover with the mouse cursor in order to view the help.

The first section is identified by the label **Capacity options** and is used to define the basic VM configuration, such as its name, allocated memory, dedicated CPU, and the number of virtual CPUs attached. The only mandatory field is **Memory**, as the other fields are retrieved from the VM Manager driver defaults. While the **Capacity options** section is configured it will appear like the following screenshot.

Capacity options

Name:	testvm
Memory:	512
CPU:	0.5
VCPU:	2

The second section, **Boot/OS options**, is used to define the VM CPU architecture and boot options. The **Boot method** field will expand itself if **Kernel** is selected, allowing us to define `custom kernel`, `initrd`, and `boot` parameters (needed for Xen paravirtualization).

Boot/OS options

Architecture:	i686
Boot method:	Driver default
Boot:	hd

The **Features** section allows us to enable or disable the **ACPI** and **PAE** features for this particular VM template. The **ACPI** feature is mainly used to handle shut-down actions from the host, and **PAE** is used to enable use of more than 4 GB of memory on an i686 VM.

Features

PAE:	Enable
ACPI:	Enable

The following section, **Add disks/images**, is used to attach one or more disks to the VM. It is possible to attach a custom disk image, by providing an absolute path, or by using an image registered in the OpenNebula repository.

Depending on the hypervisor, you have multiple choices for the **Bus** type, **Target**, and **Driver** attributes. Blank fields will default to the VM Manager driver; usually, you do not need to manually specify both **Target** and **Driver** fields.

Double-check the image path you provide, as there is no early check of accessibility when defining the template.

Once you finish defining the first disk, you should press the **Save** button and the first disk will be added on the lower textfield, as reference. If you have added a wrong disk, select it on the textfield and press the **Remove selected** button.

> This will not remove the disk; only the association with this particular VM template will be removed.

If you select **Image** instead, most fields will disappear, leaving you with a simple combobox, where you can choose from already registered disk images in the repository.

As a reminder, every VM can have one OS disk image type attached and the number of datablock disk images needed (limited to a total number of 4 when using the IDE bus). The disk image type is defined at the image template level, not here in the VM template.

—	Add disks/images
Add disk/image	◯ Disk ⦿ Image
Image:	ttylinux ▾ ❶ ⚠
Bus:	IDE ▾ ❶
Target:	❶
Driver:	❶

The next section, **Setup Networks**, is about network configurations. With the **Predefined** switch enabled, you will be able to select an already existing virtual network. You can manually specify an IP address or leave it blank and OpenNebula will automatically assign an available IP based on the network settings.

It is possible to configure VM firewalling, for example, enabling access only to SSH, HTTP, and HTTPS services, and filtering UDP ports commonly used for Windows File Sharing. Also, **Internet Control Message Protocol (ICMP)** packets (mainly used for `ping` requests) can be dropped or accepted.

—	Setup Networks
Add network	⦿ Predefined ◯ Manual
Network:	Small network ▾ ❶ ⚠
IP:	❶
Tcp firewall mode:	Port whitelist ▾
Tcp white ports:	22,80,443 ❶
Udp firewall mode:	Port blacklist ▾
Udp black ports:	135,139,445 ❶
Icmp:	Drop ▾ ❶

With **Manual** network configuration you can specify the name of the physical bridge configured on host machines (we used `green0` before) and an IP address. Also, it is possible to customize the name of the tun device that will be created on the host, for this VM, and the path to a shell script to be executed after the creation of the tun device.

The commonly required sections to create a real-life VM template are done. The following sections will permit you to fine-tune the VM.

The **Add inputs** section may be used to add an input, for the sections **Bus**: **USB** and **Type**: **Tablet** pointing device, useful if mouse movement is de-synchronized when using VNC for graphical sessions (for example, with Windows).

–	Add inputs		
Type:	Tablet	▼	ⓘ
Bus:	USB	▼	ⓘ

> In recent KVM releases, the USB tablet is added by default, and everything should work without manually specifying it.

The **Add Graphics** section should be used to configure a VNC session attached to any instance. Remember to specify the **Listen IP** field as **0.0.0.0** since it defaults to **127.0.0.1** (accessible only from the host on which it is running). The section **Keymap** should be configured only when the locale keyboard charset differs between hosts and VNC clients.

–	Add Graphics	
Graphics type:	VNC ▼	ⓘ
Listen IP:	0.0.0.0	ⓘ
Port:		ⓘ
Password:	mypassword	ⓘ
Keymap:		ⓘ

The **Add placement options** section is used to instruct the OpenNebula scheduler where a VM instance can be started.

— Add placement options	
Requirements:	ⓘ
Rank:	FREEMEMORY| ⓘ

In **Add Hypervisor raw options**, you can enter raw text that will be appended in the hypervisor-specific deployment file before booting a new instance.

— Add Hypervisor raw options	
Data:	ⓘ

In **Add context variables**, multiple context variables can be passed and made available to the contextualization script.

— Add context variables	
Name:	DNS ⓘ
Value:	8.8.8.8,8.8.4.4 ⓘ

After you click on the **Create** button on the bottom of the pop-up window, the VM template will be submitted to the repository. If you want to start again with an empty template, press the **Reset** button, and all textfields will be cleared.

The last tab in the **Create VM Template** pop-up window, named **Advanced Mode**, can be used to directly paste a template file, as you would submit it through the `onetemplate submit` file.

Unfortunately, reusing the creation form has not yet been implemented; hence editing a template after the initial creation is not possible. When you click on the **Update a template** button, a pop-up window will appear asking for the template to be edited and you will be able to edit it directly in text mode, as you would do from a text editor.

Hopefully, in the future this will get more user friendly, even if updating a template is not so frequent an operation. Maybe it is faster to create a new template and keep the old version for historical purposes.

Virtual Networks

When you open the Virtual Networks page in Sunstone, you will find a list of the active virtual networks managed by OpenNebula.

In the main table, you can see for each network the parameters, such as **ID**, **Name** of the network, **Owner**, **Group**, **Network type** (ranged or fixed), the physical **Bridge** to which it is connected, **Public** or **Private** status, and the total number of active leases (IP addresses assigned to a VM).

When you click on a row, the bottom panel will show up and, among the standard virtual networks attributes, you will be able to retrieve the list of the **IP** or **MAC** address currently assigned to a running VM (or not).

Virtual Network information	Virtual Network template

Virtual Network 0 information		Leases information	
ID	0	**0**	
Owner	oneadmin	MAC	02:00:c0:a8:42:cd
Group	oneadmin	VID	-1
Public	no	IP	192.168.66.205
		USED	0
		1	
		MAC	02:00:c0:a8:42:ce
		VID	16
		IP	192.168.66.206
		USED	1

If you click on the **New** button, you can create a new virtual network to be used in our infrastructure. The first two required fields in the **Wizard** mode are the names under which the new virtual network will be identified and the name of an existing physical bridge of the host.

Wizard	Advanced mode

Name:	public
Bridge:	red0

Depending on the type of virtual network we are going to configure, you need to provide different things. For a fixed network, if you have a bunch of public IP addresses available, you can specify them one-by-one, optionally providing a particular MAC address too (some ISPs may require it).

At a later time, if you need to add or remove an IP lease, you can use the action buttons **Add** and **Remove selected** to add or remove an IP from our fixed network.

Network type:	◉ Fixed network
	○ Ranged network
Lease IP:	130.10.0.4
Lease MAC (opt):	
	Add Remove selected
Current leases:	130.10.0.1
	130.10.0.2
	130.10.0.3
	130.10.0.4

Instead, for a ranged network such as a common LAN, it is sufficient to provide the physical **Bridge** name, as before, and a network definition, using a **Classless Inter-Domain Routing (CIDR)** notation, split between the two available fields (**Network Address** and **Network size**).

The common private networks are 192.168.0.0/24, 172.16.0.0/16, and 10.0.0.0/8.

Name:	lan
Bridge:	green0
Network type:	○ Fixed network
	◉ Ranged network
Network Address:	192.168.0.0
Network size:	24

As for the VM template creation procedure, you can switch to **Advanced Mode** and paste a working virtual network template.

Images

From the **Add disks/ images** section, you can manage the Image Repository, which contains OS images, datablocks, and CD-ROM images.

After clicking on the **New** button, both **Wizard** and **Advanced mode** options are available to create new images.

Wizard	Advanced mode

Fields marked with ⚠ *are mandatory*

Name: ubuntu-lucid-amd64 ❶ ⚠

Description: Base Ubuntu Lucid Server 10.04 install ❶

After providing a unique **Name** and a human-readable **Description**, we can configure the image type (OS, DATABLOCK, or CDROM), if it should be available to all users or only to owner, if it should be cloned or not when used by VM instances, and the default Bus type which (can be overridden in the VM template).

A path should be provided for file-based images (for example, `.raw`, `.qcow2`, `.vmdk`, and `.iso`), while a source should be provided for block-devices (for example, raw partitions and LVM logical volumes). When image **Type** is **OS** we have the following options:

Type: OS ▾ ❶

Public: ☐ ❶

Persistent: ☐ ❶

Device prefix: ❶

Bus: IDE ▾ ❶

Path vs. source:
◉ Provide a path
○ Provide a source
◉ Create an empty datablock ❶

Path: ❶ ⚠

Instead, when **DATABLOCK** is selected as image **Type** we can choose to create an empty datablock with the specified **Size** in MB and **FS type**.

Path vs. source:	○ Provide a path
	○ Provide a source
	◉ Create an empty datablock ⓘ
Size:	20480 ⓘ ⚠
FS type:	ext3 ⓘ ⚠

After confirming the creation of a new image, you may need to wait a little as the image will be copied from the source to the Image Repository. In the image table, you will find all the common image attributes, including its status (for example, INIT, READY, USED, and DISABLED) and the count of the VM currently using it.

It is possible to alter common image attributes using the different available action buttons, for example, enable, disable, publish, unpublish, make persistent, and make non-persistent.

All	ID ◇	Owner ◇	Group ◇	Name ◇	Type ◇	Registration time ◇	Public ◇	Persistent ◇	Status ◇	#VMS ◇
	0	oneadmin	oneadmin	ttylinux	OS	17:21:52 12/17/2011	no	no	USED	11

Users

The **Create user** section will permit us to easily add a new user identified with a password. From the same page, we will be able to change the group to which the user belongs or delete existing users.

Unfortunately, the current Sunstone release does not include a function to permit each user to update their passwords independently. If a user wants to change his or her password, they must use the command `oneuserpasswd<user><password>`. By default, users of the group `oneadmin` can create new users and change their passwords while unprivileged users may change only their own passwords.

Create user		✖
Username:		
Password:		
Authentication:	Core ▾	
	Create Reset	

Group

As for users, there is a simple page to manage groups from the web interface. Group membership is not managed from the **Create group** section, but it is possible to change group for each existing user from the Users page.

Create group		✖
Group name:	developers	
	Create Reset	

ACLs

The **Create ACL** section is used to manage the different privileges that can be assigned to single users or entire groups.

Even though we have not created any ACL before, OpenNebula by default creates a basic set of rules for the default group users or users of any other group we created.

Press **New** to create a new ACL. The first field, **This rule applies to**, is used to define for which specific user or group the ACL should be applied. The second field, **Affected Resources**, is used to select the resources that this ACL will cover.

The third field, **Resource subset**, is used to restrict the set of resources that the ACL will be applied to. For example, a particular resource ID or all the resources owned by a particular group, as specified in their respective textfields.

The last field required to create a new ACL is **Allowed operations**, that is used to set the operations that the user or group will be allowed to perform on the previously selected resources.

When we have finished configuring the generated ACL using the standard OpenNebula ACL syntax, an ACL String will appear in the bottom textbox, as shown in the following screenshot:

Click on **Create** and the new ACL will take effect.

Summary

In this chapter we have detailed all the OpenNebula Sunstone management functions. As this is the newest component that has appeared in the OpenNebula toolkit, do not negatively judge any poor user experience you may have felt. I am certain that a lot of work has been done, as it is already at a good level.

In this chapter, we have not covered the particular plugin architecture on which Sunstone is built, as it is too technical and may appear boring to most readers, but you can find all the technical documentation you need, to extend the Sunstone interface and functionalities, at the following pages:

- `http://opennebula.org/documentation:rel3.2:sunstone_plugin_ guide`
- `http://opennebula.org/documentation:rel3.2:sunstone_plugin_ reference`

In the next chapter, we will go a step further into managing our infrastructure effectively, by installing and configuring a monitoring tool often used in grid deployments, Ganglia. We will be able to constantly monitor our nodes and instances, getting an overview of the current health of our infrastructure, and receive e-mail alerts whenever something goes wrong.

7
Health and Monitoring

Now that we have a running OpenNebula infrastructure with a bunch of virtual machines running and a fancy web interface to manage them, we probably want to explore a bit more as to how we can keep an eye on what is going on.

As we already know, the OpenNebula Information Manager (IM) is responsible for host monitoring and resource usage gathering. It is composed by different sensors, each one acquiring different information on the monitored host: CPU usage, available memory, hostname, and so on. Besides physical resource sensors, there are the hypervisor-specific ones that are used to gather information, such as network bandwidth usage and used memory, about the running Virtual Machines (VMs).

Checking the status of the available hosts

At least one IM driver should be enabled in the `oned.conf` configuration file:

```
IM_MAD = [
  name       = "im_kvm",
  executable = "one_im_ssh",
  arguments  = "kvm" ]
```

Multiple IM drivers could be activated if you plan to use the same OpenNebula frontend for heterogeneous physical hosts.

The number of available IM drivers, bundled in the main OpenNebula packages are four, one for each supported hypervisor (KVM, Xen, and VMWare), plus a generic one using Ganglia as the underlying transport instead of the default SSH one (as we will see later in this chapter).

There is a fifth IM driver, to be used when using the EC2 integration, but it is not a real IM, since we would not be able to monitor the physical hosts running on the Amazon cloud (we will learn about it in *Chapter 8, Hybrid Cloud Computing: Extending OpenNebula*).

When a particular IM is enabled, we can use it when adding new machines to the host pool, with:

```
$ onehost create odin im_kvm vmm_kvm tm_shared.
```

Wait for the first monitoring hop to happen, and we will find updated information with the onehost list command:

```
  ID NAME            RVM TCPU FCPU ACPU TMEM FMEM AMEM  STAT
   2 thor                  5    400      43    350   2.9G   1.3G    2.6G
on
   3 odin                  5    400      46    350  3.9G   1.4G   3.6G    on
```

The odin host has five running VMs, and each of them has 10 allocated CPU units (10 * 5 = 400 - 350). For the memory, each VM is a ttylinux sytem with 64 MB allocated (64 MB * 5 = 320 MB used, so for a total of 3.9 GB, there is 3.6 GB of memory available). But what about the Free CPU (FCPU) and Free Memory (FMEM)? They represent the actual usage during the last monitoring hop, the real CPU and memory availability on the physical host.

Why is the usage higher than expected? Because there are other services running on that host, and obviously OpenNebula takes care of this, so the scheduler will never place a new virtual machine on a host that has no CPU or memory available.

Instead, if there are problems monitoring the host, you will get err in the status column:

```
  ID NAME            RVM TCPU FCPU ACPU TMEM FMEM AMEM  STAT
   2 thor                  5    400      43    350   2.9G   1.3G    2.6G
on
   3 odin             0     0      0     100   OK     0   OK    err
```

A recently added host with wrong hypervisor configuration will show zeroed stats, since the IM has never run.

We can get a detailed error message, returned by the failing IM poll for the host, using the onehost show command:

```
$ onehost show 3
MONITORING INFORMATION
ERROR=[
```

```
MESSAGE="Error monitoring host 3 : MONITOR FAILURE 3
  Could not update remotes",
TIMESTAMP="Sat Jan 21 15:26:57 2012" ]
```

If the first probe is successful, we have not missed anything in the basic hypervisor configuration on that host (further problems may appear later, during the first instance deployment, for example, wrong storage configuration).

In a working environment, if a host suddenly falls into `err` status, it means that the host is unreachable by the frontend or that the monitoring script returned an error. In this case, the instances that were running on this host are no longer reachable and need to be restarted on another available host.

For further information, we should always check `oned.log`, available in `/var/log/one` or `$ONE_LOCATION/var`:

```
[InM] [I]: Monitoring host odin (3)

InM] [I]: Command execution fail: scp -r /var/lib/one/remotes/.
odin:/var/tmp/one

[InM] [I]: ssh: Could not resolve hostname odin: nodename nor servname
  provided, or not known

[InM] [I]: lost connection

[InM] [I]: ExitCode: 1

[InM] [E]: Error monitoring host 3 : MONITOR FAILURE 3 Could not
  update remotes
```

The error messages are usually sufficiently explanatory and should help you with understanding which configuration is causing the trouble. In this specific case, there is a problem mapping the node hostname to its IP address, so maybe your DNS server configuration or your `/etc/resolv.conf` is wrong, or you should update the `/etc/hosts` file accordingly.

As an additional suggestion, always leave open a terminal with live `oned.log` streaming:

```
$ sudo tail -f /var/log/one/oned.log
```

or:

```
$ tail -f $ONE_LOCATION/var/oned.log
```

Another very common error is passwordless login not working; check the early chapters for more information.

Host monitoring and failure recovery hooks

Host monitoring takes place in every time interval configured in oned.conf, managed by the HOST_MONITORING_INTERVAL and HOST_PER_INTERVAL parameters.

In large environments, it may be necessary to increase the monitoring interval or decrease hosts per interval to reduce overhead on the frontend and the hosts. Increasing the monitoring interval will lead to more outdated information about hosts and delay the failover host hooks too.

Please ensure, when you adjust these values, HOST_MONITORING_INTERVAL is never lower than MANAGER_TIMER, which is the time in seconds that the core uses to evaluate all the periodical functions.

The same logic applies for VM_POLLING_INTERVAL and VM_PER_INTERVAL, which are used to determine how frequently the VM instances are monitored.

A oned.conf configuration for simpler infrastructures is as follows:

- MANAGER_TIMER = 10
- HOST_MONITORING_INTERVAL = 10
- HOST_PER_INTERVAL = 25
- VM_POLLING_INTERVAL = 10
- VM_PER_INTERVAL = 100

In larger environments, you can increase the HOST_PER_INTERVAL and VM_PER_INTERVAL parameters, else it will take ages to traverse the entire host and VM pool, and we may increase the monitoring interval to not constantly overload the frontend:

- MANAGER_TIMER = 30
- HOST_MONITORING_INTERVAL = 60
- HOST_PER_INTERVAL = 100
- VM_POLLING_INTERVAL = 60
- VM_PER_INTERVAL = 500

Monitoring intervals should be kept as low as possible, since they also affect the reactivity of host and VM hooks.

The Hook Manager present in OpenNebula enables the triggering of custom scripts tied to a change in state in the hosts and VM. This is very useful for system administrators that need to automatize task execution on status changes, starting with a simple automatic failover solution. Its driver is enabled by default in `oned.conf`:

```
HM_MAD = [
  executable = "one_hm" ]
```

When the HM is enabled, it is possible to define a HOST_HOOK array with the following attributes:

- **Name**: Used only for identification purposes
- **On**: Specifies when the hook should be triggered (CREATE, ERROR, DISABLE)
- **Command**: Script to be executed, absolute path or relative to remotes or hooks
- **Arguments**: Having passed to the script, available variables are $HID, containing the current host ID, and $TEMPLATE, containing the entire host template encoded in base64 and XML
- **Remote**: no (by default) will execute the script hook on the frontend, `yes` on the remote host.

The unique host hook bundled with OpenNebula is used to implement a simple host failover and can be enabled as follows:

```
HOST_HOOK = [
    name      = "error",
    on        = "ERROR",
    command   = "ft/host_error.rb",
    arguments = "$HID -r n",
    remote    = "no" ]
```

This script is available under `/usr/lib/one/remotes/hooks/ft` or in `$ONE_LOCATION/var/remotes/hooks/ft`.

The two available arguments are:

- R—Resubmit VMs running in the host
- D—Delete VMs running in the host

By default, the second argument is not used to resubmit or finalize suspended VMs; you can change this behavior using `y` instead of `n`.

Additionally, there is a corner case that in critical, production environments should be taken into account. If a network error occurs, the hook may be triggered and the VMs resubmitted. When (and if) the network comes back, there will be a potential clash between the old and the reincarnated VMs. This problem increases its potential when using shared storage, since multiple instances can issue write requests to the same disk image, corrupting it. In order to prevent this, some fencing technique should be taken into account.

To solve this problem, many cluster management softwares adopt a particular mechanism called fencing. **Fencing** is the process of isolating a node of a computer cluster, or protecting the shared resources when a node appears to be malfunctioning.

This is usually done by forcefully shutting down malfunctioning nodes, using integrated remote management interfaces (such as DRAC for Dell, Lights-Out for HP, or whatever else supporting the standard IPMI support), remotely managed UPS, or remotely managed network switches.

Since the implementation of one of these solutions will be strictly hardware-dependent, we cannot provide a general configuration. However, it will be sufficient to implement a new host hook, based on the default `host_error.rb`, to implement a basic fencing mechanism as follows:

```ruby
#!/usr/bin/env ruby
ONE_LOCATION=ENV["ONE_LOCATION"]
if !ONE_LOCATION
   RUBY_LIB_LOCATION="/usr/lib/one/ruby"
   VMDIR="/var/lib/one"
else
   RUBY_LIB_LOCATION=ONE_LOCATION+"/lib/ruby"
   VMDIR=ONE_LOCATION+"/var"
end
$: << RUBY_LIB_LOCATION
require 'OpenNebula'
include OpenNebula
if !(host_id=ARGV[0])
   exit -1
end
begin
   client = Client.new()
   rescue Exception => e
   puts "Error: #{e}"
   exit -1
end
# Retrieve hostname
```

```
host  =  OpenNebula::Host.new_with_id(host_id, client)
exit -1 if OpenNebula.is_error?(host)
host.info
host_name = host.name
puts "Executing kill command for "+host_name
system("echo kill "+host_name);
```

This custom hook can be saved as `kill_host.rb` in the same folder of `host_error.rb`. Configure it in `oned.conf`, as follows:

```
HOST_HOOK = [
    name      = "kill",
    on        = "ERROR",
    command   = "ft/kill_host.rb",
    arguments = "$HID",
    remote    = "no" ]
```

VM monitoring and failure recovery hooks

Besides host failure, VMs could also face a failure during their life cycle. There are two main types of failures:

- **VM failures**: These can occur due to a network error that prevents the image from being copied into the node, a hypervisor-related issue, or a migration problem. The common symptom is that the VM enters the FAILED state.

- **VM crashes**: A machine can crash after it has been successfully booted, due to an unexpected hypervisor or OS error. The common symptom is that the VM enters into the UNKNOWN state.

In order to deal with these errors, a VM hook can be configured to resubmit a failed VM or to delete it, depending on our needs. This is achieved by adding a VM_HOOK definition with the following attributes in `oned.conf`:

- **Name**: Used only for identification purposes
- **On**: Specifies when the hook should be triggered:
    - ° CREATE: When the VM is created
    - ° RUNNING: After the VM is successfully booted (by the hypervisor, not the OS installed on it)
    - ° SHUTDOWN: After the VM is shut down

- ○ STOP: After the VM is stopped (including VM image transfers)
- ○ DONE: After the VM is deleted or shut down
- ○ FAILED: When the VM enters the failed state

- **Command**: Script to be executed, absolute path or relative to remotes or hooks
- **Arguments**: Having passed to the script, available variables are $VMID, containing the current VM ID, and $TEMPLATE, containing the entire host template encoded in base64 and XML
- **Remote**: no (by default) will execute the script hook on the frontend, yes on the remote host

Examples of the two basic VM hooks are:

```
VM_HOOK = [
    name         = "on_failure_delete",
    on           = "FAILED",
    command  = "/usr/bin/env onevm delete",
    arguments = "$VMID" ]
VM_HOOK = [
    name         = "on_failure_resubmit",
    on           = "FAILED",
    command  = "/usr/bin/env onevm resubmit",
    arguments = "$VMID" ]
```

Obviously, only one of the two should be defined.

A custom hook: e-mail notification for each failure

The simplest hook use case could be to send an e-mail notification whenever a host or VM fails, without too much fuss:

```
VM_HOOK = [
  name         = "on_failure_email",
  on           = "FAILED",
  command  = "mail_notify.sh",
  arguments = "VM $VMID noc@libersoft.it" ]
HOST_HOOK = [
  name         = "error_email",
  on           = "ERROR",
  command  = "mail_notify.sh",
```

```
arguments = "HOST $HID noc@libersoft.it",
remote    = "no" ]
```

Place the script in `/var/lib/one/remotes/hooks` or `$ONE_LOCATION/var/remotes/` `hooks` with:

```
#!/bin/bash
TYPE=$1
ID=$2
MAIL=$3
echo "You have been warned!" | mail -s "ON: $TYPE with ID $ID has
failed!" $MAIL
```

Do not forget to make it executable with `chmod +x mail_notify.sh`.

Now, you will easily get an e-mail notification every time a host or a VM switches to FAILED status.

Sending e-mail from the frontend

To send e-mail from the frontend, you need to have a configured MTA, such as Postfix or SSMTP. There are many things to take into consideration while configuring an MTA, and the Internet has plenty of ways to go about doing it. For a test install, simply do `sudo apt-get install postfix` and in the next `debconf` screen, select either `Internet Site` or `Internet with smarthost` (depending on whether or not you have another working SMTP server).

Expanding data collected by the IM

With the modular OpenNebula architecture, it is possible to extend the default IM driver to expose new variables that could be used by the scheduler or whatever monitoring information we may need.

IM drivers are arranged in these directories:

- `/usr/lib/one/mads` or `$ONE_LOCATION/lib/mads`: The drivers' main executable files

- `/var/lib/one/remotes/im/<virtualizer>.d` or `$ONE_LOCATION/var/` `remotes/im/<virtualizer>.d`: Hypervisor-specific probes to gather every monitoring metric

Temperature attribute

For example, we can decide to introduce a new TEMPERATURE attribute for our KVM-based cloud, to be used in the RANK attribute for the scheduler. This is as simple as defining a shell script that will output one per line:

```
PARAMETER=VALUE
```

Place the new script inside the `remotes/im/kvm.d` directory, called `temperature.sh`:

```
#!/bin/bash
echo TEMP=`sensors|grep 'CPU Temperature'|awk -F' ' '{ print $3}'| sed
s/+//|sed s/\.[0-9]°C//`
```

You may need to adjust the first `grep` argument, since the sensor's description may vary from hardware to hardware.

Make it executable,and try to run it as follows:

```
$ chmod +x temperature.sh
$ ./temperature.sh
TEMP=23
```

> **Sensor's basic configuration**
>
> For those who are not accustomed to the utility of the sensor, install it through package manager (`sudo apt-get install lm-sensors`), and launch the configuration procedure with `sudo sensors-detect`. At the end of the detection procedure, if it succeeds, you will be asked to put some kernel modules in `/etc/modules`. Do it and load them manually for the first time, using the command `modprobe modulename`. To check if it is working, launch `sensors` without parameters.

Now, let OpenNebula copy this new script on all hosts with:

```
$ onehost sync
```

Wait for the next monitoring hop, and if everything is OK, we will see the new attribute in the VM instance template with:

```
$ onevm show <id>
```

The new attribute is treated as the default one, and you can use it in the VM templates.

Following our example, you can define a RANK expression with the new TEMPERATURE attribute, to prefer cooler hosts with spare CPU available:

```
RANK = FREECPU - TEMPERATURE
```

Load average attribute

Another common IM extension could be to retrieve and use in the scheduler the load average values of the hosts.

Place a new script, `loadavg.sh`, in the `remotes/im/kvm.d` directory:

```
#!/bin/sh
awk -F' ' '{ print "LOAD1="$1*100"\nLOAD5="$2*100"\nLOAD15="$3*100 }' /proc/loadavg
```

Make it executable and run it:

```
$ chmod +x loadavg.sh
./loadavg.sh
LOAD1=55
LOAD5=61
LOAD15=48
```

As with the preceding script, execute `onehost sync` and wait for the next monitoring hop.

Now we could use this new information from the hosts, using it in the RANK attribute as before:

```
RANK = - LOAD5
```

With this RANK definition, the scheduler will prefer hosts with lower value of the five minutes load average.

What is Ganglia?

Ganglia is an open source, scalable, distributed monitoring system for clusters. It was mainly used in high-performance computing systems and grids in the past, but due to the increasing size of virtualization infrastructure, it is a good candidate for our needs, as shown in the following screenshot:

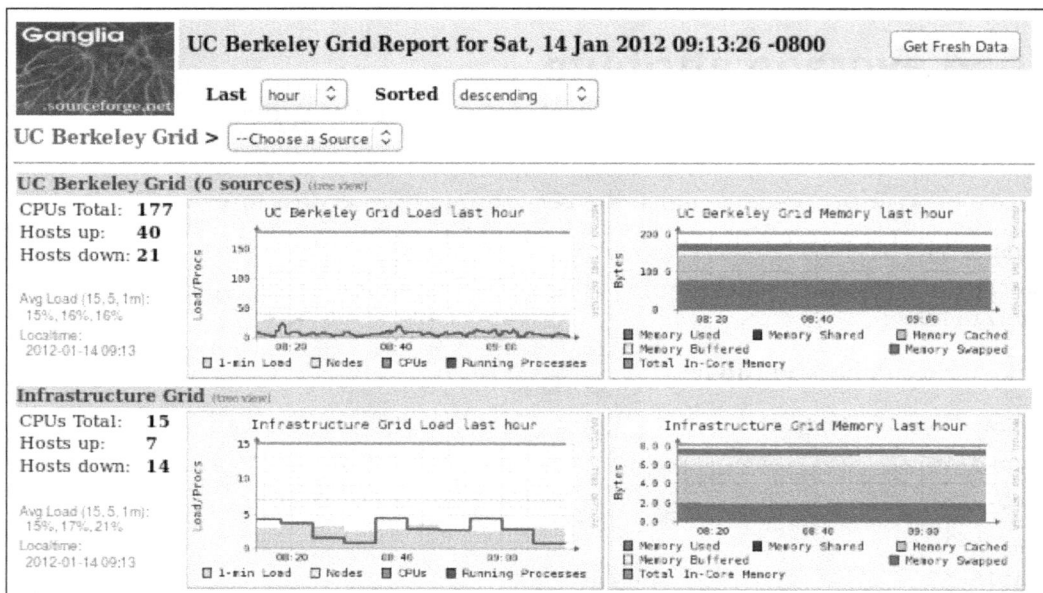

It leverages widely used technologies, such as XML for data representation, XDR for data transport, and the RRD tool for data storage and visualization. It has been developed with a focus on on achieving very low per-node overheads and high concurrency. It has been used to link clusters across university campuses and around the world and can scale to handle clusters with 2000 nodes.

Many large corporations and universities are using Ganglia to monitor their infrastructure: Berkley University (the birthplace of Ganglia), Harvard, MIT, NASA, CERN, Sun, Cisco, Motorola, HP, Microsoft, Dell, Wikipedia (`http://ganglia.wikimedia.org/`), Twitter, Flickr, last.fm, and so on.

In this chapter, we are going to cover firstly a basic Ganglia configuration to monitor the physical hosts and VMs managed by our infrastructure, and secondly, the integration with the OpenNebula IM, useful in improving monitoring performance in large clusters and getting rid of the standard SSH-based host or VM monitoring.

Ganglia architecture and deployment on the frontend

Ganglia relies on a multicast-based listen or announce protocol to monitor the state of a cluster and uses a tree of point-to-point connections amongst promoted nodes to federate clusters and aggregate their state.

The main components of a Ganglia infrastructure are three:

- Monitoring Daemon (gmond)
- Metadata Daemon (gmetad)
- PHP Web frontend

We start deploying all the three components on our OpenNebula frontend though they could be placed on a dedicated machine, whether physical or not.

Ganglia Monitoring Daemon (gmond)

gmond is the service that should run on the hosts we wish to monitor. Its features are:

- It collects monitoring data from the current host
- It announces its presence on the local network
- It may receive the state of other gmond nodes through unicast or multicast sytems.
- It replies to requests for the XML description of the cluster state

The gmond daemon is packaged in Ubuntu or Debian in the package called Ganglia-monitor:

```
$ sudo apt-get install gmond
```

The unique configuration file needed by gmond is in /etc/ganglia/gmond.conf. Since a single installation of Ganglia can potentially monitor multiple clusters inside the same physical network, the first section of the file is used to define the cluster that this node will be a member of, and on which ports it will listen, as follows:

```
cluster {
  name = "NebulaPhy"
  owner = "me"
  latlong = "unspecified"
  url = "http://mywebsite.it"
}
```

The hosts with the same cluster name will be logically grouped and showed in a separate section on the web interface.

For OpenNebula infrastructure, we may want to use a cluster for all the physical hosts (or physical hosts with the same hypervisor or Linux distribution) and a cluster for all the virtual machines. On bigger infrastructures, it may be useful to create multiple clusters, depending on the services they are hosting (such as a webserver cluster), or some hardware characteristics, for example, Dell, Proliant or OfficeA, OfficeB.

Multicast configuration

The next section is about local port configuration. The default configuration will use the multicast socket to send and receive stats from other gmonds. Multicast is easier to set up but it is practically usable only on a local network and may introduce jitters in large networks:

```
udp_send_channel {
  mcast_join = 239.2.11.71
  port = 8649
  ttl = 1
}
```

Using multicast provides redundancy, since every gmond will know the current status of the others, as they are all sharing the same multicast address:

```
udp_recv_channel {
  mcast_join = 239.2.11.71
  port = 8649
  bind = 239.2.11.71
}
```

A TCP port is required to answer XML description requests by other nodes:

```
tcp_accept_channel {
  port = 8649
}
```

Unicast configuration

To configure unicast, you should designate one or more (for redundancy) machines to be receivers, and configure all the other gmonds to send data to them.

On the receiver node (frontend), define as follows:

```
udp_send_channel {
  host = frontend
```

```
  port = 8649
  ttl = 1
}
```

This node will send collected data to itself (frontend) and receive stats from all the other gmonds on 8649 or UDP port, as follows:

```
udp_recv_channel {
  port = 8649
}
```

As done previously, we define the TCP port for XML descriptive exchange, as follows:

```
tcp_accept_channel {
  port = 8649
}
```

On all the other nodes (do not do it now; finish the basic configuration first), we will install gmond and configure it to send data to one or more receivers, as follows:

```
udp_send_channel {
  host = frontend
  port = 8649
  ttl = 1
}
```

You can define multiple udp_send_channel sections pointing to different hosts, to achieve redundancy. Remember that each receiver gmond should have enabled udp_receive_channel on the same port.

Metric modules configuration

The second part of the gmond configuration file contains definitions of the modules used to gather system statistics of the current node.

The basic configuration covers all the common metrics that a system administrator would find interesting:

- Machine type, OS version, uptime
- CPU load
- Memory usage
- Network bandwidth
- Disk space available
- Load average

Besides these common C modules included with the main Ganglia package, there are a bunch of user-contributed modules available. Since the 3.1 release, it is possible to plug in Python modules in gmond, making it easier for people to contribute.

There are two official GitHub repositories where people are encouraged to create new modules and submit them, as follows:

- `https://github.com/ganglia/gmetric`: It contains scripts (perl, bash, and so on), that use the generic Ganglia utility gmetric (a command-line binary) to push metrics for the current node to the local gmond, usually executed through cron.
- `https://github.com/ganglia/gmond_python_modules`: Python modules are embedded in gmond, like the native C modules, and they are the recommended approach if you need to develop a new module from scratch.

A few examples of the most interesting modules already available are:

- `nginx_status` (for Sunstone SSL proxy)
- `mysql` (for OpenNebula frontend DB)
- `xenstats` (for Xen hosts)
- `nfsstats` (if using NFS as shared filesystem)

How to use a gmetric script

Using or writing a gmetric script is, by far, the easiest way to inject new custom metrics on every node.

`logged_in_users.sh` is a very simple gmetric script that understands its own operation; it has been contributed by Miles Davis and can be found at `https://github.com/ganglia/gmetric/blob/master/system/logged_in_users/logged_in_users.sh`.

Let us take a look at the following code:

```
#!/bin/sh
# Report number of users logged in. Sorry it's not more exciting. :)
# Miles Davis <miles@cs.stanford.edu>
CLIENT="/usr/bin/gmetric"
# Last line in output of "who -q" is in the form "^# users=N$", so just
# grab the last line & split on the equals sign. This works on Linux, IRIX,
# Solaris, & probably most other un*xes.
USERS=`who -q | tail -1 | cut -d = -f 2`
```

```
#echo $USERS
$CLIENT -t uint16 -n users -v $USERS
exit $?
```

What he's done here is to simply gather the relevant metrics, using our favorite scripting language, and submit them using the gmetric utility (`$CLIENT`), passing a metric named `users` with a value of `$USERS`, that is, an unsigned 16-bit integer.

The possible types are: `string`, `int8`, `uint8`, `int16`, `uint16`, `int32`, `uint32`, `float`, `double`.

To keep this metric updated, you should configure a cron job to execute this script every minute or so.

$ crontab -e

* * * * * /home/oneadmin/gmetric/logged_in_users.sh

How to use a gmond Python module

Python support in gmond is enabled through Python at compile time, and we ensure that the following requirements are met before installing a new Python module:

`gmond.conf` contains `include ('/etc/ganglia/conf.d/*.conf')`. This is the directory where we should put the configuration files of each Python module as `pyconf` files.

A `modpython.conf` file exists in `/etc/ganglia/conf.d` with contents as follows:

```
modules {
  module {
    name = "python_module"
    path = "modpython.so"
    params = "@moduledir@/python_modules"
  }
}
include ("@sysconfdir@/conf.d/*.pyconf")
```

We have `modpython.so` in `/usr/lib64/ganglia`.

The directory `/usr/lib64/ganglia/python_modules` exists. This is the directory where Python modules should be placed as `.PY` files.

If we were using Xen on our hosts, we would probably be interested in the available xenstats Python module here: `https://github.com/ganglia/gmond_python_modules/tree/master/xenstats`.

Each module is usually structured in three folders, as follows:

- `conf.d`: Copy its contents to `/etc/ganglia/conf.d`, on the host
- `graph.d`: Copy its contents to `/usr/share/ganglia-webfrontend/graph.d`, on the Ganglia web frontend
- `python_modules`: Copy its contents to `/usr/lib64/ganglia/python_modules`

Restart Ganglia monitor, and the new Xen-related metrics gathering will start.

For updated information on how to install or create new Python modules for Ganglia, containing configuration notes for different systems, take a look at `http://sourceforge.net/apps/trac/ganglia/wiki/ganglia_gmond_python_modules`.

Ganglia Meta Daemon (gmetad)

Gmetad periodically polls a collection of child data sources, parses the collected XML, saves all numeric, volatile metrics to round-robin databases, and exports the aggregated XML over a TCP socket to clients. Child data sources could be multiple gmond daemons representing specific clusters, or other gmetad daemons representing sets of clusters.

The XML data will be used by the web interface to generate pages and graphs. A single gmetad is sufficient to manage multiple clusters that can be deployed on the OpenNebula frontend host.

Install it on Ubuntu or Debian as follows:

```
$ sudo apt-get install gmetad
```

Its configuration file is placed in `/etc/ganglia/gmetad.conf`, and contains a list of multiple `data_source` definitions, one for each managed cluster, followed by a list of data source hosts (gmonds or gmetads):

```
data_source "my cluster" [polling interval] address1:port addreses2:port
...
```

As we probably installed gmond on the frontend too, we can simply point gmetad to `localhost`, as follows:

```
data_source "NebulaPhy" localhost:8649
NebulaPhy
```

Please note that a single gmetad can actually gather and process data for multiple clusters, and you can decide to deploy more than one, on different machines, for redundancy.

Ganglia PHP web frontend

The Ganglia web frontend is used to show all the data collected by a gmetad in a simple way for system administrators and users.

Its operations are quite simple: call the gmetad to get the constructed XML tree describing hosts and their associated data, and show them in a bunch of HTML pages. Since the XML tree can become quite big in large environments, the web interface XML parsing can easily become a bottleneck when browsing the web interface.

Since the web interface has been developed in PHP, we need a web server with PHP support to use it. The package present in the Ubuntu or Debian repositories bundles an Apache2 configuration script (through `debconf`), as shown next, so configuring it takes a few seconds:

```
$ sudo apt-get install ganglia-webfrontend apache2-mpm-prefork
libapache2-mod-php5
```

Make sure that Apache2 gets configured for running Ganglia:

```
$ sudo dpkg-reconfigure ganglia-webfrontend
```

Since we have already configured `nginx` to serve SSL-enabled Sunstone, and we probably want to install Ganglia web interface on the OpenNebula frontend, enabling PHP support in nginx through FastCGI can be a good idea, but it requires non-trivial configuration steps, depending mainly on the availability of PHP-FPM (the simplified PHP FastCGI manager) only on very recent distributions (neither in Ubuntu 10.04 nor in Debian Squeeze).

Another alternative, easier and faster to configure, is to use the standard Apache2 to execute PHP, and nginx acting as an SSL-enabled reverse proxy in front of it (like we previously did for Sunstone).

We need to change the default Apache2 listening port (*:80), so as not to conflict with nginx, in `/etc/apache2/ports.conf`:

```
Listen 127.0.0.1:8000
```

Reload Apache2, as follows:

```
$ sudo /etc/init.d/apache2 reload
```

Now, we can configure a new nginx virtual host in `/etc/nginx/sites-available/ganglia`, similar to how we did for Sunstone:

```
upstream ganglia {
  ip_hash;
  server 127.0.0.1:8000;
}
```

This is a reference to Apache2 with PHP support listening on 127.0.0.1.

```
server {
    listen    444;
    server_name localhost;
```

Here, I have switched to a different port than the default 443 that we already dedicated to Sunstone. To prevent this kind of conflict, you can configure a dedicated subdomain on your DNS, for example, ganglia.yourdomain.com, switch back to the default 443 port, and insert that subdomain here:

```
ssl on;
ssl_certificate server.crt;
ssl_certificate_key server.key;
```

We reuse the same self-signed SSL certificate as for Sunstone:

```
error_page   500 502 503 504  /50x.html;
location = /50x.html {
root   /var/www/nginx-default;
}
```

Indeed, we provide the custom page for 50x errors:

```
location / {
    rewrite ^ https://$http_host/ganglia/
permanent;
    }
location /ganglia {
    index index.php;
    proxy_pass http://ganglia;
    }
}
```

Since Ganglia is served by Apache2 only for /ganglia requests, we need to first use a location to redirect all requests to /ganglia, and /ganglia requests to the backend Apache2.

Activate the new virtual host and reload nginx:

```
$ sudo ln -s /etc/nginx/sites-available/ganglia /etc/nginx/sites-enabled/
ganglia
$ sudo /etc/init.d/nginx reload
```

Now, accessing https://front-end:444 should redirect you to https://front-end:444/ganglia, and you should reach the Ganglia web interface.

Deploying gmond on the remaining hosts

Now that we have a working Ganglia web interface, serving stats gathered by gmetad (that contains only sensor data about itself) on the frontend, we should start to install the Ganglia monitor (gmond) component on all the other nodes.

It is sufficient to follow the same directives when installing gmond on the frontend node:

1. Install the Ganglia monitor package.
2. Configure it in `/etc/ganglia/gmond.conf`, as follows:
    ° Cluster name
    ° `udp_send_channel` section, either multicast or unicast, pointing to the gmetad in the frontend
3. Reload gmond.

Once you have configured a new node, it will immediately be displayed in the web interface with empty stats.

Multiple Ganglia cluster configuration (for VMs)

After we configure all the hosts to join the same monitoring cluster (NebulaPhy), we may want to set up a new cluster for all the VMs running on our hosts.

We should simply install the package Ganglia-monitor, as we did for the hosts:

```
$ sudo apt-get install ganglia-monitor
```

We need to change the cluster definition in `/etc/ganglia/gmond.conf`, providing a different cluster name as follows:

```
cluster {
  name = "NebulaVirt"
  owner = "LiberSoft"
  latlong = "unspecified"
  url = "http://libersoft.eu"
}
```

The communication port needs to be changed as well, so that it does not conflict with the already existing NebulaPhy cluster communication:

```
udp_send_channel {
  mcast_join = 239.2.11.71
  port = 8650
  ttl = 1
}
udp_recv_channel {
  mcast_join = 239.2.11.71
  port = 8650
  bind = 239.2.11.71
}
tcp_accept_channel {
  port = 8650
}
```

Do not forget to restart the service:

```
$ sudo /etc/init.d/ganglia-monitor restart
```

Now tell the gmetad on the frontend to poll and aggregate stats for this cluster too:

```
data_source "NebulaVirt" ubuntu-1.local:8650 ubuntu-2.local:8650
```

As you can see, this time we cannot point to localhost since the gmond running on the frontend does not belong to the *NebulaVirt* cluster, and for this reason, it does not have any information about it.

Please note that you do not need to specify here all the foreign cluster nodes but only a bunch of them; since we configured udp_recv_channel on every gmond, everyone has full stats for each gmond.

As a last step, since our Ganglia is managing multiple clusters, we may want to make changes in /etc/ganglia/gmetad.conf:

```
gridname "LiberSoft"
```

This is used only in the web interface, for aesthetic reasons.

Ganglia PHP web frontend usage

Now, our effort in configuring Ganglia will be rewarded, having an unique interface reporting resource usage for both physical and virtual servers, beautifully left open on a big monitor inside our NOC.

Open your browser and point it to `https://front-end:444/ganglia`, and you will hopefully find our Ganglia web frontend home page, as follows:

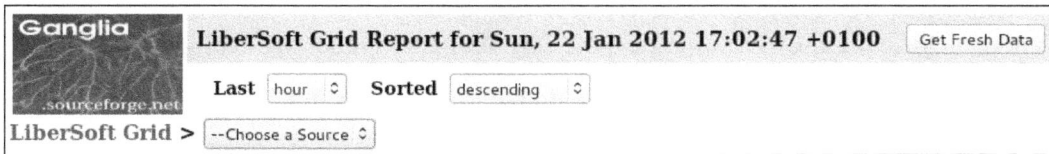

In the header at the top, you will see the date of the last refresh, with a **Get Fresh Data** button on the right-hand side, to gather updated statistics.

Under this, the two drop-down menus are used to select the time frame of the displayed statistics (**Last hour, day, week, month, year**, and so on) and to select the sorting of the objects displayed (**by name, by host up, by host down**, and so on).

On the bottom part of the header, there is the hierarchical breadcrumb trail of the current page. Starting from the main grid, we can dig into available clusters and hosts.

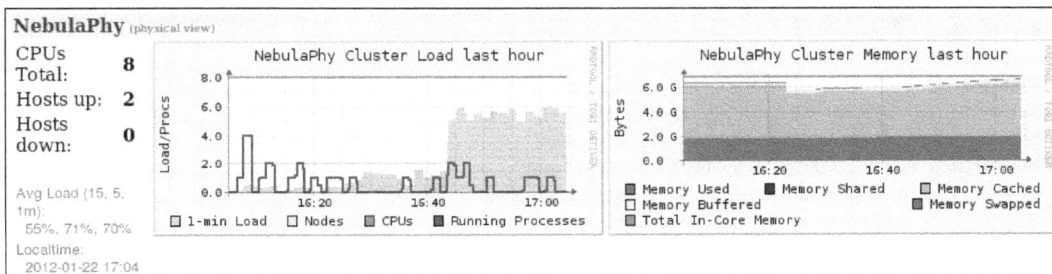

For the grid (the sum of all clusters) and each of the available clusters, we can find a section on the home page, showing a count of the available and unavailable hosts, a snap of the current average load of all the hosts, and two graphs that highlight the current resource usage of the cluster:

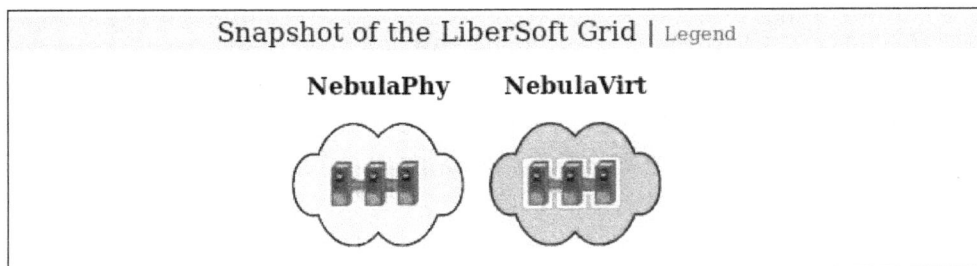

After the main cluster table, at the bottom of the page, there is a small section containing a cute graphical representation of the available clusters, with the cloud color ranging from azure to red, according to the actual cluster average load.

When clicking on one of them, or on the earlier clusters table, we will get access to the cluster detail page that follows:

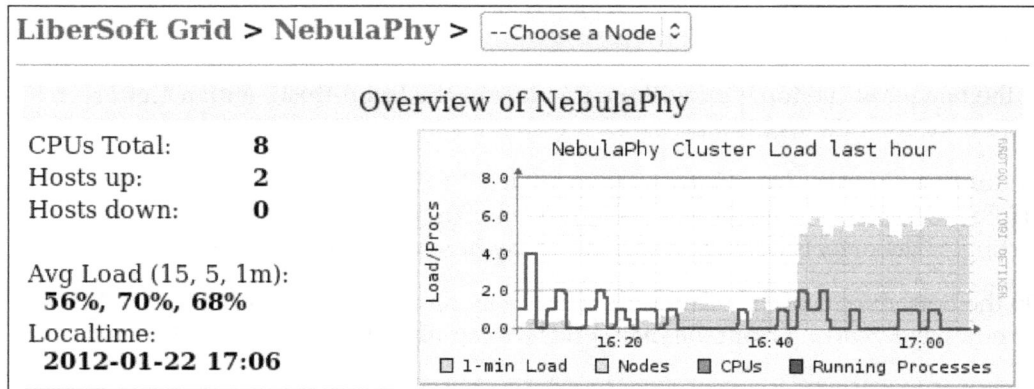

In the cluster overview page, we can find more graphs about CPU and network usage history, besides the previous ones of load average and memory usage.

Remember that, from the bottom bar, it is possible to switch the time frame of the graphs (**last hour**, **day**, **week**, **month**, **year**, and so on):

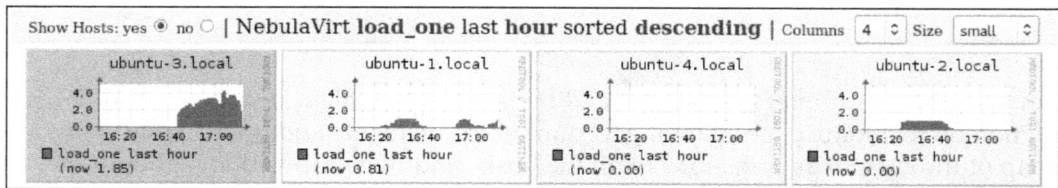

On the bottom of the cluster overview page, you can find a colored grid showing each of the hosts in the current cluster. By default, the graph shows the load average of the last minute, but we can switch metrics by using the **Metric** drop-down at the top of the page.

With the **Columns** and **Size** drop-downs, we will be able to change the arrangement and the resolution of each host graph.

If we click on a specific node graph on the **hosts** panel, or if we select a node from the upper **Choose a Node** drop-down, we will get access to the host info page, providing information and graphs for the current host only.

Please note that, on this page, there is not only resource usage information available but also software information (the current operating system, kernel, boot time, and so on) and hardware information (CPU number and frequency, total RAM, most full disk partition, and so on):

This host is up and running.

Time and String Metrics

Last Boot Time	Sun, 22 Jan 2012 13:56:38 +0100
Gexec Status	OFF
Gmond Started	Sun, 22 Jan 2012 15:01:02 +0100
Last Reported	0 days, 0:00:19
Machine Type	x86
Operating System	Linux
Operating System Release	2.6.32-37-generic
Uptime	0 days, 3:15:14

If we go back to the cluster overview page, we can find in the upper-right corner a **Physical View** link, which will move us to a new page that does not contain any graphs but only text metrics, particularly useful in showing all the nodes of a very large cluster in one page.

When in the host **Info** page, there is an alternative view as well, called **Node View**, a clean and concise page with information and metrics about the current host:

odin Info

odin

Load: 4.10 4.04 3.62

1m 5m 15m

Location: Unknown

Cluster local time Sun Jan 22 18:03:06 2012
Last heartbeat received 4 seconds ago.
Uptime 0 days, 8:03:36

CPU Utilization: 25.1 0.9 45.7

user sys idle

Hardware
CPUs: 4 x 2.60 GHz
Memory (RAM): 3.86 GB
Local Disk: Using 41.047 of 490.287 GB
Most Full Disk Partition: 28.0% used.

Software
OS: Linux 2.6.32-5-amd64 (x86_64)
Booted: January 22, 2012, 9:59 am
Uptime: 0 days, 8:03:36
Swap: Using 17.1 of 1905.9 MB swap.

Physical View | Reload

Ganglia integration with OpenNebula IM

Besides the basic Ganglia configuration for monitoring OpenNebula hosts and resource usage of VMs, we can configure the OpenNebula frontend to use information about hosts and VMs collected by Ganglia, rather than the default Information Manager drivers.

The Ganglia drivers for OpenNebula should reduce the monitoring overhead in a large deployment as they do not rely on SSH connections to the nodes to get all the information. On the other side, cron jobs must be installed on the nodes to provide VM information to the Ganglia system in a not-so-fashionable way, as we will see later.

To enable the Ganglia Information Manager driver defined in `oned.conf`:

```
IM_MAD = [
  name        = "im_ganglia",
  executable  = "one_im_sh",
  arguments   = "ganglia" ]
```

To enable the Ganglia information polling, append `-l poll=poll_ganglia` to the existing parameters listed in the `arguments` attribute of the VM manager driver in `oned.conf`:

```
VM_MAD = [
    name        = "vmm_kvm",
    executable  = "one_vmm_ssh",
    arguments   = "-t 15 -r 0 kvm -l poll=poll_ganglia",
    default     = "vmm_ssh/vmm_ssh_kvm.conf",
    type        = "kvm" ]
```

Stop and start one daemon as usual:

```
$ one stop
$ one start
```

Pointing to the local gmond

Both the `im_ganglia` and vmm `poll_ganglia` scripts need to communicate with the gmond daemon running on all the available hosts.

Make sure that the scripts:

```
remotes/im/ganglia.d/ganglia_probe
remotes/vmm/kvm/poll_ganglia
remotes/vmm/xen/poll_ganglia
```

Point to the correct gmond TCP port, used for retrieving the XML description file:

```
###############################
##        CONFIGURATION GOES HERE            ##
###############################
# host and port where to get monitoring information
GANGLIA_HOST='localhost'
GANGLIA_PORT=8649
```

Setting cron for updating VM information

The `poll_ganglia` script will search for active VM information from a host in a particular Ganglia host attribute called `OPENNEBULA_VMS_INFORMATION`. Obviously, this is not a native Ganglia attribute and should be populated by every host using the gmetric utility, every minute.

For doing this, we need one of the following sets of scripts:

- `/var/lib/one/remotes/vmm/xen/poll`

- `/var/lib/one/remotes/vmm/kvm/poll`

or:

- `$ONE_LOCATION/var/remotes/vmm/kvm/poll`

- `$ONE_LOCATION/var/remotes/vmm/xen/poll`

are available on each host. If you are not using a shared filesystem, you need to manually copy them somewhere on every host.

Assuming that we have our `$ONE_LOCATION` script in the oneadmin home directory that is placed on a shared filesystem between all the nodes, I need to configure a cron tab through the following:

```
$ crontab -e
   * * * * * gmetric -n OPENNEBULA_VMS_INFORMATION -t string -v `$HOME/
   one/var/remotes/vmm/kvm/poll -kvm`
```

This cron job will run every minute and will update the `OPENNEBULA_VMS_INFORMATION` attribute for the current host, with a `base64` string containing the current status of the active VM.

You can test it with:

```
$ echo `$HOME/one/var/remotes/vmm/kvm/poll --kvm`| base64 -d
```

You should see a block similar to the following for every active VM in the current host:

```
one-35:
  :state: a
  :nettx: 0
  :usedcpu: "1.9"
  :name: one-35
  :usedmemory: 65536
  :netrx: 955849
```

> **Bug in the poll_ganglia in OpenNebula 3.x**
>
> There is a bug inside the `poll_ganglia` script that will cause VM information polling to fail with the error in `oned.log`: `remotes/vmm/kvm/poll_ganglia:73: undefined method `[]' for nil:NilClass`. I have opened a bug report at `http://dev.opennebula.org/issues/1060`; the bug should be fixed when you read this, but who knows; this is an open source project.

For Xen host, there is an additional required cron job, involving two scripts:

- `/usr/share/one/scripts/ganglia/push_ganglia`
- `/var/lib/one/remotes/im/xen.d/xen.rb`

or:

- `$ONE_SOURCES/share/scripts/ganglia/push_ganglia`
- `$ONE_LOCATION/var/remotes/im/xen.d/xen.rb`

Put them in a cron job with:

```
$ crontab -e
  * * * * $HOME/one/var/remotes/im/xen.d/xen.rb | ./push_ganglia
```

Adding new hosts using im_ganglia

Now, if everything has been configured correctly, you should remove the hosts (if you had already configured them before Ganglia) and add them as follows:

```
$ onehost create <hostname> im_ganglia vmm_kvm tm_shared
```

For Xen hosts:

```
$ onehost create <hostname> im_ganglia vmm_xen tm_shared
```

If no errors are returned after the next monitoring hop, and if VM information is retrieved correctly, then the Ganglia integration with OpenNebula IM is working correctly.

Web interface glitch fix

Now, since we have configured the new custom metric OPENNEBULA_VMS_INFORMATION, it will appear in the host detail page on the Ganglia web interface, and since this is a very long base64-encoded string, we should definitely get rid of it.

Edit /usr/share/ganglia-webfrontend/host_view.php and place it at line 37, right before foreach ($metrics as $name => $value) that cycles the instruction.

unset($metrics['OPENNEBULA_VMS_INFORMATION']) will do the trick.

Sending alerts when a metric reaches a user limit

The following solution will not substitute an appropriate alert system for network and software application monitoring, such as the well-known Nagios. There is a contributed Perl daemon that connects to gmetad and, using a rule-based configuration file, sends alerts to a specified e-mail address.

Download Ganglia-alert from https://github.com/ganglia/ganglia_contrib/tree/master/ganglia-alert. There is also an init.d script for Debian and Ubuntu, contributed by me, as follows:

```
$ wget https://github.com/ganglia/ganglia_contrib/tarball/master -O
ganglia_contrib.tar.gz
$ tar xzf ganglia_contrib.tar.gz  --wildcards ganglia-ganglia_contrib-*/
ganglia-alert
$ cd ganglia-ganglia_contrib-*/ganglia-alert
```

Copy the ganglia-alert script in /usr/bin, and make it executable, as follows:

```
$ sudo cp ganglia-alert /usr/bin
$ sudo cp init.d-debian /etc/init.d/ganglia-alert
$ sudo chmod +x /usr/bin/ganglia-alert /etc/init.d/ganglia-alert
$ sudo update-rc.d ganglia-alert defaults
```

Now, create a new configuration file in `/etc/ganglia-alert.conf`, as follows:

```
email_from: alert@frontend.domain.com
email_to: monitoring@yourdomain.com
pid_file: /var/run/ganglia-alert.pid
group_by: host  # or alert
sleep_secs: 5    # how frequently poll gmetad
digest_secs: 30 # how long buffer multiple alerts
log_file: /var/log/ganglia-alert.log
!disk_full: $disk_free < .05 * $disk_total
!high_load: $load_one > $cpu_num*2
!very_high_load/5: $load_one_tn > 5000
```

Alerts are defined as `alert[/threshold]: expression` or `!name[/thresh]: expression`.

The threshold is the number of consecutive times the expression is `true` (non-zero) before sending an alert. It is optional and defaults to `1`.

A hackish way to retrieve the available metric is to analyze the XML description file returned by gmetad, opening a connection to the 8651 or TCP port:

```
$ telnet localhost 8651|grep "METRIC NAME"| awk -F' ' '{ print $2 $3 }'
```

Here is a table containing the default available metric internal variables:

boottime	disk_free	mem_total
bytes_in	disk_total	os_name
bytes_out	gexec	os_release
cpu_aidle	load_fifteen	part_max_used
cpu_idle	load_five	pkts_in
cpu_nice	load_one	pkts_out
cpu_num	machine_type	proc_run
cpu_speed	mem_buffers	proc_total
cpu_system	mem_cached	swap_free
cpu_user	mem_free	swap_total
cpu_wio	mem_shared	

Summary

In this chapter, we have learned how to effectively monitor and manage host and VM failures for our infrastructure. We used the Ganglia monitoring system initially to gather statistics from all of our nodes and VMs, to extend it through third party or our own modules, and finally to visualize all the gathered data in the PHP web frontend.

When running a large OpenNebula deployment, we saw how it is possible to install and configure an alternative OpenNebula Information Manager that relies on Ganglia monitors instead of using the default Ruby probes executed through SSH.

Finally, we discovered how to configure a simple e-mail alerting script that could warn us if some particular Ganglia metric is out of our predefined ranges.

In the next chapter, we will see how it is possible with OpenNebula not to rely only on on-premises hosts and to use an external cloud provider to offload our resource to it.

8
Hybrid Cloud Computing: Extending OpenNebula

A Hybrid Cloud is a natural extension to our deployed Private Cloud, and consists of combining local resources with others from the external Cloud providers. The remote provider could either be a commercial Cloud service (such as Amazon Web Services), or another OpenNebula infrastructure.

In this chapter, we are going to see how it's possible to off-load instances to the Amazon Web Services, detailing all the necessary steps for getting started with it.

Why use an external Cloud provider?

We surely know that managing an IT infrastructure requires resources and skills, for example, planning, choosing the hardware, waiting for the delivery process, environmental control inside the data center, hardware maintenance, and so on.

Often there are chances that you may need more flexibility other than having a virtualized infrastructure: to withstand a peak demand period during a new product presentation on a world expo or as a result of unexpected multiple hardware failures.

Also, relying on an external Cloud provider may provide the following benefits:

- **Cost-effective resources**: You pay for what you use (usually price per hour, without the requirement of a long-term commitment), without infrastructure and hardware maintenance overhead

- **Instant Elasticity**: You can request for multiple instances of multiple sizes at any time (more or less), and even for a few hours

- **Security**: Most Cloud providers undergo many industry-recognized certifications and audits, and have multiple layers of operational and physical security

What is AWS

Among all the Cloud providers around the world, we chose to detail **Amazon Web Services** as it is one of the first Cloud pioneers and is a well-established service running since 2006. They are the authors of the EC2 API, which nowadays has become a de facto standard for Cloud API.

In a few words, AWS is a bunch of **Infrastructure as a Service** (**IaaS**) manageable via remote API, ranging from networking, storage, and VM instances, to databases (both relational and document-oriented), content delivery network, and load-balancers. There are apps-related services available such as messaging queues and accounting/billing services.

Of all the services available in AWS, we will examine carefully the EC2 service, which will deliver to us VM instances as per our needs. There are other services and functions that interact with EC2 that are worth knowing:

- **Simple Storage (S3)**: This provides the basic, non-persistent image store for instances and can be used to archive snapshots or any data.
- **Elastic Block Storage (EBS)**: This is used to provide persistent data disks to instances, for both OS and data partitions.
- **Elastic IP**: This is a persistent IP address across VM instances, as even rebooting an instance may change its floating public and private IP.
- **Load Balancer**: This provides a manageable balancer in front of an application's server pool (but cannot be managed directly with OpenNebula). It's very useful for providing high-availability to a particular web application (but can be used for every TCP service too).
- **Security Groups**: This acts as a firewall for one or more started instances, specifying permitted source address, TCP/UDP ports, and ICMP.

How EC2 works

This is an EC2 VM instance's common life-cycle:

1. Select a base template image (called AMI) provided by Amazon, or build a custom one.
2. Configure firewall access policy for a particular instance.

3. Configure a preferred Availability Zone, an optional elastic IP address, or multiple persistent storage blocks.

4. Launch the instance and keep it running, make snapshots, launch more instances from snapshots.

5. Terminate the instance when no longer needed.

As you can notice, this is practically equivalent to the OpenNebula VM life-cycle to which we are already accustomed.

EC2 Locations (Regions and Availability Zones)

AWS has different datacenters spread all over the world, called **regions**.
The currently available AWS regions are:

- us-east-1 (Northern Virginia)
- us-west-2 (Oregon)
- us-west-1 (Northern California)
- eu-west-1 (Ireland)
- ap-southeast-1 (Singapore)
- ap-northeast-1 (Tokyo)
- sa-east-1 (São Paulo)

There is an eighth region, called **GovCloud**, which is dedicated to the US government agencies and contractors that want to move their sensitive workloads into the cloud while addressing their specific regulatory and compliance requirements.

Usually, we want to use a region closer to us for lowering network latency, and prefer using different regions to increase general availability of a service. Prices vary from region to region, reflecting infrastructure costs in the different areas.

Be aware that each region is divided into **Availability Zones (AZ)**, which are distinct locations that are engineered to be insulated from failures in other AZ (but provide a low latency network connectivity to other AZ in the same Region). By launching different VM instances in separate AZ, we can be pretty confident that they will not fail together.

Instance types by purchasing options

There are three different instance types, related to the different purchasing options:

- **On-demand instances**: We pay for computing capacity by the hour with no long-term commitments or upfront payments. This is the recommended option as it is the most flexible for us.

- **Reserved instances**: We make a one-time advanced payment for an instance, keeping it available for medium to long term. This is the recommended option for production instances, and to help lower costs.

- **Spot instances**: We configure a maximum hourly price and the instance will be started and terminated automatically, depending on the fluctuation of supply and demand for instances in a particular Region/Availability Zone. This is recommended for batch processing instances on low prices.

> OpenNebula can launch and manage on-demand instances only.

You will find more and updated information on instance types at `http://aws.amazon.com/ec2/purchasing-options/`.

Instance types by size

CPU power and memory are not directly configurable as we do in OpenNebula templates, but there are predefined sets of instances, some for general usage and others for particular workloads.

Following is a list of the available instance types, with their API name in brackets, and a reference to the hourly price of Linux instances in the us-east-1 region (the cheapest we can find in the EC2 offer).

The standard instances suited for most workloads are:

- **Small instance (m1.small, $0.085)**: 1.7 GB memory, 1 EC2 Compute Unit (1 virtual core with 1 EC2 Compute Unit), 160 GB instance storage, 32-bit platform, I/O Performance: Moderate

- **Large instance (m1.large, $0.34)**: 7.5 GB memory, 4 EC2 Compute Units (2 virtual cores with 2 EC2 Compute Units each), 850 GB instance storage, 64-bit platform, I/O Performance: High

- **Extra Large instance (m1.xlarge, $0.68)**: 15 GB memory, 8 EC2 Compute Units (4 virtual cores with 2 EC2 Compute Units each), 1,690 GB instance storage, 64-bit platform, I/O Performance: High

Recently, a micro instance has been introduced. This type is well suited for lower-throughput applications and websites, but that may consume significant compute cycles periodically (for example: scheduled backups or maintenance):

- **Micro instance (t1.micro, $0.02)**: 613 MB memory, Up to 2 EC2 Compute Units (for short periodic bursts), EBS storage only, 32-bit or 64-bit platform, I/O Performance: Low

Moving to the specialized instances types, we can find high-memory instances, suitable for running instances with large memory, high throughput applications, including database and memory caching applications:

- **High-Memory Extra Large (m2.xlarge, $0.50)**: 17.1 GB memory, 6.5 EC2 Compute Units (2 virtual cores with 3.25 EC2 Compute Units each), 420 GB of instance storage, 64-bit platform, I/O Performance: Moderate
- **High-Memory Double Extra Large (m2.2xlarge, $1.00)**: 34.2 GB memory, 13 EC2 Compute Units (4 virtual cores with 3.25 EC2 Compute Units each), 850 GB of instance storage, 64-bit platform, I/O Performance: High
- **High-Memory Quadruple Extra Large (m2.4xlarge, $2.00)**: 68.4 GB memory, 26 EC2 Compute Units (8 virtual cores with 3.25 EC2 Compute Units each), 1690 GB instance storage, 64-bit platform, I/O Performance: High

For compute-intensive applications, there is a set of high-CPU instances that have proportionally more CPU resources than memory (RAM):

- **High-CPU Medium (c1.medium, $0.17)**: 1.7 GB memory, 5 EC2 Compute Units (2 virtual cores with 2.5 EC2 Compute Units each), 350 GB instance storage, 32-bit platform, I/O Performance: Moderate
- **High-CPU Extra Large (c1.xlarge, $0.68)**: 7 GB memory, 20 EC2 Compute Units (8 virtual cores with 2.5 EC2 Compute Units each), 1690 GB instance storage, 64-bit platform, I/O Performance: High

Arriving at the latest, highly-specialized instance types, we can find high CPU resources with increased network performance that are well suited for **High Performance Compute** (**HPC**) applications, and other demanding network-bound applications (used by scientists and engineers to solve complex science, engineering, and business problems):

- **Cluster Compute Quadruple Extra Large (cc1.4xlarge, $1.30)**: 23 GB memory, 33.5 EC2 Compute Units (2 x Intel Xeon X5570, quad-core "Nehalem" architecture), 1690 GB instance storage, 64-bit platform, I/O Performance: Very High (10 Gigabit Ethernet)

- **Cluster Compute Eight Extra Large (cc2.8xlarge, $2.40)**: 60.5 GB of memory, 88 EC2 Compute Units (eight-core 2 x Intel Xeon), 3370 GB of instance storage, 64-bit platform, I/O Performance: Very High (10 Gigabit Ethernet)

Finally, there is a very specialized instance type providing general purpose **Graphics Processing Units** (**GPUs**), with proportionally high CPU, and increased network performance for applications benefiting from highly parallelized processing (for example, 3D rendering and media processing applications):

- **Cluster GPU Quadruple Extra Large (cg1.4xlarge, $2.10)**: 22 GB memory, 33.5 EC2 Compute Units (2 x Intel Xeon X5570, quad-core "Nehalem" architecture), 2 x NVIDIA Tesla "Fermi" M2050 GPUs, 1690 GB instance storage, 64-bit platform, I/O Performance: Very High (10 Gigabit Ethernet)

Amazon has put in a lot of effort and research when choosing each instance size, to better fit customer demand and also considering competitive prices. You can check the updated instance size information at `http://aws.amazon.com/ec2/instance-types/`.

Available Amazon Machine Images (AMI)

As uploading a disk image for each instance we need to launch is expensive in terms of bandwidth and time, AWS offers a wide range of updated machine templates, supporting many Linux flavors and Windows:

- **Standard Linux**: Ubuntu, Debian, Fedora, Gentoo

- **Enterprise Linux**: RedHat, Oracle, SUSE

- **Amazon Linux**: A CentOS derivative, with Amazon tools already included

- **Windows Server**: 2003 r2, 2008 r2, with or without SQL server

There are images with application stacks or databases already installed, such as IBM DB2, MySQL Enterprise, Oracle 11g, Hadoop, Apache HTTP, IIS/Asp.net, Webshpere, JBOSS and many others. Check carefully if the image you need is already available before starting!

> We can search in the AMI database at `http://aws.amazon.com/amis`. Try to make a search for `ubuntu server-10.04 lts`, and you will find the two (32-bit and 64-bit) official images of Ubuntu, maintained directly from Canonical (the company responsible for Ubuntu).

For each AMI, we can find detailed information—from the Changelog to the list of the AMI IDs to be used in different regions.

> **Proprietary Software Licensing**
>
> One of the inborn capabilities of running instances in Amazon with proprietary software is that, you don't need to buy licenses for the software you need, as they are already included in the hourly cost of the instance!
>
> In practical terms, a small Linux instance costs 0.095 $ per hour, while a small Windows instance $ 0.12 per hour (EU region).

BitNami AMIs

BitNami (`http://bitnami.org/`) is a third party project that provides VM templates bundled with a lot of high quality, ready-to-use open source software packages, which are directly available in Amazon EC2.

Just to name a few of them: SugarCRM, Alfresco, Redmine, Drupal, Wordpress, Joomla, phpBB. Along with the application stacks, BitNami offers infrastructure stacks, including: LAMP, Postgres, Ruby, Django, Tomcat, and JBoss.

Always make a search on `http://bitnami.org/stacks` to see if you can find an AMI that is already configured, to speed-up your deployment process.

When we find an image that interests us, we simply need to reach the application page, to see the list of available AMI ID in each region (for example: `http://bitnami.org/stack/drupal`).

Drupal 6.22-0 (Ubuntu 10.04)	64 bits	EBS	ami-68956e01	ami-b76133f2	ami-1ef5782e	ami-4c93a338	ami-2c5c247e	ami-ec02a8ed	
Drupal 7.12-0 (Ubuntu 10.04)	64 bits	EBS	ami-dfda0ab6	ami-735c0536	ami-707df040	ami-e9ebd59d	ami-6841053a	ami-dc67d1dd	ami-4c449b51
Drupal 6.22-0 (Windows Server 2008.r1.sp2) Beta	32 bits	EBS	ami-128d747b	ami-971341d2		ami-3abb8d4e	ami-ead6afb8	
Drupal 7.12-0 (Windows Server 2008.R2.SP1) Beta	64 bits	EBS	ami-0fdb0b66	ami-d55c0590	ami-7e7df04a	ami-69e8d61d	ami-32410560	ami-fe65d3ff	ami-44449b59

AWS signup and first login

In order to use the OpenNebula integration with EC2 AWS, you need to register an account at `http://aws.amazon.com/`, and sign up for S3 and EC2 services.

1. On the main page, click on the **Sign Up** button at the top (it's free); you will be directed to the following screen:

If you already have an account at `amazon.com` (for example, if you bought books on `amazon.com/.uk/.de/.it`) you can use the same credentials for logging into AWS.

If you are a new user, you will be asked for personal details, and a valid credit card. In order to increase the protection of your account, you may be interested in using the **AWS Multi-Factor Authentication** available in both a software edition for Android/iPhone/BlackBerry, and as a hardware OTP generator (`http://aws.amazon.com/mfa/`).

2. After completing the registration process correctly, you will receive a confirmation e-mail.

3. Once you have received the e-mail, you may log in to **AWS Management Console** by clicking on the **My Account/Console** link at the top (`https://console.aws.amazon.com/console/home`).

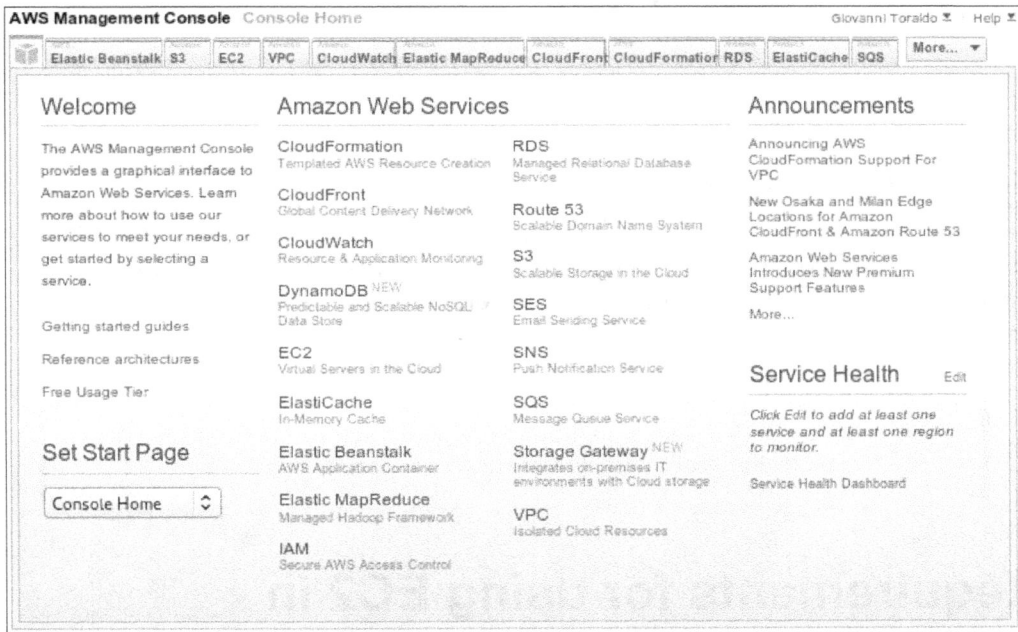

The dashboard will present itself as the default homepage for the console. Always take a look at the **Service Health** section to see if there are any ongoing problems on the infrastructure, and to check for the latest Amazon Announcements.

For our purposes, we need to sign up at least for the S3 and EC2 services (sign up is free, we pay for effective resource usage only), and wait for the confirmation e-mail, which states that all the services are available for our account.

1. First click on the **S3** service tab, and verify that there aren't any messages stating that the S3 service is not available yet (you don't need to create any bucket for OpenNebula to work).

2. Next, check that the EC2 service is available too. Click on the **EC2** tab, and you should get the interface to administer instances.

In the EC2 dashboard page, you will be able to switch between the various available Regions, using the combo-box on the left. In the central box, you will see a big **Launch Instance** button, along with a summary of the actual available resources.

Free usage tier

To help the new AWS customers get started in the Cloud, AWS introduced a free usage tier. New AWS customers will be able to run a free EC2 Micro Instance for one year, along with S3, EBS, and data transfer. This is great for testing and becoming confident with AWS without paying anything!

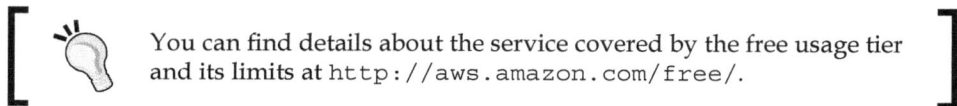

> You can find details about the service covered by the free usage tier and its limits at http://aws.amazon.com/free/.

Requirements for using EC2 in OpenNebula

Before starting with the OpenNebula configuration, we should set up an SSH Key Pair, an X.509 certificate, and the Amazon EC2 API Tools.

Setting up an SSH Key Pair

The first requirement to access our future EC2 instances is to create a new SSH Key Pair (or import your existing ~/.ssh/id_rsa.pub generated via ssh-keygen). The key pair will be used to identify yourself when connecting via ssh to a Linux-based AMI, or to decrypt the default administrator password in a Windows-based AMI.

1. From the **EC2** tab on the Management Console, access the **Key Pairs** section.

2. Either click on **Create Key** and save it somewhere on your desktop/laptop, or click on **Import Key Pair** to proceed with uploading your public SSH key.

For highest security, you should create a new SSH Key Pair on your local machine, and only submit the public key to AWS. However, letting Amazon generate a new key pair is easy and the private key is downloadable for one time only (if you lose it, you need to invalidate it and generate a new one).

Setting up an X.509 Certificate

The second requirement is to generate an X.509 certificate, which is used to identify the OpenNebula frontend with your current credentials, while using the remote EC2 API.

1. Click on the upper right corner of the screen with your full name, and select **Security Credentials** (https://aws-portal.amazon.com/gp/aws/securityCredentials).

2. On the new page, scroll down to **Access Credentials.** Select the **X.509 Certificates** tab, and click on **Create a New Certificate** or **Upload your Own Certificate**.

3. Download and take care of the private key; you cannot re-download it afterwards as it isn't stored by Amazon for security purposes.

The two files (the certificate and the private key) should be kept readable on the OpenNebula frontend: copy them to /etc/one or $ONE_LOCATION/etc and configure permission as read-only for the oneadmin user:

```
$ chmod 400 pk-*.pem cert-*.pem
$ chown oneadmin:oneadmin pk-*.pem cert-*.pem
```

Downloading and configuring Amazon EC2 API Tools

The API tools are used as a client interface to the Amazon EC2 web service, and are used to register and launch new instances by the OpenNebula EC2 Drivers.

1. Download the latest package from http://aws.amazon.com/developertools/351.

2. Unpack it somewhere on the OpenNebula frontend, for example, in /opt/local/ec2-api-tools or $ONE_LOCATION/share/ec2-api-tools.

3. The Amazon EC2 API Tools require the Java JRE package to be available on the frontend (we probably want to use the headless edition as the OpenNebula frontend doesn't have a desktop interface):

```
$ sudo apt-get install openjdk-6-jre-headless
```

4. Make sure that the environment variable JAVA_HOME is available for the oneadmin user:

```
$ echo $JAVA_HOME
/usr/lib/jvm/java-6-openjdk
```

5. If not present, put it in oneadmin ~/.profile as we did in the early chapters for $ONE_LOCATION:

```
export JAVA_HOME=/usr/lib/jvm/java-6-openjdk
```

6. Remember to reload your .profile:

```
$ source ~/.profile
```

OpenNebula configuration

Now that the prerequisites are satisfied, we can start with the OpenNebula configuration. The two drivers needed to manage remote EC2 instances are:

- **im_ec2**: This driver simulates an ephemeral physical host, reporting available CPU and memory, depending on the max number of instances we want to run at the same time on EC2
- **vmm_ec2**: This invokes deploy and shutdown actions, using the Amazon EC2 API Tools

Uncomment the two drivers in oned.conf:

```
IM_MAD = [
    name       = "im_ec2",
    executable = "one_im_ec2",
    arguments  = "im_ec2/im_ec2.conf" ]

VM_MAD = [
    name       = "vmm_ec2",
    executable = "one_vmm_ec2",
    arguments  = "vmm_ec2/vmm_ec2.conf",
    type       = "xml" ]
```

Before restarting the frontend, we need to take a look at the available configuration files.

IM_EC2 configuration

Take a look at the available configuration parameters in /etc/one/im_ec2/im_ec2.conf or $ONE_LOCATION/etc/im_ec2/im_ec2.conf:

```
#-------------------------------------------------------------------
-----------
# Max number of instances that can be launched into EC2
#-------------------------------------------------------------------
-----------

SMALL_INSTANCES=5
LARGE_INSTANCES=
EXTRALARGE_INSTANCES=
```

As, while using a remote Cloud provider, we cannot talk directly to the remote host that will run our instances and there aren't any hardware limits (free CPU and free memory), the idea here was to define the maximum number of concurrent instances launched on the remote Cloud provider, in the configuration file.

These parameters are used to calculate an ephemeral available CPU and memory, to effectively stop the scheduler from deploying more instances when those limits are reached.

Unfortunately, as you can see from the configuration file, in the current OpenNebula release, only three standard instance types are taken into consideration.

VMM_EC2 default template attributes configuration

Take a look at the available configuration parameters in /etc/one/vmm_ec2/vmm_ec2.conf or $ONE_LOCATION/etc/vmm_ec2/vmm_ec2.conf:

```
<TEMPLATE>
  <EC2>
    <KEYPAIR>my-keypair</KEYPAIR>
    <AUTHORIZEDPORTS>22</AUTHORIZEDPORTS>
    <INSTANCETYPE>t1.micro</INSTANCETYPE>
  </EC2>
</TEMPLATE>
```

The default template parameters used, when omitted in the VM template, are kept here.

The `KEYPAIR` tag is used to define the name of the default key pair that should be able to `SSH` remotely when the new instance is launched (`<KEYPAIR>gt</KEYPAIR>` in my case).

You can generate a new key pair with the **Create Key Pair** button or import your existing `OpenSSH` public key using the **Import Key Pair** button in the **Key Pairs** page.

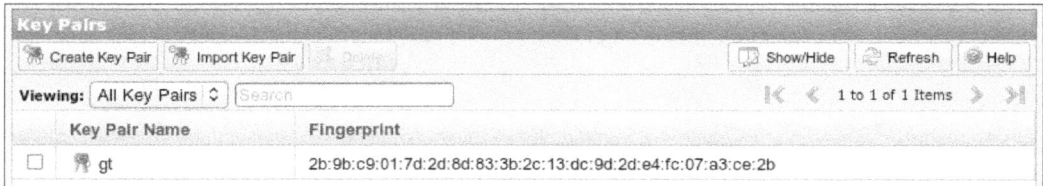

Key Pairs		
Create Key Pair Import Key Pair Delete	Show/Hide Refresh Help	
Viewing: All Key Pairs ⬍ Search	⏮ ◀ 1 to 1 of 1 Items ▶ ⏭	
Key Pair Name	**Fingerprint**	
☐ 🔑 gt	2b:9b:c9:01:7d:2d:8d:83:3b:2c:13:dc:9d:2d:e4:fc:07:a3:ce:2b	

> Remember that each AWS Region is independent from each other, and you need to import your first key pair in each region you are going to use!

The `AUTHORIZEDPORTS` tag is used to define the list of ports that should be present in the **default** security group.

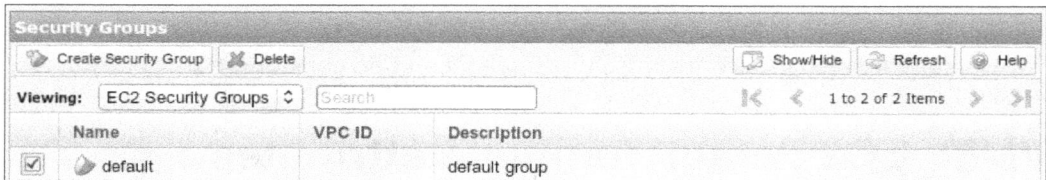

Security Groups			
Create Security Group Delete	Show/Hide Refresh Help		
Viewing: EC2 Security Groups ⬍ Search	⏮ ◀ 1 to 2 of 2 Items ▶ ⏭		
Name	**VPC ID**	**Description**	
☑ default		default group	

The **default** security group, if not present, will be automatically created and shared among all the launched instances.

The `INSTANCETYPE` tag is used to define the default size of an instance, unless specified in the VM template.

You can find all the available instance types earlier in this chapter, or at `http://aws.amazon.com/ec2/instance-types/`, along with their `API Name` that should be used here.

EC2 API Tools configuration

We should have already unpacked the Amazon EC2 API Tools somewhere in the frontend, and now we need to configure them.

1. In /etc/one/vmm_ec2/vmm_ec2rc or $ONE_LOCATION/etc/vmm_ec2/vmm_ec2rc:

    ```
    #-----------------------------------------------------------------
    -----------
    # EC2 API TOOLS Configuration.
    #-----------------------------------------------------------------
    -----------
    EC2_HOME="$ONE_LOCATION/share/ec2-api-tools"
    EC2_PRIVATE_KEY="$ONE_LOCATION/etc/pk.pem"
    EC2_CERT="$ONE_LOCATION/etc/cert.pem"
    ```

2. EC2_HOME should point to the unpacked folder of the EC2 API Tools:

    ```
    $ ls $ONE_LOCATION/share/ec2-api-tools

    bin  lib  license.txt  notice.txt  THIRDPARTYLICENSE.TXT
    ```

3. Now, it's time to use the already downloaded X.509 certificate and its private key. EC2_PRIVATE_KEY points to the private key of our X.509 certificate (pk-*.pem), while EC2_CERT points to the X.509 certificate (cert-*.pem).

    > Here I have copied both of them inside the etc folder, but they could be kept anywhere, it's enough that they are readable from the oneadmin user on the frontend.

4. For debugging purposes, we may want to put the EC2_* environment variables in our ~/.profile, so we can easily execute the tools outside the OpenNebula drivers:

    ```
    export EC2_HOME=$ONE_LOCATION/share/ec2-api-tools
    export EC2_PRIVATE_KEY=$ONE_LOCATION/etc/pk.pem
    export EC2_CERT=$ONE_LOCATION/etc/cert.pem
    PATH=$EC2_HOME/bin:$PATH
    ```

5. Reload .profile:

    ```
    $ source ~/.profile
    ```

6. For security reasons, check that the current private key permissions are read-only for oneadmin!

```
$ chown oneadmin:oneadmin $ONE_LOCATION/etc/pk.pem

$ chmod 400 $ONE_LOCATION/etc/pk.pem

$ ls -1 $ONE_LOCATION/etc/pk.pem

-rw------- 1 oneadmin oneadmin 928  1 feb 16.58 /var/cloud/one/
etc/pk.pem
```

7. Check that the EC2 configuration is correct by executing one of the tools included in the package, such as:

```
$ ec2-describe-availability-zones

AVAILABILITYZONE      us-east-1a     available      us-east-1

AVAILABILITYZONE      us-east-1b     available      us-east-1

AVAILABILITYZONE      us-east-1c     available      us-east-1

AVAILABILITYZONE      us-east-1d     available      us-east-1
```

8. If no errors are printed, the EC2 API Tools are correctly configured.

Later in the configuration file, there are some Java-related driver tuning options:

```
#--------------------------------------------------------------------
--------
# Driver configuration
#--------------------------------------------------------------------
--------
# Arguments for the JAVA Virtual Machine
EC2_JVM_ARGS="-Xms16m -Xmx64m"

# Number of concurrent EC2 operations (not instances)
EC2_JVM_CONCURRENCY=10
```

The -Xmx argument defines the max memory size that the heap can reach for the JVM. A low value can cause OutOfMemoryExceptions, or a very poor performance if the heap memory is reaching the maximum heap size.

The -Xms argument sets the initial heap memory size for the JVM. This means that, when EC2 API Tools start, the JVM will allocate this amount of memory instantly. This avoids the JVM from constantly increasing the heap and gain some performance.

Defaults are optimal values for most workloads and should be changed only when getting memory management errors on larger infrastructures.

EC2_JVM_CONCURRENCY defines the maximum number of parallel tasks that are executed within during our session. On large infrastructures, it could be increased if we need better responsiveness when busy.

Adding the first EC2 host

Now that all the configuration requirements are met, we can add a new host using the onehost command to finally start using the remote Cloud provider:

```
$ onehost create ec2 im_ec2 vmm_ec2 tm_dummy dummy
```

Check if it's working with the onehost list and show commands:

```
$ onehost list
  ID NAME     RVM    TCPU    FCPU    ACPU    TMEM    FMEM    AMEM    STAT
   4    ec2      0     500     500     500            8.5G    8.5G
8.5G        on


oneadmin@odin:~$ onehost show 4
HOST 4 INFORMATION
ID               : 4
NAME             : ec2
STATE            : MONITORED
IM_MAD           : im_ec2
VM_MAD           : vmm_ec2
VN_MAD           : dummy
TM_MAD           : tm_dummy
LAST MONITORING TIME   : 1328129974
```

Now we have successfully configured OpenNebula and we are ready to launch our first instance on EC2!

Known Limitations

As there is no direct access to the host that is running the instance, it cannot be monitored against failures (we do not know where the VM is running on the EC2 cloud). However, there is a monitoring service integrated in AWS—**CloudWatch**—that can be configured to check for availability of instances and report back any malfunctioning.

In addition, the usual OpenNebula functionality of snapshotting, restoring, or live migration from one host to another is not available with EC2.

Launching the first VM instance on EC2

Now it's time to start our first instance on Amazon EC2 Cloud.

1. Let's define a basic template ec2.one:

```
EC2 = [
    AMI="ami-4a0df923",
    INSTANCETYPE=t1.micro
]
```

Impressed? The unique mandatory attribute is the AMI ID, to be used for launching a new instance.

When choosing the right AMI for your instance, you should remember that there are two types of AMI images available:

*   **Instance Store**: This type is an inexpensive and non-persistent root device
*   **Elastic Block Store**: This type is a faster root device and persistent across reboots and failure

The first is mainly useful for testing instances or cloned ones (such as an application server), while the second is advisable for production instances (especially for file servers and databases), data persists across user reboots or EC2 crashes, and its price is around $0.10 per GB per month and $0.10 per 1 million I/O requests.

The full browsable catalog is available at http://aws.amazon.com/amis.

As example, the official Canonical AMIs for **Ubuntu 10.04 amd64 Server** are:

Instance Store	EBS
ap-southeast-1: ami-14067846	ap-southeast-1: ami-06067854
eu-west-1: ami-1e34016a	eu-west-1: ami-f6340182
us-east-1: ami-da0cf8b3	us-east-1: ami-4a0df923
us-west-1: ami-860c5cc3	us-west-1: ami-880c5ccd

Please note that there are different AMI images for each different region, even for the same image, as each region is completely independent from the others. For this reason, you need to pick the right AMI depending on the region where you are planning to deploy the instance (the default is us-east-1).

1. Now submit the VM template and wait for the instance start-up:

```
$ onevm create ec2.one
```

The instance will go rapidly into the RUNN state, but this only means that the request has been successfully submitted to EC2 and you need to wait for the real boot-up process.

2. After a while, check with the onevm show if the EC2 drivers have successfully retrieved the public IP of the instance:

```
$ onevm show 56

..

VIRTUAL MACHINE TEMPLATE
EC2=[
    AMI=ami-4a0df923,
    INSTANCETYPE=t1.micro ]
IP=ec2-50-17-89-79.compute-1.amazonaws.com
NAME=one-56
VMID=56
```

Yes, it's online!

3. Now, try to SSH to the public IP address you see, using the private key of the associated key pair (not the private key of the X.509 certificate!):

```
$ ssh root@ec2-50-17-89-79.compute-1.amazonaws.com -i ~/gt.pem
The authenticity of host 'ec2-50-17-89-79.compute-1.amazonaws.com
(50.17.89.79)' can't be established.
RSA key fingerprint is 36:05:95:dc:b4:a6:49:3f:bf:96:24:22:ae:27:d
2:1a.
Are you sure you want to continue connecting (yes/no)? yes
Warning: Permanently added 'ec2-50-17-89-79.compute-1.amazonaws.
com,50.17.89.79' (RSA) to the list of known hosts.
Please login as the ubuntu user rather than root user.
Connection to ec2-50-17-89-79.compute-1.amazonaws.com closed.
```

Why this restriction? Most AMIs are configured to not allow remote root login, but each one has a particular deprivileged user with sudo privileges. As stated in the previous message, connect back using the ubuntu user instead of root:

```
$ ssh ubuntu@ec2-50-17-89-79.compute-1.amazonaws.com -i ~/gt.pem
Linux ip-10-243-109-8 2.6.32-309-ec2 #18-Ubuntu SMP Mon Oct 18 21:00:50
UTC 2010 x86_64 GNU/Linux
Ubuntu 10.04.1 LTS
Welcome to Ubuntu!
```

Nice, we are in! Remember that AMI images are often outdated, and for this reason you should always remember to do an upgrade as the first thing after connecting:

```
$ sudo apt-get update && sudo apt-get dist-upgrade
```

As there is nearly always a kernel update, reboot the instance when you finish to upgrading the system.

```
$ sudo reboot
```

> By default, each AMI should use the repositories managed by Amazon's internal facilities, so updating a system don't waste precious bandwidth.
>
> Obviously, you should be using an EBS-based image, or rebooting will simply reset your instance to its initial state.

EBS Snapshots

After writing data to an EBS volume, we can periodically create a snapshot of the volume to use as a baseline for new instances or for data backup.

Unfortunately, OpenNebula doesn't directly support snapshotting, but we can easily create a new snapshot using the EC2 Tools.

1. We need to discover the volume ID. List all the available volumes with:

   ```
   $ ec2-describe-volumes

   VOLUME   vol-b07281d8   10   snap-4c1f0324  eu-west-1a   in-use

   ATTACHMENT   vol-b07281d8   i-569ad31f   /dev/sda1   attached
   ```

2. Pick the volume name and queue the snapshot creation with:

   ```
   $ ec2-create-snapshot -d 'Testing snapshot' vol-b07281d8
   ```

3. Retrieve the list of the available snapshots with:

   ```
   $ ec2-describe-snapshots eu-west-1

   SNAPSHOT       snap-db7e9bb0 vol-b07281d8  pending        2012-02-
   12T14:39:40+0000            061356295859 10    Testing snapshot
   ```

   The snapshot creation is in `pending` state, and is not yet ready.

When the snapshot reaches the `completed` state, it's possible to create a volume that could be attached to an existing instance, or be converted as an AMI that could be used to bootstrap a new instance.

To create a new volume, larger than the initial volume (10 GB), in a different availability zone (original volume was in eu-west-1a):

1. Run the following command:

```
$ ec2-create-volume -s 12 --snapshot snap-db7e9bb0 -z eu-west-1b
```

2. Check if the new volume has been created:

```
$ ec2-describe-volumes
VOLUME vol-6275860a 12      snap-db7e9bb0 eu-west-1b     available
2012-02-12T14:53:12+0000
```

The resulting volume could be attached to an existing instance by using the Management Console—access the **Volumes** section in the **EC2** tab, and click on **Attach Volumes**.

Creating a new AMI from a snapshot

1. The creation of a new AMI from a snapshot is available from the Management Console: Go to the **Snapshots** section, select your snapshot and click on the **Create Image** button.

2. A pop-up window will appear, asking you to fill some details about the new AMI—Name, Description, OS architecture, Kernel ID, RAM Disk ID, and Root Device Name.

It's important to specify the right kernel—it should be the same that was used in the original AMI; using the wrong kernel may lead to unsuccessful boot.

Nowadays, most AMIs use **pv-grub** (including the ones maintained by Canonical), which permits us to boot kernels and `initrd` bundled in the AMI. PV-grub is available as both, 32-bit and 64-bit versions, with a different kernel ID for each region:

Region	pv-grub i386	pv-grub x86_64
us-east-1	aki-805ea7e9	aki-825ea7eb
us-west-1	aki-83396bc6	aki-8d396bc8
us-west-2	aki-c0e26ff0	aki-94e26fa4
eu-west-1	aki-64695810	aki-62695816
ap-southeast-1	aki-a4225af6	aki-aa225af8
ap-northeast-1	aki-ec5df7ed	aki-ee5df7ef
sa-east-1	aki-bc3ce3a1	aki-cc3ce3d1

> You will find a complete reference, and a list of the available pv-grub kernel ID at: `http://docs.amazonwebservices.com/AWSEC2/latest/UserGuide/UserProvidedkernels.html`.

1. Click on **Yes, Create**, and wait for a few seconds.
2. Then move to the **AMIs** section and adjust the filter — **Viewing: Owned by Me**, after which you should find the newly created AMI.

    The AMI ID could be used in any new instance and should bootstrap successfully our snapshotted system.

> By clicking on the **Permissions** button, you can grant another AWS user access to the newly created AMI or make it public, so everyone else can actually find and use it.

A more complex template example

We see that defining a template suitable to run on EC2 is simple, and needs only the AMI name to start up correctly.

Here follows a complete list of all the available EC2 attributes:

- **AMI**: The AMI name that will be launched.
- **KEYPAIR**: The RSA key pair name that will be used to configure remote access to newly launched instances. The private key pair will be used later, to execute commands such as `ssh -i id_keypair` or `scp -i id_keypair`.
- **ELASTICIP**: The elastic IP address you want to assign to the instance launched (we need to request one from the AWS console before using it).
- **AUTHORIZED_PORTS**: This attribute is passed to the `ec2-authorize` command along with the parameter `-p port`, and can be a single number (for example: `22`) or a range (for example: `22-1024`).
- **INSTANCETYPE**: The type of instance to be launched in EC2. As already said, the most used instance types are: t1.micro, m1.small, m1.large, m1.xlarge, c1.medium, and c1.xlarge.

An interesting feature is the possibility to combine both the standard VM attributes and EC2-specific ones, in a unique VM template. Depending on the deployment host, OpenNebula will automatically take into account the correct attributes.

Use the following as a simple example:

```
NAME     = ubuntu-vm-ec2-enabled

# Standard VM attributes
MEMORY = 600
CPU = 0.5
VCPU = 1
DISK = [ IMAGE_ID  = 2 ]
DISK = [ TYPE = swap,
         SIZE = 1024 ]
NIC = [ NETWORK_ID = 1 ]

# EC2 attributes
EC2 = [ AMI="ami-4a0df923",
            KEYPAIR="gt",
            ELASTICIP="75.101.155.97",
            AUTHORIZED_PORTS="22",
            INSTANCETYPE=t1.micro]
```

Memory and CPU attributes should be similar to the ones available with the defined EC2 instance type, to achieve similar performances when running.

After the template is submitted, the instance is put in the PENDING state, waiting for the scheduler. The scheduler will take care of the instance and may use an existing RANK attribute or use defaults (usually, based on free CPU).

If you want to force the deployment on the EC2 host, you can use either of the following two options:

- Run the onevm deploy command while the instance is in the PENDING state:

  $ onevm deploy vm-id host-id

- Add a requirements attribute to the VM template to always force the deployment on the ec2 host:

  ```
  REQUIREMENTS = 'NAME = "ec2"'
  ```

Using Elastic IP addresses

Elastic IP addresses are static IP addresses associated with the AWS account (and not specific instances) that you can float around multiple instances until you explicitly release them.

They can be used to mask instance or Availability Zone failures by rapidly remapping the Elastic IP addresses to any instance. If an instance is serving a public service that is reachable by a domain (for example: blog.mysite.org), then pointing that instance to an Elastic IP is a very good idea.

To use an Elastic IP, we must first request a new one from the AWS Management Console:

1. Click on the **EC2** tab and then on **Elastic IPs**.

2. Click on **Allocate New Address**. Confirm the request for an EC2 Elastic IP with **Yes, Allocate**.

3. Now you should receive a new Elastic IP that can be used in your instance templates.

Within the same **Elastic IPs** section, it's possible to unlink the Elastic IP from an active instance using the **Disassociate Address** button. After disassociating an Elastic IP, it's possible to re-attach it to another instance using the **Associate Address** button.

Remember that Elastic IPs are free while in use, and you pay only for the non-attached Elastic IP. The main reason for this is to prevent people from taking too much Elastic IPs that aren't actually being used. Always remember to use Release Address, when an Elastic IP is not needed anymore!

Multi-region (or provider) support

Until now, we launched instances only into the default EC2 region—us-east-1 (Virginia). With a minimal effort, it is possible to define and manage multiple EC2 hosts separately within the same frontend, pointing to different EC2 regions or to a completely different cloud provider.

1. In oned.conf, add a new VM_MAD definition using a unique name, and add a -u parameter, followed by the remote endpoint of a new EC2 region:

    ```
    VM_MAD = [
        name        = "vmm_ec2_ireland",
        executable  = "one_vmm_ec2",
        arguments   = "-u https://ec2.eu-west-1.amazonaws.com/ vmm_ec2/
    vmm_ec2.conf",
        type        = "xml" ]
    ```

2. Restart oned and define a new host with:

    ```
    $ onehost add ec2_ireland im_ec2 vmm_ec2_ireland tm_dummy dummy
    ```

Every instance deployed on this host will be started on the wanted EC2 region (Ireland).

A list of the endpoints for each region is as follows:

Region	Endpoint	1-Hour Cost Extra-Large
US East (Northern Virginia)	ec2.us-east-1.amazonaws.com	$0.68
US West (Oregon)	ec2.us-west-2.amazonaws.com	$0.68
US West (Northern California)	ec2.us-west-1.amazonaws.com	$0.76
EU (Ireland)	ec2.eu-west-1.amazonaws.com	$0.76
Asia Pacific (Singapore)	ec2.ap-southeast-1.amazonaws.com	$0.76
Asia Pacific (Tokyo)	ec2.ap-northeast-1.amazonaws.com	$0.80
South America (São Paulo)	ec2.sa-east-1.amazonaws.com	$0.92

When choosing a region, the price needs to be taken in account; use the third column as an affordability reference for each available region (it's the hourly cost of an Extra-Large Linux instance).

When using multiple EC2 hosts, it's very useful to specify the CLOUD attribute in the VM template, so you can use the right AMIs in the right region.

For example, to launch an Ubuntu 10.04 LTS 64-bit on the eu-west-1 region, you will pick the right AMI (http://aws.amazon.com/amis/4348), and specify the OpenNebula host name inside the CLOUD attribute:

```
EC2 = [ AMI="ami-f6340182" ,
          CLOUD="ec2_ireland" ]
```

In this way, the VM will always be launched on the chosen region.

Windows instances

Using Windows instances on EC2 doesn't involve any particular attention, except the retrieval of the administrator password required to connect to a newly launched instance, via RDP.

The administrator password is automatically generated during the instance startup, and is added inside a <Password> element in the VM template, encrypted with your public key.

Retrieving password from the command line

One way to retrieve the administrator password is by using the EC2 Tools from the command line .

1. First, you need to discover the instance deploy ID via the `onevm show` command:

```
$ onevm show 59
VIRTUAL MACHINE 59 INFORMATION
ID                  : 59
NAME           : one-59
USER            : oneadmin
GROUP        : oneadmin
STATE          : ACTIVE
LCM_STATE    : RUNNING
HOSTNAME   : ec2
START TIME   : 02/12 11:32:04
END TIME      : 02/12 11:32:21
DEPLOY ID     : i-5679301f
```

2. Now you can issue the `ec2-get-password` command, specifying the correct `--region` or `-U URL`, along with your private key of the correct key pair used for this instance:

```
$ ec2-get-password --region eu-west-1 -k .ssh/id_rsa  i-5679301f
```

3. If the following error message appears, you need to wait a few more minutes, or you have specified the wrong deploy ID:

```
No <Password> element was found for this instance.
```

4. When the password is correctly displayed, you can use it to connect to the remote instance via the Remote Desktop client, as an administrator.

Retrieving password from Management Console

An alternative way to retrieve the administrator password for Windows instances is directly from the AWS Management Console.

1. In the **EC2** tab, click on **Instances** on the menu to the left, or **Running Instances** on the right.

2. Locate the instance and right-click on it, and select **Get Windows Password**.

   A new pop-up window will appear, asking to either select your private key on your PC or paste it in the text box.

3. Click on **Decrypt Password**, wait a few seconds and the Administrator password should appear.

> If the password is not ready yet, a warning message will appear and you are invited to retry 15 to 30 minutes later.

Adding storage to a running instance

The AMI sizes are just enough to accommodate the base system and the most commonly used applications (a few gigabytes in total).

If we simply want to keep our data separated from the system image, or we need more storage, we can create a new EBS volume and attach it to existing instances.

Unfortunately, this is not yet manageable with OpenNebula and thus, we need to use the AWS Management Console or the EC2 Tools.

1. Find the instance ID and its Availability Zone:

   ```
   $ ec2-describe-instances
   INSTANCE i-4e25b229 ami-baba68d3 ec2-23-22-50-12.compute-1.
   amazonaws.com ip-10-243-61-174.ec2.internal runninggt 0
   t1.micro 2012-04-15T13:52:38+0000 us-east-1d aki-825ea7eb
   monitoring-disabled 23.22.50.12 10.243.61.174 ebs     paravirtual
   xen  sg-dc74b3b4 default
   ```

2. Create the new volume (20 GB) inside the same Availability Zone:

   ```
   $ ec2-create-volume -s 20 -z us-east-1d
   VOLUME vol-669e3b09 20            us-east-1d    creating      2012-
   04-15T13:57:37+0000
   ```

3. Wait a few seconds for completion and then attach the newly created volume to the running instance:

   ```
   $ ec2-attach-volume vol-669e3b09 -i i-4e25b229 -d /dev/sdo
   ATTACHMENT   vol-669e3b09 i-4e25b229   /dev/sdo      attaching
   2012-04-15T14:01:22+0000
   ```

4. In the Management Console, access the **Volumes** section under the **Elastic Block Store** section, in the **EC2** tab.

5. Click on the **Create Volume** button. A pop-up will appear asking for the size of the new volume and the Availability Zone.

Availability Zones for EBS

EBS volumes can be attached to running instances within the same AZ.

Create Volume   Cancel ✕

Size: [20] [GiB ↕]

Availability Zone: [eu-west-1a ↕]

Snapshot: [--- No Snapshot --- ↕]

[Cancel] [Yes, Create]

6. After clicking on **Yes, Create**, the new EBS volume is created and ready to be used.

7. Select the new volume and click on **Attach Volume**.

8. In the new pop-up window, select an active instance, along with a device name, ranging from /dev/sdf to /dev/sdp.

Attach Volume   Cancel ✕

Volume: vol-8659a5ee in eu-west-1a

Instances: [i-7ea3f437 - ubuntu-test (running) ↕] in eu-west-1a

Device: [/dev/sdo]

Linux Devices: /dev/sdf through /dev/sdp
Note: Newer linux kernels may rename your devices to /dev/xvdf
through /dev/xvdp internally, even when the device name entered
here (and shown in the details) is /dev/sdf through /dev/sdp.

[Cancel] [Yes, Attach]

9. The status of the selected volume will change from **available** to **in-use**.

Mounting an EBS volume on Linux-based instances

Now, on your instance, you should find a new block device. Check the latest kernel messages with the following command:

```
dmesg | tail -n2
```

```
[  867.315861] blkfront: regular deviceid=0x850 major,minor=8,80,
assuming parts/disk=16
[  867.316324]  xvdf: unknown partition table
```

Because this is a block device, you need to create a filesystem on it before you can begin using it. Obviously this is required only the first time after creating a new volume.

1. To create a new file system, run the following command:

   ```
   $ sudo mkfs.ext4 /dev/xvdf
   ```

2. Create a new mountpoint and mount the new filesystem:

   ```
   $ sudo mkdir /mnt/ebs
   $ sudo mount /dev/xvdf /mnt/ebs
   ```

3. Check if everything is OK:

   ```
   $ df -h
   Filesystem          Size  Used Avail Use% Mounted on
   /dev/xvdf           20G   44M   19G   1% /mnt/ebs
   ```

4. You may want to add an entry into /etc/fstab to automatically mount it on boot:

   ```
   /dev/xvdo              /mnt/ebs      ext4    defaults        0 0
   ```

Mounting an EBS volume on Windows-based instances

On Windows, we need to use Disk Management to mount an EBS volume.

1. Launch **Disk Management** by executing `compmgmt.msc`, or by browsing through **Server Management** | **Storage** | **Disk Management**.

2. The initial disk status will be **Offline**.

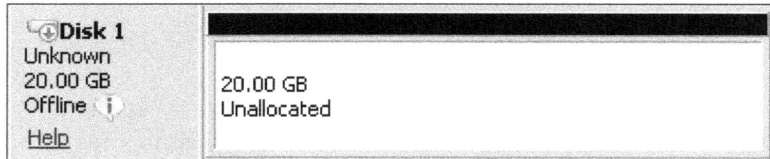

3. In order to enable it, right-click on **Disk 1** and select **Online**.

4. Now we need to initialize it—create a new partition table by right-clicking on **Disk 1** and selecting **Initialize Disk**. Then select **MBR** and hit **OK**.

5. Now right-click on the white area and select **New Simple Volume**, a new dialog window will appear.

6. Follow the wizard to create a unique partition. Choose to create an NTFS file system and make it available on a new drive letter (for example: `D:`).

Moving data around different AZ

Each EBS volume is available only to instances in the same Availability Zone. If you need to move data around different Availability Zones, you need to use the **Snapshot** function to create a new copy on the correct AZ, and then delete the old one.

1. Select the volume to be snapshotted.

2. Create a new snapshot using the **Create Snapshot** button in the **Volumes** section. The operation will be queued and executed without downtime; check for completion in the Snapshots section.

3. Next, in the **Volumes** section, use the **Create Volume** button as before, but this time select the snapshot created before, select the AZ where you want this volume to be available, and click on **Yes, Create**.

   The size of the new volume should be sufficient to contain all the data captured by the snapshot.

4. Once the disk has been created, you can attach it to a running instance as before.

> **Attaching indefinitely**
>
> Sometimes operations get stuck during EBS attaching, depending on various issues on the Amazon side. If EBS attaching isn't working in a couple of minutes, `Force Detach` and reboot the instance. When rebooted, try to `Attach Volume` again, and this time it should work.

A very simple EBS backup script

When there is a bunch of running instances, you would want to make sure to keep backups of your precious data.

There are a lot of backup solutions out there, but it is preferable to use a very simple script that can be configured as a daily `cronjob` on the OpenNebula frontend to create a new snapshot for each attached EBS volume and keep at most six backup copies of them, deleting the older ones.

```
#!/bin/bash
COUNT_TO_KEEP=6
VOLUME_LIST=$(ec2-describe-volumes | grep ATTACHMENT | awk {'print
$2'})

for VOLUME in $(echo $VOLUME_LIST); do
 echo ">>> Searching $VOLUME snapshots to remove"
 ec2-describe-snapshots | grep Autobackup | grep $VOLUME | sort -r -k
5 | sed 1,${COUNT_TO_KEEP}d | awk '{print ">>> Deleting snapshot: "
$2}; system("ec2-delete-snapshot " $2)'
 echo ">>> Create a new snapshot for $VOLUME"
 ec2-create-snapshot -d Autobackup_$VOLUME $VOLUME
done
```

It will not delete the snapshots generated without this script which is marked as **Autobackup** in the description.

Monitoring active instances

Amazon provides freely a basic instance monitoring, which includes a **System Status Check**, an **Instance Status Check** and a graph generated for each hour of instance activity.

In the **Instances** section, click on an active instance and expand the bottom window for the **Status Check** panel.

System Status Check monitors the AWS systems involved with the current instance and ensures they are functioning properly, while the **Instance Status Check** monitors the network reachability of the instance (with ping).

When both checks are returned as success, then you should be able to reach the instance without any problem.

Status checks detect problems that may impair this instance from running your applications.	
System Status Checks	**Instance Status Checks**
These checks monitor the AWS systems required to use this instance and ensure they are functioning properly.	These checks monitor your software and network configuration for this instance.
⊘ System reachability check passed. more info	⊘ Instance reachability check passed. more info

In the **Monitoring** section, you can find a bunch of statistics graphs, generated every 60 minutes, which can be used to monitor CPU, disk, and network usage.

Enable detailed monitoring for your Amazon EC2 instance to get these metrics at 1-minute frequency, plus additional metrics. Learn more.	**Enable Detailed Monitoring**

If you enable the additional **CloudWatch** service, you can use the **Enable Detailed Monitoring** button to get more interactive graphs that get updated every minute, and the ability to receive e-mails when predefined conditions occurs.

Click on the **Create Alarm** button to configure your first alarm for a running instance.

The first thing to configure is the recipient of the notification messages generated by CloudWatch, usually an e-mail address.

With every available metric, it's possible to configure a threshold before an alert is raised and sent to the user. For example, define a new alarm when the Average CPU Utilization is greater than 50%, for at least 3 consecutive periods of 1 minute each.

When an instance with the current alert is activated, the user will receive an e-mail notification, and a message will also be displayed in the **Instance Details** section.

Create Alarm for i-48adfa01		Cancel ×

You can use CloudWatch alarms to be notified automatically whenever metric data reaches a level you define.
To create an alarm, first choose whom to notify and then define when the notification should be sent

☑ **Send a notification to:** `HighCPU`

With these recipients: `gt@libersoft.it`

Whenever: `Average ◇` of `CPU Utilization ◇`

Is: `>= ◇` `50` Percent

For at least: `3` consecutive period(s) of `1 minute ◇`

Name this alarm: `awsec2-i-48adfa01-High-CPU-Utilization` cancel

CPUUtilization (Percent)

Cancel | Create Alarm

Summary

In this chapter, we saw how it is possible to rapidly increase our Cloud capacity by using a third-party Cloud provider, which supports the EC2 API interface. We have acquired specific knowledge on how Amazon EC2 works, being able to manage and troubleshoot instances from the OpenNebula standard interfaces, and via the AWS Management Console.

In the next chapter, we are going to learn how it's possible to act as a Cloud provider, and expose an OpenNebula infrastructure using standard interfaces such as EC2 and OCCI, and how to manage multiple OpenNebula installations centrally, using the oZone component.

9
Public Cloud Computing and High Availability with OpenNebula

In the last chapter, we saw how it is possible to extend our private cloud relying on an external cloud provider, and be able to get new resources instantly to cope with our computing needs.

In this chapter, we will learn how to set up a bunch of OpenNebula facilities to promote our private cloud to a fully-fledged public cloud. It means that the external users will be able to access our resources using standard industry API, as we did with Amazon EC2.

The most common use cases for a public cloud are:

- **Cloud providers**: Sell resources to customers
- **Collaboration**: Give external access to business partners
- **Optimize costs**: Sell to others your current surplus resources

Setting up the EC2 Query interface

The **EC2 Query interface** is an OpenNebula component that will permit to launch and manage virtual machines using the **Amazon EC2 Query API** within our OpenNebula installation, with any third-party tool already compatible with those APIs.

The current implementation (econe-server), a lightweight standalone web application on top of the **OpenNebula Cloud API**, includes: image upload and registration, launching of new instances, describe and terminate operations.

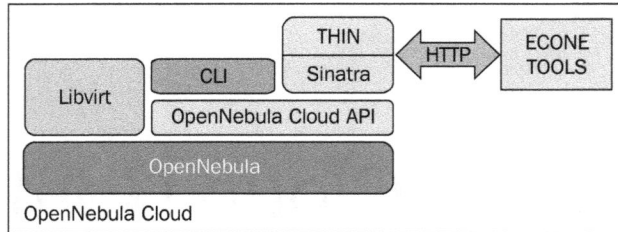

Installing econe-server

The OpenNebula components necessary to run econe-server should already be available in our installation, as they are included in the main distribution package.

Double-check that all the required Ruby gems are already installed using the well-known install_gems utility. You can use either of the following two commands for installing the gems:

```
$ sudo /usr/share/one/install_gems cloud
$ sudo $ONE_LOCATION/share/install_gems cloud
```

Configuring econe-server

The service is configured through the econe.conf file available under /etc/one or $ONE_LOCATION/etc, where we will need to adjust the following settings:

```
# OpenNebula sever contact information
:one_xmlrpc: http://localhost:2633/RPC2
```

:one_xmlrpc is used to point econe-server to our running oned on the OpenNebula frontend.

```
# Host and port where econe server will run
:server: odin.local
:port: 4567
```

`:server` should be a FQDN (host.domain.tld, not an IP address), the same that will be used by the EC2 clients to connect, otherwise the authentication will fail.

```
# SSL proxy that serves the API (set if is being used)
#:ssl_server: ssl.odin.local
```

If every client reaches the server via a reverse proxy, you should configure its FQDN here; otherwise the authentication will fail.

```
# Authentication driver for incoming requests
#   ec2, default Access key and Secret key scheme
#   x509, for x509 certificates based authentication
:auth: ec2


# Authentication driver to communicate with OpenNebula core
#   cipher, for symmetric cipher encryption of tokens
#   x509, for x509 certificate encryption of tokens
:core_auth: cipher
```

The basic authentication will use the standard OpenNebula username/password pairs, but it's possible to switch to x.509 certificates (the SSL proxy should be configured accordingly).

```
# VM types allowed and its template file (inside templates directory)
:instance_types:
  :m1.small:
    :template: m1.small.erb
```

Like with Amazon EC2, it is necessary to configure a defined set of instance types that will be available to the EC2 interface users.

In the `etc` folder, under `ec2query_templates`, we can find an example file describing a small instance (`m1.small.erb`):

```
NAME    = eco-vm

CPU     = 0.2
MEMORY  = 256

DISK = [ IMAGE_ID   = <%= erb_vm_info[:img_id] %> ]

# Put here the ID of the VNET with the IPs for the EC2 VMs
NIC=[NETWORK_ID=0]

IMAGE_ID = <%= erb_vm_info[:ec2_img_id] %>
INSTANCE_TYPE = <%= erb_vm_info[:instance_type ] %>
```

```
<% if erb_vm_info[:user_data] %>
CONTEXT = [
        EC2_USER_DATA="<%= erb_vm_info[:user_data] %>",
        TARGET="hdc"
        ]
<% end %>
```

ERB is a templating system available within the Ruby standard library, and here it is used to generate the final OpenNebula VM template, keeping it clean and easily readable.

Each template is processed by the EC2 service to include specific data as received from the client, and you probably don't need to make changes to the `<%= %>` compounds.

The unique requirement is to configure the predefined network to which the instances created by users will be attached, into the NIC attribute. Don't put static declarations such as an IP address here, or else the deployments will fail.

Feel free to adjust the CPU and MEMORY attributes depending on the size of each available instance type, and to add new attributes that will be included in each new instance (for example: RANKING or REQUIREMENT).

Starting and stopping econe-server

As with many of the other OpenNebula components, we can start econe-server service:

1. Run the following command:

   ```
   $ econe-server start
   ```

2. Check in the logs folder for the econe-server.log file.

3. To stop the EC2 service, do:

   ```
   $ econe-server stop
   ```

Using the EC2 Interface

The fastest way to try our new EC2 Query interface is to use the econe tools bundled in OpenNebula. They are already installed on our frontend, but you can install them on a dedicated machine (for example: your workstation) using the source distribution and passing the -c parameter to the install.sh script:

```
$ ./install.sh -d ~/one-cli -c
```

Remember to install the required Ruby gems along with the econe tools, with the usual script available in the main source distribution under `share/install_gems/install_gems`:

```
$ ./install_gems cloud
```

Before using the econe tools, it's highly recommended that you set up a few environment variables in our `~/.profile`, so that we don't need to specify the URL, username, and password in each command:

```
export EC2_URL="http://odin.local:4567/"
export EC2_ACCESS_KEY="oneadmin"
export EC2_SECRET_KEY="f1d0d84347460a9cf457beab926f7a226e7e"
```

`EC2_URL` is where the EC2 Query interface is reachable (directly on `4567` port or via the SSL reverse proxy). The `EC2_ACCESS_KEY` is an already existing user created via the `oneuser` utility, and `EC2_SECRET_KEY` is the password hash of that user (retrievable via `oneuser show username`).

The available econe tools commands are:

- **econe-describe-images**: This command is used to list all the available images
- **econe-describe-instances**: This command is used to list all the active instances
- **econe-upload**: This command is used to upload a new image
- **econe-register**: This command is used to register a previously uploaded image
- **econe-run-instances**: This command is used to launch new instances
- **econe-terminate-instances**: This command is used to terminate a running instance

EC2 example user session

With the environment variables correctly configured, we should be already able to communicate with the EC2 Query interface.

If running each one of the following commands leads to a `User not authorized` error message, then please be aware that in order to authenticate using EC2, a signature must be generated in both client and server. For building this signature, the `EC2_URL` variable is used on the client side, and therefore, the same URL must be used in the econe-server configuration.

1. We start uploading a new raw disk image using the
   `econe-upload` command:

   ```
   $ econe-upload ubuntu-base.raw
   Success: ImageId ami-00000004
   ```

   > The disk image should be in raw format, with contextualization scripts already bundled.

2. If successful, we will find the new disk image available in the catalog, along with any public image already, running the `econe-describe-images` command:

   ```
   $ econe-describe-images
   oneadmin ami-00000000 available 56c142fba67f483cf54426af642707cc
   oneadmin ami-00000001 available 5a828c77785d860dbe0c6a17b243eba9
   oneadmin ami-00000002 available 0ce6b8134fc79eb9824baeb5d8e7fdbe

   oneadmin ami-00000004 available d3fa1e8bc247242f0ebc530c4057a0e8
   ```

3. Now we can try to launch a new small instance using the latest uploaded image:

   ```
   $ econe-run-instances -t m1.small ami-00000004
   oneadmin ami-00000004 i-66 m1.small
   ```

4. The acknowledgment message will assure us that the command has been processed correctly, and that our instance is going to be started in the next few seconds.

5. This instance will be visible from the OpenNebula frontend too, using the standard utilities such as `onevm`:

   ```
   $ onevm list | grep 66
   66 oneadmin oneadmin eco-vm runn 10 256M thor 00 00:01:55
   ```

6. The `econe-describe-instances` command will be used to retrieve the status of the instances and their IP address:

   ```
   $ econe-describe-instances
   oneadmin    i-66         ami-00000004   running   192.168.66.205
   m1.small
   ```

7. In order to shutdown a running instance, we will use the `econe-terminate-instances` command:

```
$ econe-terminate-instances i-66
Success: Terminating i-66 in running state
```

ElasticFox example user session

ElasticFox is a **Mozilla Firefox** extension for managing an Amazon EC2 account that can be used to monitor and launch new instances on our OpenNebula EC2 Query interface.

> Browse at `http://aws.amazon.com/developertools/609`, download and install it, and restart Firefox.
>
> You will find ElasticFox in the **Tools** menu; clicking on it will open it in a new tab.

1. The first thing to configure is our local EC2 Query interface URI, by clicking on **Regions** and entering our details.

Endpoint Name	Endpoint URL	🖳
us-east-1	https://ec2.us-east-1.amazonaws.c....	
eu-west-1	https://ec2.eu-west-1.amazonaws....	
us-west-1	https://ec2.us-west-1.amazonaws....	
odin	http://odin.local:4567	

Region Name: `odin`

Endpoint URL: `http://odin.local:4567`

[Remove] [Add] [Close]

2. The second required configuration step is to enter our user credentials by clicking on the **Credentials** button and entering our username as **AWS Access Key**, and our hashed password as **AWS Secret Access Key** (this can be retrieved with the `oneuser show` command).

Account Name	AWS Access Key ID	
oneadmin	oneadmin	

Account Name: `oneadmin`

AWS Access Key: `oneadmin`

AWS Secret Access Key: `••••••••••••••••••••••••••••••••••••••••••`

Remove	Add		Close

If everything goes smoothly, you should be able to navigate in the **Instances** and **Images** sections to see the running instances and the available disk images.

Obviously, most of the actions will not be available as AWS EC2 provides a lot of custom features that are currently (and probably never will be) not implemented in `econe-server`, but we can easily monitor and issue basic commands within this graphical interface.

Instances	Images	KeyPairs	Security Groups	Elastic IPs	Volumes and Snapshots	Bundle Tasks	Reserved Instances	Virtual Priva

Your Instances

☐ Don't show Terminated Instances

Reserva...	Own...∨	Instan...	AMI	AKI	ARI	State	Private DNS	
default	oneadmin	i-70	ami-00000004	eki-EA801065	eri-1FEE1144	pending	... 192.168.66.209	...
default	oneadmin	i-71	ami-00000004	eki-EA801065	eri-1FEE1144	pending	... 192.168.66.210	...
default	oneadmin	i-72	ami-00000004	eki-EA801065	eri-1FEE1144	pending	... 192.168.66.211	...
default	oneadmin	i-73	ami-00000004	eki-EA801065	eri-1FEE1144		192.168.66.212	
default	oneadmin	i-74	ami-00000004	eki-EA801065	eri-1FEE1144	pending	... 192.168.66.213	...

OCCI Interface

Along with the EC2 Query interface, OpenNebula natively includes a second remote interface, called **OCCI**.

The **Open Cloud Computing Interface** (OCCI) is a RESTful protocol, and a comprehensive API for managing cloud resources. Unlike the Amazon EC2 Query interface, OCCI is being developed through the **Open Grid Forum** (http://www.ogf.org/), which actually maintains a lot of standards, mainly for the Grid interoperability environments (http://en.wikipedia.org/wiki/ Open_Grid_Forum#Standards).

If you do not need EC2 compatibility, or if you are starting from scratch in developing ad-hoc integrations with OpenNebula, using the OCCI interface is highly recommended for its openness.

Like the EC2 Query interface, the OCCI service is implemented upon the OpenNebula Cloud API (**OCA**) and Sinatra, a widely used lightweight Ruby web framework.

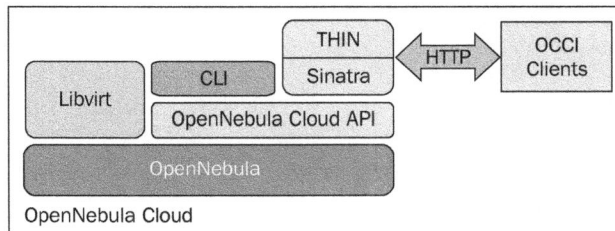

The OCCI interface included in the OpenNebula 3.x distribution does not implement the latest OCCI specification, but it is based on the draft 0.8 of the OGF OCCI specification (http://forge.ogf.org/sf/docman/do/downloadDocument/ projects.occi-wg/docman.root.drafts/doc15731/3). The implementation of the latest specification is being developed by TU-Dortmund in a separated ecosystem project (http://www.opennebula.org/software:ecosystem:occi).

Setting up the OCCI interface

The OCCI interface is implemented by the occi-server component, and its configuration is very similar to econe-server.

Installing occi-server

The OpenNebula components necessary to run occi-server should already be available as they are included in the main distribution packages.

Double-check that required Ruby gems are installed as well, using the well-know `install_gems` utility. They can be installed by running any one of the following commands:

```
# /usr/share/one/install_gems cloud
```

```
# $ONE_LOCATION/share/install_gems cloud
```

Configuring occi-server

The service is configured through the `occi-server.conf` file inside `/etc/one` or `$ONE_LOCATION/etc`, where we will need to configure the following settings:

```
# OpenNebula sever contact information
:one_xmlrpc: http://localhost:2633/RPC2
```

`one_xmlrpc` is used to point the `occi-server` to our running `oned` on the OpenNebula front-end.

```
# Host and port where OCCI server will run
:server: 0.0.0.0
:port: 4567
```

`:server` should be a FQDN (host.domain.tld, not an IP address), the same that will be used by the OCCI clients to connect, otherwise the authentication will fail.

> The `4567` port is also used as the standard port in the default configuration file of `econe-server`; remember to change at least one of them if you plan to run both services.
> ```
> # SSL proxy that serves the API (set if is being used)
> #:ssl_server: fqdm.of.the.server
> ```

If every client reaches the server via a reverse proxy, you should configure its FQDN here, otherwise the authentication will fail:

```
# Authentication driver for incoming requests
#    occi, for OpenNebula's user-password scheme
#    x509, for x509 certificates based authentication
:auth: occi

# Authentication driver to communicate with OpenNebula core
#    cipher, for symmetric cipher encryption of tokens
#    x509, for x509 certificate encryption of tokens
:core_auth: cipher
```

The basic authentication will use the standard OpenNebula username/password pairs, but it's possible to switch to x509 certificates (the SSL proxy should be configured accordingly).

```
# Life-time in seconds for token renewal (that used to handle
OpenNebula auths)
:token_expiration_delta: 1800
```

Upon successful login, an authentication token is sent to the client. The authentication token will be valid for this configured life-time. If the token expires, the client should start a new login procedure before operations can continue.

```
# VM types allowed and its template file (inside templates directory)
:instance_types:
  :small:
    :template: small.erb
    :cpu: 1
    :memory: 1024
  :medium:
    :template: medium.erb
    :cpu: 4
    :memory: 4096
  :large:
    :template: large.erb
    :cpu: 8
    :memory: 8192
```

Like with EC2, we need to configure a bunch of predefined VM templates that will be operated by those using the OCCI Interface.

Configuring OCCI VM and network templates

Within the `occi_templates` directory, which is either inside /etc/one or $ONE_ LOCATION/etc, we will find a bunch of predefined templates:

- **common.erb**: This is the base template that gets included in every OCCI VM template, where it's possible to add common attributes that will be valid for every instantiated VM

- **custom.erb**: This template is used when the user opts to instantiate a custom VM template

- **network.erb**: This template contains specific network configuration for every VM instance

- **small.erb, medium.erb, large.erb**: These are a predefined set of customized VM templates

The unique configuration required in the OCCI VM templates is to set the correct network device for the newly created VM instances at the end of `network.erb`:

```
#BRIDGE = NAME_OF_DEFAULT_BRIDGE
#PHYDEV = NAME_OF_PHYSICAL_DEVICE
#VLAN   = YES|NO
```

With our configuration, it will be sufficient to define the default bridge name available on the hosts:

```
BRIDGE = lan0
```

Besides the network configuration, we can easily customize the OCCI templates to suit our needs by either editing the existing `small.erb`, `medium.erb` or `large.erb`, or creating a new one from scratch (remember to add a reference in the `occi-server.conf`) by simply defining:

```
CPU    = 2
MEMORY = 768
```

Starting and stopping occi-server

Follow the steps specified here to start and stop `occi-server`:

1. Start `occi-server` by executing:

   ```
   $ occi-server start
   ```

2. Check in the logs folder for the `occi-server.log` file.

3. To stop the OCCI service, run:

   ```
   $ occi-server stop
   ```

Using the OCCI interface

As for the EC2 Query interface, the OpenNebula source package also includes a simple OCCI client implementation that is ready to use.

They are already installed on our frontend, but you can install them on a dedicated machine (for example: your workstation) using the source distribution and passing the `-c` parameter to the `install.sh` script:

```
$ ./install.sh -d ~/one-cli -c
```

Remember to install the required Ruby gems with the usual script, available in the main source distribution under `share/install_gems/install_gems`:

```
$ ./install_gems cloud
```

Before using the OCCI client, it's highly recommended that you set up a bunch of environment variables in our `~/.profile`, so that we don't need to specify the URL, username, and password in each command:

```
export OCCI_URL="http://odin.local:4567/"
export ONE_AUTH=$HOME/.one/one_auth
```

OCCI_URL is where the OCCI interface is reachable (directly on 4567 port or, via the SSL reverse proxy).

ONE_AUTH will point to a text file containing the username:password credential of an existing OpenNebula user, on a single line.

The available OCCI client tools commands are:

- **occi-compute**: This command is used to show, create, update, and delete VM instances
- **occi-network**: This command is used to show, create, update, and delete virtual networks
- **occi-storage**: This command is used to show, create, update, and delete VM images

OCCI example user session

With the environment variables correctly configured, we should already be able to communicate with the OCCI interface.

1. We start uploading a new raw disk image by preparing an OCCI template with the following contents:

    ```
    <STORAGE>
        <NAME>ubuntu-occi</NAME>
        <DESCRIPTION>Ubuntu 10.04 desktop example image</DESCRIPTION>
        <TYPE>OS</TYPE>
        <URL>file:///home/scorp/ubuntu-base.raw</URL>
    </STORAGE>
    ```

    And submit it via:

    ```
    $ occi-storage create image.occi
    ```

2. Wait for the upload to finish.

3. Now configure a dedicated virtual network that we will use in our test OCCI instance:

```
<NETWORK>
    <NAME>occi-network</NAME>
    <ADDRESS>192.168.69.0</ADDRESS>
    <SIZE>10</SIZE>
    <PUBLIC>NO</PUBLIC>
</NETWORK>
```

And submit it with:

```
$ occi-network create network.occi
```

4. The last step is to create a COMPUTE resource, referencing the STORAGE and NETWORK that we have just created using their own ID, using a representation as shown here:

```
<COMPUTE>
    <NAME>occi-vm</NAME>
    <INSTANCE_TYPE>small</INSTANCE_TYPE>
    <DISK>
        <STORAGE href="http://odin.local:4567/storage/4"/>
    </DISK>
    <NIC>
        <NETWORK href="http://odin.local:4567/network/1"/>
        <IP>192.168.69.12</IP>
    </NIC>
    <CONTEXT>
        <HOSTNAME>MAINHOST</HOSTNAME>
        <DATA>DATA</DATA>
    </CONTEXT>
</COMPUTE>
```

We can retrieve the URL of the available storage objects with:

```
$ occi-storage list
<STORAGE_COLLECTION>
  <STORAGE href='http://odin.local:4567/storage/0' name='ttylinux'/>
  <STORAGE href='http://odin.local:4567/storage/1' name='test-
datablock'/>
```

```
  <STORAGE href='http://odin.local:4567/storage/2' name='ubuntu-base'/>
  <STORAGE href='http://odin.local:4567/storage/4' name='ec2-5d8b0fd6-
f3c2-4225-b50f-80ffe631c414'/>
  <STORAGE href='http://odin.local:4567/storage/5' name='ubuntu-occi'/>
</STORAGE_COLLECTION>
```

With `econe-describe-images`, we will not only get a list of all the images uploaded using the OCCI interface, but also of all the available images for the current user.

To retrieve the available virtual network we can issue the following command:

```
$ occi-network list
<NETWORK_COLLECTION>
  <NETWORK href='http://odin.local:4567/network/0' name='Small network'/>
  <NETWORK href='http://odin.local:4567/network/1' name='occi-network'/>
</NETWORK_COLLECTION>
```

When the VM description is ready to be submitted, use the `occi-compute` command to push it to the OCCI server, as shown here:

```
$ occi-compute create vm.xml
```

If successful, the command will return the XML description of the full compute object, which is useful for debugging basic template changes too.

To list the available VM, run the following command:

```
$ occi-compute list
<COMPUTE_COLLECTION>
  <COMPUTE href='http://odin.local:4567/compute/70' name='eco-vm'/>
  <COMPUTE href='http://odin.local:4567/compute/71' name='eco-vm'/>
  <COMPUTE href='http://odin.local:4567/compute/73' name='eco-vm'/>
  <COMPUTE href='http://odin.local:4567/compute/74' name='eco-vm'/>
  <COMPUTE href='http://odin.local:4567/compute/75' name='occi-vm'/>
</COMPUTE_COLLECTION>
```

To get the VM instance details such as the current STATE or the assigned IP, use the show command followed by the VM id:

```
$ occi-compute show 75
<COMPUTE href='http://odin.local:4567/compute/75'>
  <ID>75</ID>
  <CPU>1</CPU>
```

```
<MEMORY>1024</MEMORY>

<NAME>occi-vm</NAME>

<INSTANCE_TYPE href='http://odin.local:4567/instance_type/
small'>small</INSTANCE_TYPE>

<STATE>ACTIVE</STATE>

<DISK id='0'>

    <STORAGE href='http://odin.local:4567/storage/5' name='ubuntu-occi'/>

    <TYPE>DISK</TYPE>

    <TARGET>hda</TARGET>

</DISK>

<NIC>

    <NETWORK href='http://odin.local:4567/network/1' name='occi-
network'/>

    <IP>192.168.69.11</IP>

    <MAC>02:00:c0:a8:45:0b</MAC>

</NIC>

<CONTEXT>

    <DATA>DATA1</DATA>

    <HOSTNAME>MAINHOST</HOSTNAME>

    <TARGET>hdb</TARGET>

</CONTEXT>

</COMPUTE>
```

Updating the already submitted resources

When using the OCCI interface, it's necessary to prepare an XML snippet to update a particular attribute of a storage, network or compute object.

Take a look at the following example (save it as `image-udpate.occi` or whatever) to set the previously submitted storage image as public:

```
<STORAGE href='http://odin.local:4567/storage/5'>
    <ID>5</ID>
    <PUBLIC>YES</PUBLIC>
</STORAGE>
```

Submit this snippet using the `update` command:

```
$ occi-storage update image-update.occi
```

As before, if the operation is successful, we will receive the updated storage object in the output.

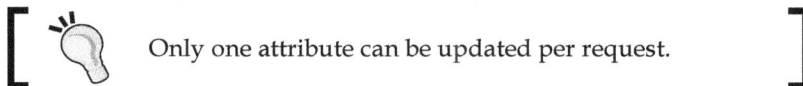

[💡 Only one attribute can be updated per request.]

In order to publish a network entity so that other users can use it, we can update the resource using the following snippet (`network-update.occi`), very similar to the previous one:

```
<NETWORK href='http://odin.local:4567/network/5'>
    <ID>0</ID>
    <PUBLIC>YES</PUBLIC>
</NETWORK>
```

And submit it as before:

```
$ occi-network update network-update.occi
```

Finally, for computing objects in addition to changing the descriptive attributes, it's possible to operate at the instance level control by altering the STATE attribute, with one of the following options:

- STOPPED
- SUSPENDED
- RESUME
- CANCEL
- SHUTDOWN
- REBOOT
- DONE

For example, to shut down our running instance, prepare the following XML snippet (`vm-shutdown.occi`):

```
<COMPUTE href='http://odin.local:4567/compute/75'>
    <ID>75</ID>
    <STATE>SHUTDOWN</STATE>
</COMPUTE>
```

Once the snippet is submitted, OpenNebula will take care to alter the execution status accordingly:

```
$ occi-compute update vm-shutdown.occi
```

OpenNebula Zones and VDC

By enabling the EC2 Query interface and/or OCCI interface, we are opening our infrastructure to a wider audience that can lead to a higher demand of resources. This can be satisfied only by increasing our physical hardware availability.

To cope with the manageability of a larger infrastructure, we may want to split it up into smaller, independent parts to simplify its administration or to achieve partitioning for a number of reasons; these reasons will become apparent later.

For this reason, the **oZones** component of OpenNebula allows the centralized management of multiple running OpenNebula instances that will be called zones. This module allows the oZones administrators to monitor each zone, and enables them to grant access to the different zones to particular users, from a centralized CLI and web GUI.

In addition, inside each zone, it's possible to define multiple Virtual Data Centers (**VDC**) that contain a set of virtual resources (images, VM templates, virtual networks, and virtual machines) and users that use and control those virtual resources.

For each VDC, there is a special privileged user (VDC administrator), who can create new users inside the VDC, as well as manage all the virtual resources. But this user cannot access other resources inside the same zone, or even directly access physical hosts used in the VDC. The VDC admin and VDC users access its resources through a reverse proxy, so they don't actually know what the real endpoint of the zone is, but rather the address of the oZones module and the VDC to which they belong.

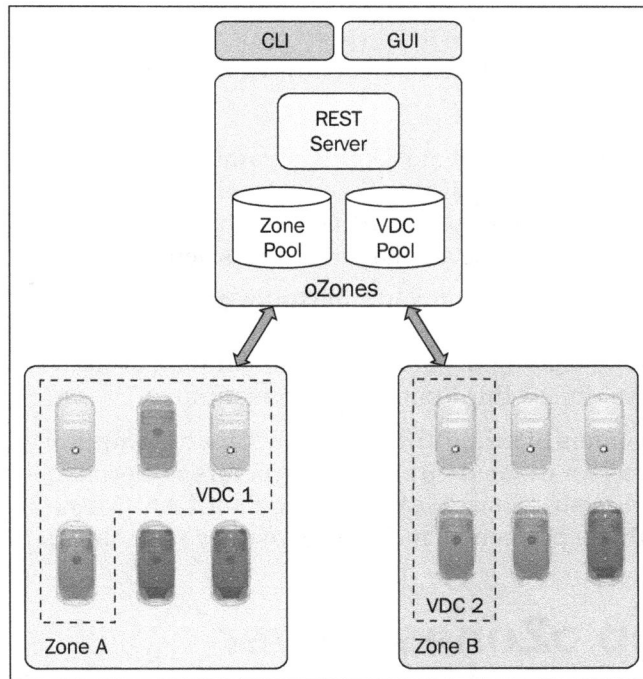

Why Zones?

In large infrastructures, and especially for enterprise use cases, the oZone component makes it possible to achieve:

- Complete isolation of users, organizations or workloads in different physical facilities, with different performance grades, security or high-availability optimal performances, execution of different workloads profiles on different physical clusters, with varying hardware and software components

- Centralized management of multiple OpenNebula clusters may be hosted in different physical data centers, to build a geographically distributed cloud

Why VDC?

In addition to the early advantages, VDC allows advanced on-demand provisioning scenarios such as:

- On-premise multiple Private Clouds separating multiple scientific projects, departments, units, or partners, each one with an independent management of the access privileges to the virtual and physical infrastructure, and to dynamically allocate the available resources across them.

- In these scenarios, the cloud administrator could create a VDC for each department by dynamically allocating physical hosts according to their needs, and delegating the internal administration of the VDC to the project, department, unit or third-party IT administrator.

- Cloud Providers offering Virtual Private Cloud Computing. Enterprises may prefer to buy an isolated virtual infrastructure rather than individual VM instances directly connected via VPN to their LAN. This combines a Public Cloud with the protection and control usually seen only in Private Clouds.

Setting up oZones server

To get started with zone and VDC, we need to configure and start the `ozones-server` component, already available on the frontend, with the standard installation procedure.

If you plan to use a dedicated installation (maybe inside a VM instance running on one of the managed OpenNebula clusters) rather than on one of the available OpenNebula frontends, you can install only the oZones components by passing the `-o` parameter to the `install.sh` script from the sources package. Don't forget to run the `install_gems` script!

The `ozone-server` component will permit us to define new zones and VDCs, and manage them from a bird's eye view with the integrated web GUI and CLI. Also, a `.htaccess` file will be automatically generated to configure a local running Apache server to act as a proxy to hide the VDC details to end users.

Configuring the Apache2 reverse-proxy

In the early chapters, we used `nginx` as a SSL proxy for the Sunstone interface as it is more lightweight than a full-fledged Apache2 proxy. Unfortunately, the current version of OpenNebula supports the dynamic generation of proxy rules for reaching each VDC only for Apache2 (although the native support for any other web server or a simple converter implementation is quite easy to achieve).

1. Install the Apache2 web server on the same host that will run
   `ozones-server`:

   ```
   $ sudo apt-get install apache2-mpm-worker
   ```

2. Enable the necessary modules:

   ```
   $ sudo a2enmod rewrite and proxy_http
   ```

3. Edit `/etc/apache2/sites-available/default` to allow the `.htaccess`
   functionality:

   ```
   <Directory /var/www/>
       Options Indexes FollowSymLinks MultiViews
       AllowOverride All
       Order allow,deny
       allow from all
   </Directory>
   ```

4. Finally, restart Apache2:

   ```
   $ sudo /etc/init.d/apache2 restart
   ```

Configuring ozones-server

The main configuration file for `ozones-server` is `$ONE_LOCATION/etc/ozones-server.conf` or `/etc/one/ozones-server.conf`.

1. The current version of `ozones-server` only supports SQLite as a
   backend database:

   ```
   :databasetype: sqlite
   ```

2. The `.htaccess` functionality will be kept updated in the following location,
   which should be inside the `DocumentRoot` configure in the Apache2
   virtual host:

   ```
   :htaccess: /var/www/.htaccess
   ```

3. Keep SQL query debugging off:

   ```
   :dbdebug: no
   ```

4. Specify the port on which the service will bound:

   ```
   :host: 0.0.0.0
   :port: 6121
   ```

5. Make sure that the user account that will execute `ozones-server` is able to
   update the `.htaccess` file inside `DocumentRoot`:

   ```
   $ sudo touch /var/www/.htaccess
   $ sudo chown oneadmin:oneadmin /var/www/.htaccess
   ```

6. To configure the credentials of the administrative account that will be able to create the new zones and VDC, we need to export the $OZONES_AUTH environment variable containing the path to a text file, which contains the username and password, separated by colon, on a unique line in our ~/.profile (as we already did for the oned daemon in the first chapter):

7. export OZONES_AUTH=$HOME/.one/ozones_auth, and reload it:

    ```
    $ source ~/.profile
    ```

8. Create the file, with credentials as per your preference:

    ```
    ozadmin:thepassword
    ```

9. Finally, start the server:

    ```
    $ ozones-server start
    ```

Managing the zones

A zone is a group of interconnected physical hosts, running different hypervisors, and controlled by a unique OpenNebula frontend. A zone can be added and managed through the oZones server by simply providing valid oneadmin credentials and the remote XMLRPC endpoint URL.

The onezone utility can be used to create, delete and list zones. In order to use it, make sure that the current user has the following environment variables correctly configured in its ~/.profile:

*   **$OZONES_AUTH**: It points to the file containing the credentials for logging on to ozones-server
*   **$OZONES_URL**: This variable contains ozones-server XMLRPC endpoint, defaults to http://localhost:6121/

Adding a new zone

The procedure to add a new zone is as follows:

1. As with every other OpenNebula utility, we should create a template file (for example: host.ozone) containing:
    *   NAME=odinZone
    *   ONENAME=oneadmin
    *   ONEPASS=password
    *   ENDPOINT=http://odin.local:2633/RPC2
    *   SUNSENDPOINT=http://odin.local:9869

Make sure that you specify the correct `oneadmin` credentials and that both the two remote endpoints (`oned` and `sunstone`) are not bound on `127.0.0.1`, or it won't work.

2. Submit the new zone with the following command:

```
$ onezone create host.ozone
```

3. Verify whether everything went smoothly with the following command:

```
$ onezone list
    ID            NAME                              ENDPOINT
    1          odinZone              http://odin.local:2633/RPC2
```

4. And show the details:

```
$ onezone show 1
ZONE odinZone INFORMATION
ID                    : 1
NAME              : odinZone
ZONE ADMIN     : oneadmin
ZONE PASS       : YPXQyA/ziCzt6Rc/8jgjfw==
ENDPOINT        : http://odin.local:2633/RPC2
# VDCS          : 0
```

5. Repeat this step for every OpenNebula cluster you manage and also for the ones you want to monitor with the oZones GUI.

Managing Virtual Data Centers

With a few zones correctly configured, we can start defining multiple VDCs inside them.

A VDC is a logic grouping of multiple hosts inside the same zone that can be used by multiple users, even with administrative access, but without directly accessing the host's configuration that remains visible only to the original `oneadmin` user of that zone.

The nice part of a VDC, which distinguishes itself from a standard, unprivileged group of users, is that all the requests for the VDC get proxied by the Apache2 running on `ozones-server` (actually hiding the real endpoint of the zone), and a complete isolation between the different VDCs (for example: public images can be seen only inside the same VDC and not on all the zones as usual).

Adding a new VDC

The `onevdc` utility can be used to create, delete, and list VDC. Like with the `onezone` utility, we need the two environment variables `$OZONES_AUTH` and `$OZONE_URL` correctly defined.

1. Create a VDC template file with the following contents:
   - `NAME=odinVDC`
   - `VDCADMINNAME=odinvdcadmin`
   - `VDCADMINPASS=odinvdcpass word`
   - `ZONEID=1`
   - `HOSTS=1`

   `NAME` will identify this VDC, and it will be used in the URL of the proxy.

   `VCADMIN`, as defined here, can be used to access this VDC, with full privileges like the `oneadmin` account.

   `ZONEID` is the identification number of the zone where this VDC will be placed, as seen in the `onezone list` output.

   `HOSTS` is a comma-separated list of hosts id that exists in the specified zone.

2. Submit the template with `onevdc`:

   ```
   $ onevdc create vdc.ozone
   ```

3. After successful submission, a few actions are automatically executed on the affected zone:
   - A new group called `odinVDC` will be created
   - A new user identified with `odinvdcadmin` will be created
   - A set of ACLs to allow users from the group `odinVDC` to deploy VM on the selected hosts, and to allow `odinvdcadmin` to create new users and manage resources created in the group will be created

4. Check for the correct VDC creation with the following command:

   ```
   $ onevdc list
     ID            NAME                                    ZONEID
      1          odinVDC                                      1
   ```

5. Check the VDC details with the following command:

   ```
   $ onevdc show 1
   VDC  INFORMATION
   ID               : 1
   ```

```
NAME            : odinVDC
GROUP_ID    : 100
ZONEID        : 1
VDCADMIN   : odinadmin
HOST IDs     : 1
```

6. Now that a VDC has been created, check for the updated content of the `.htaccess` file:

```
RewriteEngine On
RewriteRule ^odinVDC http://odin.local:2633/RPC2 [P]
RewriteRule ^sunstone_odinVDC/(.+) http://odin.local:9869/$1 [P]
RewriteRule ^sunstone_odinVDC http://odin.local:9869/ [P]
```

These rules will instruct the Apache2 proxy module where to redirect every user request concerning the `odinVDC` XMLRPC and Sunstone endpoint.

Sharing hosts between VDCs

Normally, a check is enforced to ensure that the different VDCs don't share the same physical hosts inside the same zone. If you want to relax this check, it's possible to add the following attribute in the VDC template:

```
FORCE=yes
```

In any case, a VDC administrator can only terminate its own instances and, sharing or not, physical hosts between VDCs is only an operational choice.

Adding or removing hosts in a VDC

Hosts belonging to a particular VDC can be changed after the initial creation using the `onevdc` utility, and the `addhost` and `delhost` commands:

```
onevdc addhost <vdc-id> <range>
onevdc delhost <vdc-id> <range>
```

Remember that the `host` should have already been added via the `onehost` utility in the relevant zone.

Using a VDC

To use a VDC we have to cope with the standard client-side requirements of OpenNebula, except that we will not directly use an XMLRPC endpoint; we will need to point the CLI utilities to the oZones proxy.

Command line access

In order to use a VDC through the command line:

1. The VDC administrator will need to define the following environment variables, inside his `~/.profile` file, to connect to our `odinVDC`:

    ```
    export ONE_XMLRPC=http://ozones.local/odinVDC
    export ONE_AUTH=$HOME/.one/vdc_auth
    ```

2. The `vdc_auth` file will contain the login credentials of the VDC administrator:

    ```
    odinadmin:odinpass
    ```

Now try to issue some of the standard OpenNebula CLI utilities such as:

```
$ oneuser list
    ID     GROUP        NAME          AUTH            PASSWORD
     2    odinVDC    odinadmin       core
77cb2959a4d9b[..]
```

You should see only your VDC administration account, and you can start creating any user account you may want, which will have access only to their VDC resources.

Add a new user with the following command:

```
$ oneuser create odinuser userpass
```

This new user will be able to access the VDC and manage its own resources and other VDC user's resources (if marked as group-accessible).

Also try to execute a non-supported command such as:

```
$ onehost create dummyHost im_kvm vmm_kvm tm_shared dummy
[HostAllocate] User [2] : Not authorized to perform CREATE HOST.
```

Sunstone access

The reverse proxy in Apache2 should have been automatically configured when the VDC was created. So we should be able to point our web browser to: `http://ozones.local/sunstone_odinVDC/`, and be able to reach the login page. Once we log in successfully, we have access to our well-known Sunstone interface, where it's possible to manage every resource within this VDC.

Even if there are many other VM instances running on the host to which this VDC belongs, the VDC administrator and any other user created within it will see only their own resources.

Using the oZones GUI

The oZones GUI can be used to monitor every running resource among all the managed zones and perform management tasks regarding zones and VDC configuration.

1. Open your browser and point to `http://ozones.local:6121/`.

2. Login with the credentials configured in the file pointed from $ONE_AUTH at the first `ozones-server` start.

After a successful login, you will be introduced to a **Dashboard** section. This section will contain all the information regarding the total amount of hosts, virtual machines, virtual networks, images, users, and templates in every configured zone.

Going deeper in the dashboard, you will find a section for every resource type, listing all the resources in detail. The results can be easily filtered using the top-right textbox in each page.

Zone ID	Zone Name	ID	Owner	Group	Name	Status	CPU	Memory	Hostname	Start Time
1	odinZone	0	oneadmin	oneadmin	ubuntu-1	RUNNING	0	256M	odin	17:54:55 03/18/2012
1	odinZone	1	oneadmin	oneadmin	ubuntu-2	RUNNING	0	256M	odin	18:07:04 03/18/2012
1	odinZone	2	oneadmin	oneadmin	ubuntu-3	RUNNING	0	256M	odin	18:07:09 03/18/2012
1	odinZone	3	oneadmin	oneadmin	ubuntu-4	RUNNING	0	256M	odin	18:07:12 03/18/2012
1	odinZone	4	oneadmin	oneadmin	ubuntu-5	RUNNING	3	256M	odin	18:07:15 03/18/2012
2	thorZone	0	oneadmin	oneadmin	ubuntu-1	RUNNING	0	400M	thor	18:16:51 03/18/2012
2	thorZone	1	oneadmin	oneadmin	ubuntu-2	RUNNING	0	400M	thor	18:18:36 03/18/2012
2	thorZone	2	oneadmin	oneadmin	ubuntu-3	RUNNING	0	400M	thor	18:18:38 03/18/2012
2	thorZone	3	oneadmin	oneadmin	ubuntu-4	RUNNING	0	400M	thor	18:18:46 03/18/2012
2	thorZone	4	oneadmin	oneadmin	ubuntu-5	RUNNING	0	400M	thor	18:18:50 03/18/2012

Leaving the **Dashboard** section and moving on to the **Zones** section, it's possible to see all the currently configured zones, with their own XMLRPC URL endpoint.

When clicking on a particular zone, the bar at the bottom will pop up, showing a series of tabs containing zone information, hosts, templates, virtual machines, virtual networks, images and users, with every configured resource available in the current zone.

With the buttons at the top, it's possible to create a new zone by just entering the few needed details (Name, XMLRPC endpoint, oneadmin credentials, Sunstone endpoint), or even delete any among the existing ones.

Proceeding to the **VDCs** section, it's possible to examine all the currently configured VDCs or to create a new VDC by simply providing a Name, the VDC administrator credentials, the Zone and their associated Hosts. The flag—**VDC host sharing**—can be enabled to relax the restriction on not using the same hosts among different VDCs.

Please note that in the oZones GUI, resources coming from a VDC are not shown, and we need to use the Sunstone as usual to monitor them.

Summary

In this chapter, we learnt how to configure and use the two standard public interfaces for OpenNebula—the EC2 Query interface and the OCCI interface—opening our infrastructure to a wider integration with any of the existing tools implementing these protocols.

Later, with the oZones component, we were able to monitor and centrally manage multiple OpenNebula instances, residing on different data centers, and subdivide them into multiple VDC, with complete privileges separation.

Index

Symbols

A

enable button 158
enable <id> attribute 123
epilog (epil) 125
ept, CPU flag 18
ERB 246
ESX support
  Libvirt, installing with 77
eu-west-1 (Ireland) region 211
examples
  VMware example 139
  Xen HVM example, virtual machine template 139
  Xen pygrub example, virtual machine template 139
exec_and_log function 83
executable parameter, image manager driver configuration 42
external Cloud provider
  about 209
  benefits 209
extra Large instance (m1.xlarge, $0.68) 213

F

failed (fail) 126
fail_timeout parameter 150
FCPU 178
Features section 164
federation, hybrid cloud 11
fencing 182
Filesystem in Userspace. *See* FUSE
Firefox 146
fix_paths function 83
FMEM 178
FORMAT attribute, disks section 130
Free CPU. *See* FCPU
Free Memory. *See* FMEM
free usage tier
  URL 218
frontend software requisites, OS installation 25
full virtualization 62
FUSE 96
fw, network drivers
  configuring 58

G

Ganglia
  about 188
  components 189
  Ganglia Meta Daemon (gmetad) 194
  Ganglia Monitoring Daemon (gmond) 189
  Ganglia PHP web frontend 196
  Ganglia web frontend 195, 196
  integrating, with OpenNebula IM 202
  multiple Ganglia cluster configuration (for VMs) 197, 198
  PHP web frontend usage 198-201
Ganglia-alert
  downloading, URL for 205
Ganglia, components
  Ganglia Meta Daemon (gmetad) 194
  Ganglia Monitoring Daemon (gmond) 189
  Ganglia PHP web frontend 195
Ganglia, integrating with OpenNebula IM
  about 202
  cron setup, for updating VM information 203, 204
  daemon, starting 202
  daemon, stopping 202
  Ganglia Information Manager driver, enabling 202
  Ganglia information polling, enabling 202
  local gmond, pointing to 202
  new hosts adding, im_ganglia used 204
  Web interface glitch, fixing 205
Ganglia Meta Daemon. *See* gmetad
Ganglia-monitor 189
Ganglia Monitoring Daemon. *See* gmond
Ganglia PHP Web frontend
  about 195
  usage 198-201
  virtual host reload nginx, activating 196
Ganglia web frontend. *See* Ganglia PHP Web frontend
Gemius SA
  URL 99
generic contextualization 141-143
GlusterFS
  about 91
  CIFS client 95

public cloud, use cases
  cloud providers 243
  collaboration 243
  optimize costs 243
PUBLIC parameter, ranged network 118
pv-grub 229
PXE environment 22
pygrub bootloader 129
Python 2.5 146
python_modules 194

Q

QA 8
QEMU
  about 13
  features 13
  VirtIO 13
  wiki, URL 13
Quality Assurance. *See* QA
Quick Emulator. *See* QEMU
Quickstart tab 154
quota libraries 31
quotas
  configuring 48
  cpu quota 48
  default quotas 48
  enabling 49
  -f flag 49
  memory quota 48
  num_vm quota 48
  onequota utility 48
  representing 48
  storage quota 48
  types 48
Quramnet 12

R

RAID
  4G file filled with zeroes, writing 20
  about 19
  hardware-RAID, benefits 20
  hdparm utility, used for checking disk per-
    formances 20
  Linux software-RAID 20
  RAID 0 (striping) 19
  RAID 1 (mirroring) 20

RAID 5 20
RAID 10 (or RAID 1+0) 20
read and write test, performing on mounted
    filesystem 20
software-RAID, benefits 20
RAID 0 (striping) 19
RAID 1 (mirroring) 20
RAID 5 20
RAID 10 (or RAID 1+0) 20
ranged network
  about 118
  NAME parameter 118
  PUBLIC parameter 118
Rank attribute 125
RANK attribute, placement section 135
R argument 181
RAW section, virtual machine
  DATA attribute 138
  TYPE attribute 138
READONLY attribute, disks section 130
Red Hat
  URL 91
Redundant Array of Independent Disks. *See*
    RAID
registered template
  listing, command for 143
  new instance launching, command for 143
  removing, command for 143
  updating, command for 143
release <vm-id> 126
Remember me option 153
remote machine support, Libvirt 14
remote user login
  about 44, 45
remove-brick operation 97
Remove selected action button 171
Remove selected button 165
REPLICATIONS_DELAY_DISCONNECT
    option 103
REPLICATIONS_DELAY_INIT option 103
requirements attribute 231
REQUIREMENTS attribute, placement sec-
    tion 135
Research Group
  URL 6
reserved instance 212
resource ID. *See* RID column

[PACKT] open source
PUBLISHING — community experience distilled

Thank you for buying
OpenNebula 3 Cloud Computing

About Packt Publishing

Packt, pronounced 'packed', published its first book "*Mastering phpMyAdmin for Effective MySQL Management*" in April 2004 and subsequently continued to specialize in publishing highly focused books on specific technologies and solutions.

Our books and publications share the experiences of your fellow IT professionals in adapting and customizing today's systems, applications, and frameworks. Our solution based books give you the knowledge and power to customize the software and technologies you're using to get the job done. Packt books are more specific and less general than the IT books you have seen in the past. Our unique business model allows us to bring you more focused information, giving you more of what you need to know, and less of what you don't.

Packt is a modern, yet unique publishing company, which focuses on producing quality, cutting-edge books for communities of developers, administrators, and newbies alike. For more information, please visit our website: www.packtpub.com.

About Packt Open Source

In 2010, Packt launched two new brands, Packt Open Source and Packt Enterprise, in order to continue its focus on specialization. This book is part of the Packt Open Source brand, home to books published on software built around Open Source licences, and offering information to anybody from advanced developers to budding web designers. The Open Source brand also runs Packt's Open Source Royalty Scheme, by which Packt gives a royalty to each Open Source project about whose software a book is sold.

Writing for Packt

We welcome all inquiries from people who are interested in authoring. Book proposals should be sent to author@packtpub.com. If your book idea is still at an early stage and you would like to discuss it first before writing a formal book proposal, contact us; one of our commissioning editors will get in touch with you.

We're not just looking for published authors; if you have strong technical skills but no writing experience, our experienced editors can help you develop a writing career, or simply get some additional reward for your expertise.

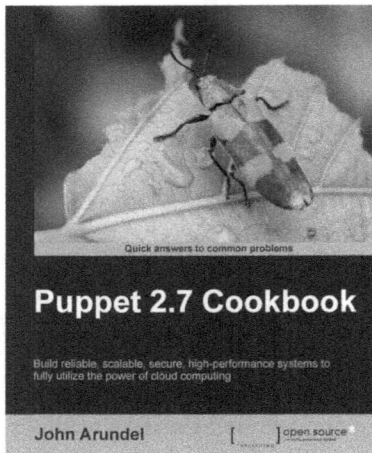

Puppet 2.7 Cookbook

ISBN: 978-1-84951-538-2   Paperback: 300 pages

Build reliable, scalable, secure, high-performance systems to fully utilize the power of cloud computing

1. Shows you how to use 100 powerful advanced features of Puppet, with detailed step-by-step instructions

2. Covers all the popular tools and frameworks used with Puppet: Dashboard, Foreman, MCollective, and more

3. Includes the latest features and updates in Puppet 2.7

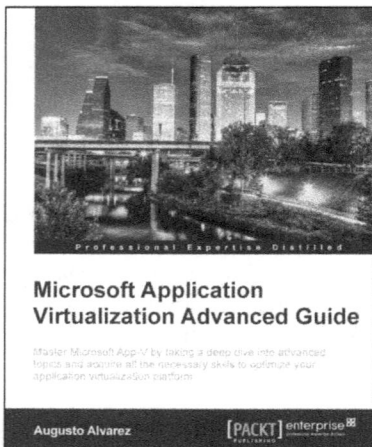

Microsoft Application Virtualization Advanced Guide

ISBN: 978-1-84968-448-4   Paperback: 474 pages

Master Microsoft App-V by taking a deep dive into advanced topics and acquire all the necessary skills to optimize your application virtualization platform

1. Understand advanced topics in App-V; identify some rarely known components and options available in the platform

2. Acquire advanced guidelines on how to troubleshoot App-V installations, sequencing, and application deployments

3. Learn how to handle particular applications, adapting companys' policies to the implementation, enforcing application licenses, securing the environment, and so on

Please check **www.PacktPub.com** for information on our titles

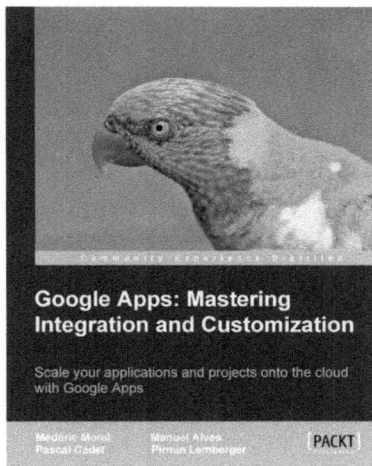

www.ingramcontent.com/pod-product-compliance
Lightning Source LLC
Chambersburg PA
CBHW082108220326
41598CB00066BA/5768